ROB-

THANKS SO MUCH FOR YOUR HELP & ELOQUENT ENDORSEMENT!

YOUR FRIEND,

Seizing Share

Seizing Share

The Semper Fortis Strategy
for Building a World-Class Solution Selling Organization
and Lasting Competitive Advantage

Bob Sakalas

Belcroft Books
Dallas Texas USA

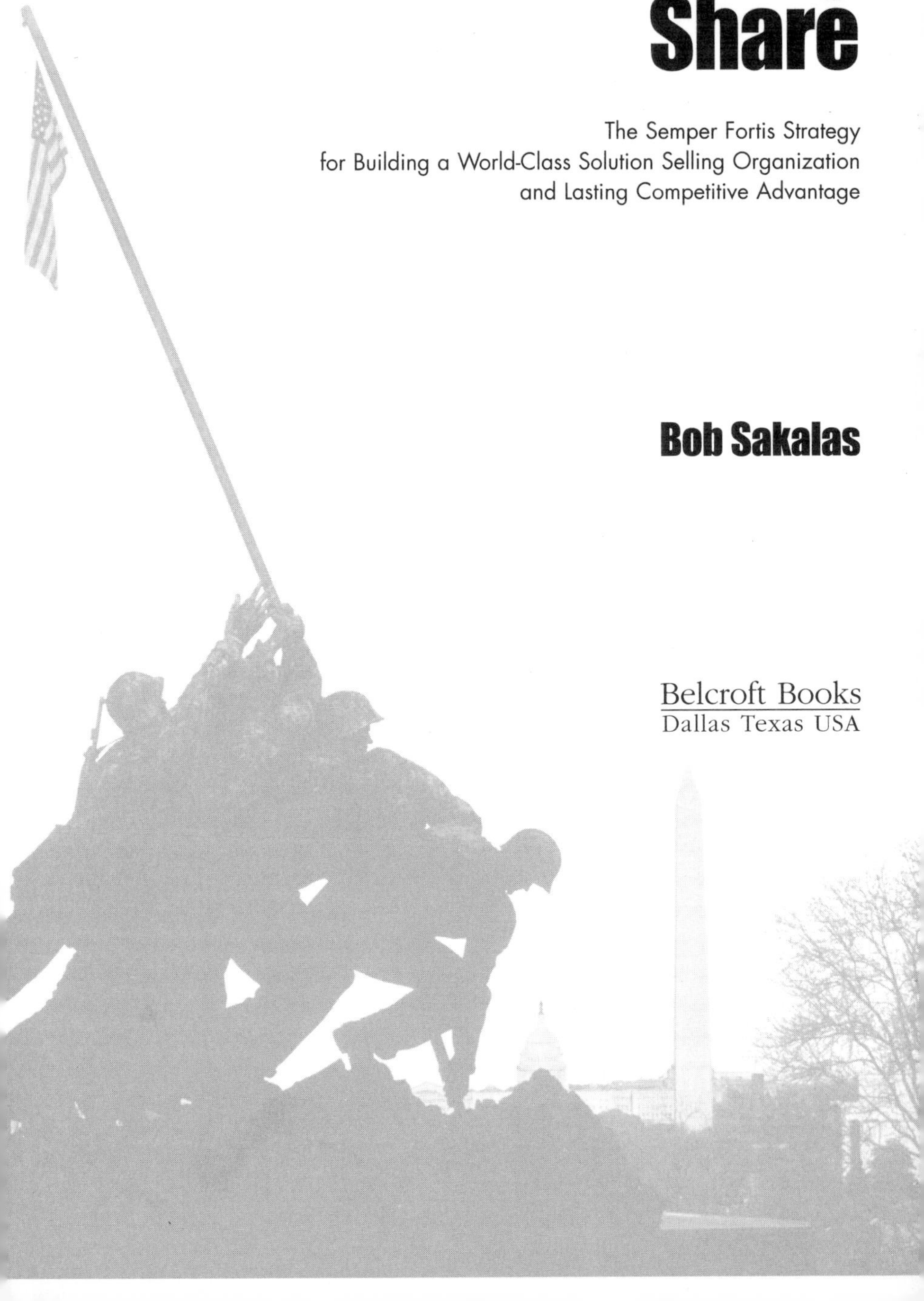

For permission requests, write to the publisher:
Copyright.Permissions@belcroft.com (e-mail), or

Belcroft Books
Attn: Copyright Permissions
P.O. Box 2921
Coppell, Texas 75019

Ordering Information

Special discounts are available on quantity purchases by corporations, associations, and others. For details, please contact Belcroft Books via e-mail at:
Quantity.Purchasing@belcroft.com (e-mail), or

Belcroft Books
Attn: Quantity Purchasing
P.O. Box 2921
Coppell, Texas 75019

Individual Sales

This book is available through online booksellers such as amazon.com, bn.com, borders.com, and others.

Printed in Dallas, Texas, USA

First Edition, April 2004

The paper used in this publication meets the requirements of the American National Standard for Permanence of Paper for Publications and Documents in Libraries and Archives Z39-48-1992.

Sakalas, Bob

Seizing Share: The Semper Fortis strategy for building a world-class solution selling organization and lasting competitive advantage / by Bob Sakalas
p. cm.
Includes Bibliographical references.

Library of Congress Control Number: 2004101835

ISBN 0-9742838-1-9

1. Business strategy. 2. Leadership in Business. 3. Business Management 4. Solution Selling. I. Title

04 03 02 01 00 5 4 3 2 1

Dedication

~ ~ ~ ~ ~ ~

This book is dedicated to my grandfather,
Stanley Dimgaila.

Thanks for being there everytime I needed you
and thanks for watching over me today.

I'll bet it's a great view from up there.

Seizing Share

Table of Contents

Introduction: Seizing Share

The status quo in professional selling is powerful and oppressive. My goal is to change the beliefs so much of the profession is built upon, with an argument rooted in common sense and front-line experience. This book does not address selling at the individual level; instead, the focus is on developing a superior selling team that is strategic, nimble, and works far better than today's model.

Many executives put little thought into the development, organization, and readiness of their sales force. This is a costly mistake. Competitive advantage is available for those whose eyes and minds are open. Changes in the competitive landscape and a shift of power from the vendor to the customer demand either the evolution or the extinction of current sales models. Why not develop the best sales organization in an industry niche, especially when so few companies are focused on improving their capabilities in the selling field?

The goal of this book is not to offer conventional thinking or mere comfort to the masses in American business. Executives with little experience in direct sales may not immediately embrace the Semper Fortis message. But experienced sales professionals and executives who are close to their customers will definitely get an "ah, ha!" and see the wisdom of breaking out to a higher plateau.

I have a unique perspective. My sales roots start at NCR, a company revered for inventing professional selling and formal corporate sales education, which dates back to John H. Patterson in the early 1900's. In my career, I have worked closely with a number of mainstream sales forces with companies such as NCR, Teradata, IBM, HP, Sun Micro, Symbol Technology, and a great number of sales groups from smaller enterprises. Much of the time, I was fortunate enough to be inside a smaller, nimbler organization whose sales professionals ran business franchises. The potential for improvement became clear as I observed the dramatic contrast between nimble franchises and lumbering bureaucracies.

In developing the ideas for this book, I researched sales operations at a number of leading solution-selling companies, interviewing scores of salespeople and sales managers. By focusing the investigation on the field level and specifically seeking out top-tier producers, I have great confidence that the ideas offered here ring true and will work well in most complex selling environments.

Target Audience

There is a broad spectrum in selling. At one end is the "Straight-Forward, One-Product Commodity-Selling Environment" while at the other end, we find the "Complex Corporate Solution Environment."

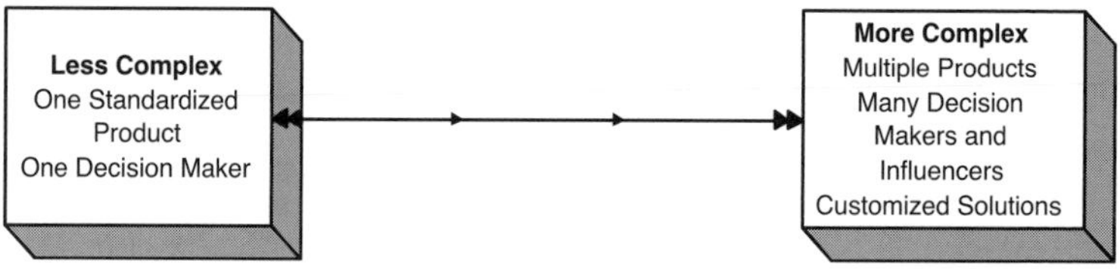

Contrary to the word "straight-forward," neither end is "easy." It can be very difficult to sell stringently specified corn syrup to a food manufacturer, but this "one commodity product" sold to one corporate buyer is simply not targeted by the Semper Fortis strategy.

Semper Fortis specifically addresses selling in the Complex Corporate Solutions Environment (CCSE). Characteristics of these types of arenas include the following:

- Corporate-to-corporate selling,
- Complex, political selling environment,
- Consultative problem-solving,
- Often, but not always, customized solutions for each client,
- Often, but not always, complex solution sets, and
- High-stakes wins and losses.

Organization of the Book

Part One forms the "executive overview"—a book within the book. In our hurried society, some do not have the time to fully explore topics, so I've offered the "Cliff's Notes" form. The first four chapters outline the core of the message, the opening argument for conversion to the Semper Fortis success formula.

These first chapters paint in broad strokes the vision of the retooled, re-cultured sales force, offering a solid understanding of the formula and steps needed to achieve a lasting sales competitive advantage. Semper Fortis also targets departments outside direct sales. In fact, a highly professional selling culture, focused on profitability, must permeate the entire organization.

Book Organization

Part One: High Level Overview
- Chapters 1 – 4
- The complete concept at a high level.

Part Two: Detailed Discussion
- Sections 1 – 8 / Chapters 5 – 25
- Complete discussion of the eight-part model and sixteen implementation steps.

Part Three: Making it Happen
- Chapters 26 – 28
- The role of leadership and measuring progress.

Additional Information

In Part Two, eight sections explore in detail the eight core foundation pillars of Semper Fortis. A company must implement all eight foundation pillars and sixteen key substructures to achieve balance, momentum, and, ultimately, the breakthrough moment of "fusion" in the program.

Much of the activity involves changing or adding to a company's culture. Clearly, cultural change starts at the top. Unless a company's top tier of executives buy actively and publicly into the plan, and actively change their personal approaches, the Semper Fortis discipline will not take hold, and competitive advantage and market share gains will remain elusive. Semper Fortis cannot be implemented with only the support of the sales management team.

Part Three ties it all together in a final summation, the closing argument that a company should commit to the Semper Fortis strategy. Unlike some strategies, Semper Fortis can coexist with other management schemes such as the Balanced Scorecard and Six Sigma. It does, however, require two to three years of commitment and focus before a world-class, unbending winning tradition can be built.

Semper Fortis Defined

Semper Fortis means "**Always Strong**" in Latin. The sales force should be built to dominate its competitors, overwhelming all with superior strategy, tactics, and resources, ultimately winning all close battles, never yielding ground with existing customers, and seizing share in its industry each year.

Indirect marketing may work miracles for a few, but competitive advantage can best be achieved with a close knit team of Sales Olympians. The phenomenal growth of the Internet, the emergence of greater sophistication on the part of the buyer, and the slow evolution of thought surrounding the sales discipline have lulled executives to sleep regarding the possibilities of state-of-the-art sales team capabilities.

Marketing through advertising and public relations, and interfacing with customers through the Internet is much like a basketball team with only jump shooters—it's tough winning without the outside shot, but it is impossible to win championships without a combination of outside shooting, great defense, solid rebounding, a dominant inside game, and reliable free-throw shooting.

Semper Fortis is a strategy that creates a corporate sales "ground" force on par with the exemplary U.S. Marine Corps. Any company relying on a minimal life support force of one-man representatives with antiquated training and few weapons stands no more chance against a Semper Fortis sales force than did Iraq's Army, strong in numbers but not in methods, against the precisely trained, superbly outfitted U.S. regiments.

Many companies rely on innovation, low-cost producer status, or marketing dominance as their core advantage. There is great risk in our high-velocity environment that a sudden breakthrough moment or event by a competitor will dramatically tilt the balance of power and momentum. Companies thus invest heavily to stay in front, counting on breakthroughs of their own to antiquate their own product offerings.

Companies following the principles of Semper Fortis do not require breakthroughs to maintain advantage in the marketplace. Semper Fortis companies forge field excellence, have superior intelligence flow from key customers, have close-knit relationships with decision makers throughout their industry, and better understand the individual problems each customer faces. There is no risk of a competitive sales capability breakout, as sales excellence can be built only over considerable time. Excellent leadership, superior recruiting, finely-honed methods, training investment, uncompromising support, and a winning culture results in forging an elite Semper Fortis force.

To my knowledge, no major Fortune 500 company today has completely achieved this level of capability. But one doesn't have to look far to see the potential. IBM has long focused on strong consultative sales representation as a critical initiative. Today, competitors, often with superior price performance products, win far fewer deals than they estimated, stymied as IBM convinces customers to wait for the "blue" solution, coming in just months. IBM's Signature Selling training methods are well regarded. The Semper Fortis strategy goes well beyond and explores the power of account management by profitability, compensation plans aligned with shareholder values, true teamwork, the use of elite special forces as needed, and more.

Semper Fortis is all about "seizing share" from competitors. Seizing market share is much more difficult than keeping market share. Once won, dislodging a Semper Fortis force from a customer's side often requires huge expenditures on the part of the attacking vendor. Many companies focus on either winning new customers or maintaining existing ones. Semper Fortis instills discipline to gain ground and hold on to it with ferocity, for the best profit usually comes from attaining vendor-of-choice status, winning the lion's share of a customer's available budget, and partnering closely for many years.

Why count on innovation breakthroughs alone? Executives who adopt the Semper Fortis strategy will sleep well at night, knowing their sales force is vigilant and on a mission to seize and keep market share.

Part One

High Level Overview

"Progress has everything to do with one's heading,
and nothing to do with the rate of travel."
- Bob Sakalas

Chapter 1: The Opportunity

Most presidents and CEOs of the Fortune 1000 have a Texas-sized blind spot.

For a number of reasons, the vast majority of America's mightiest corporations have missed building a strong competitive advantage that, with proper care and feeding, can be maintained for a decade or more, and perhaps indefinitely.

The destructive myth that exists today is the thought that "*all sales forces are basically the same*." Most companies seem to be playing to tie their competitors in the sales game—a kind of corporate Cold War brinkmanship without an ever-escalating arms race—while fighting each other with product innovation, advertising and public relations, operational advances, supply chain and procurement improvement, and service delivery and execution.

A number of factors are driving this intentional sales force détente. They include

- Lack of investment in training, often conveniently blamed on the high turnover ratio found in most sales forces,
- Little investment in advanced information systems technologies that help the sales force,
- The false perception that sales skill is something that someone is born with,
- The misguided idea and accepted practice that sales is an individual sport,
- The fact that few executives hail from the sales discipline and therefore do not understand the complexities and subtleties of the profession, and
- The reality that current "business guru" thought and publishing has been focused elsewhere for the last two decades.

Few working executives have the time to create and publish new business theories. In fact, many have little time to create new programs for their own companies, often looking to the hottest concepts in business management—ideas such as Six Sigma Quality, managing to the Balanced Scorecard, and the Hedgehog Principle found in the bestseller Good to Great. The result is that new business theory is most often driven by business authors, who mainly hail from academia and the closely-related consulting professions.

To my surprise, I have been unable to find any top-tier business guru drawing attention to the sales force in any substantive manner. Given that millions of professional salespeople work for just the Fortune 500 corporations, the topic should have more attention.

Business "Gurus" Shun Professional Selling

Pursuing this research, I looked at all the articles published in the *Harvard Business Review* for the last decade—and got a bit of a shock. The *Harvard Business Review*, arguably the leading periodical on new business thought, which published more than one thousand articles from 1993 through 2002, did not publish one article that focused on sales force organization, leveraging the sales force in a strategic way, or even improving the capabilities of a company's sales force. The one article indexed over the decade as "sales management" focused on negotiation training.

Summary of HBR's Focus

Topic (subset)	# of Articles
Finance & Acct.	31
Leadership	74
Human Res.	61
Innovation	44
Management	100
Marketing	54
New Economy	41
Sales Mgt.	1
Strategy	108
Info. Technology	51

Source: *Harvard Business Review* (annual indexes of feature-length articles) See www.SeizingShare.com/hbr for complete summary table)

Taking a step back, perhaps this is not as earth-shattering a discovery as I first thought. The *Harvard Business Review* serves as a leading publication of *academic* business thinking. Even the consultants who are often published in this magazine have deep roots at leading business schools. Yet when one looks at the fields of study at any leading business school, there are no Sales 101 classes, let alone master's degrees or Ph.D.'s in the subject. Academia, generally, does not deem selling "professional" enough for detailed study.

The reason that professional selling is such a stepchild to most academics is that it truly cannot be learned exclusively in a classroom setting. This means there are no professional salespeople turned Ivy League sales professors, which in turn means professional selling remains academia's stepchild. It's a vicious "what comes first—chicken-or-the-egg" circle.

The best sales schools in the world are found at corporations such as NCR, the company acknowledged for inventing modern sales training nearly 100 years ago. There, the curriculum requires much time spent out in the field with customers and prospects, and typically it takes two years before a trainee graduates as an associate account manager, the NCR equivalent of an undergraduate degree. Advanced selling studies follow, only after several more years of real-world experience.

There are faint signs that academia is starting to consider "selling" but it appears that most universities will never awaken from their coma. Universities, more than any other group, encourage publication. Academics are the most published business authors. Most primetime consultants, the only other group encouraging publication, have roots and MBA degrees from the best dozen business schools. Unfortunately, virtually all academics and consultants have no experience in professional selling. Therefore, it is not surprising that fresh business theory regarding sales organization strategy is missing in action.

Addressing the Black Hole

The shelves of the local Barnes & Noble or Borders book store are overflowing with "how to" books regarding selling, all targeted at the individual salesperson. Everything from "*How... to sell more... to close... to cold-call... to ask good questions... to plan your sales day*" are there. Yet few books look at the sales force in the context of the entire corporation, and none, in my assessment, outline how executives can make the sales force exponentially more effective and have it become a true competitive advantage.

This book will do just that. Many who do not believe it can be done often cite high turnover rates of sales professionals as the single most important factor preventing improvement. Turnover is not an impossible hurdle, and turnover can be reduced. Consider the following analogy:

> In college football, players enter the system and depart within four or five years. Using the accepted myth that "sales forces should play to tie because consistently winning the majority of contests is impossible over the longer term," one could draw a parallel and say that it is impossible for a college football program to win more than 50 percent of its games over one or two decades.
>
> After all, 100 percent of your "employees" or in this case players, turnover in less than five years—especially your stars—who often disappear in the NFL football draft in three.
>
> Yet all of us know that programs such as Florida State, Miami, Oklahoma, Nebraska, and a few select others are always in the hunt for undefeated seasons, primetime bowl bids, and the national championship.

Once a winning sales force program is in place, it becomes possible, even easier, to maintain a winning tradition, much the same as found in football or basketball. There are an extraordinary number of parallels between what works in team sports and what works in professional selling. Yet corporate teams today rarely follow these time-proven winning formulas. Superior attitude, superior recruiting, comprehensive practice and training, a belief that you should always win every game, excellent intelligence gathering, careful planning, a discipline of empowerment, and flawless execution all play a part. Once the "system" is in place, the success momentum takes on a life of its own.

Some readers will question whether lasting competitive advantage can be achieved since so many business strategies promising lasting advantage have come and gone. The maintenance of this advantage is very much in line with military strategy. If an elite team of the U.S. Navy's SEALs takes over and secures a small fortress, a new group of equally capable special forces would have great difficulty taking the fortress back. The SEALs would have the advantage of holding a fortified position and could be defeated only by expending vastly larger resources.

A highly-trained sales team becomes difficult to dislodge, once it has established its position and holds a dominant-share, incumbent position with a key customer. A new vendor would be required to invest much more time, resources, and capital than is often justifiable to replace the capable incumbent holding its position at the customer "fortress." In most cases, the concerted and expensive effort never takes place.

Sales professionals make an extraordinary difference in the success or failure of companies. Too many folks believe that products sell themselves. They do not. A well-trained, well-managed, self-motivated, highly professional sales team can double the sales growth rate of most companies that currently have only an average sales force for their industry segment.

Chapter 2: The Status Quo

In the last few decades, American business has experienced more change than it did over the previous one hundred years. The pace of change is continuing to accelerate in an exponential fashion. Every customer's expectations have become near real-time. The demands of the environment are becoming more relentless.

Today, the planet is much smaller. Communications are instantaneous worldwide for voice, e-mail, fax, enterprise-to-enterprise data interchange, workflow routing, and on-line collaboration.

We live in an environment of quick idea propagation. The time from idea creation in Boston or London, to physical creation at one of the new centers of heavy lifting, places such as Taiwan, Mexico, India, Korea, or the granddaddy of cheap labor, China, is measured in days. Near real-time idea communication has enabled fast mimicking of successful products by competitors.

Companies have compressed delivery by innovating along the supply-chain, cutting out steps, decreasing inventories, and consolidating or eliminating middle-men. Supply-chain initiatives are succeeding, eliminating billions in capital tied up in inventories and helping to speed up cycles, but not without growing pains and reminders that these processes are far from perfected.

A great example of these pains was seen with the implosion of the telecom equipment companies in 2000 and 2001. Executives had too much confidence in supply-chain advances and didn't ask how real the implementation was. The severe contraction occurred primarily because companies still kept substantial inventory safety margins at the various steps of each supply-chain. When business slowed, companies in the supply-chain did not have the ability to step on the brakes fast enough or hard enough, and soon their warehouses were full of rapidly depreciating technology. This clearly shows that supply-chain advances must continue to evolve before they will be able to match the nimbleness of communications, development, and manufacturing.

Relentless Competition

The trends toward relentless competition seem unstoppable. The situation from the supplier side is tough:

- There are more competitors vying in each product category.
    - Globalization has enabled many overseas original equipment manufacturers to enter foreign markets.
    - Additionally, there are a great number of service firms that compete for the "general contract" based on integration competence, then subcontract components to low-cost providers.
    - A third area of increased competition is coming from outsourcers, who fight to convince executives to completely turn over the keys to departments or business processes in exchange for relentless cost savings and contract-specified performance levels.
    - Finally, corporate downsizing has spawned a great number of small but nimble startup competitors in certain niche markets.

- Because of more entrants, there is less differentiation at the introduction of a product or service than in the past.

- Differentiation half-life has been shortened by a factor of five or more—innovations are mimicked quickly and efficiently.

- Patent protection has become less daunting to overcome as more technologies compete for many opportunities—many times, the slowness of the legal process ensures patent resolution does not come before a product is yesterday's news.

- The marketable lifespan of most products has been cut in half as compared to just two decades ago.

- Companies that do develop a successful product cannot rest and reap profits—the best protection is inventing the product that antiquates the company's own successful one before the competition does.

- Supply and demand are out of balance. The supply side is now and perhaps permanently overbuilt because a great number of manufacturing "outsourcing" firms, such as Solectron, Flextronics, and Taiwan Semiconductor, are in a race to become the back-end of many businesses.

- Sustainable margins have dramatically decreased, especially in relation to the continuing consolidation of the customer enterprises into highly demanding mega-corporations.

- Companies' cost reduction responses to decreased margins often make them more vulnerable to attack. Unbundling of customer service, warranties, and so forth decreases the loyalty of the customer.

- As customer loyalty decreases, the profitability of accounts decreases. The best profits for a vendor typically are realized once a vendor becomes the incumbent with the greatest share of a customer's business, usually year four or longer in the vendor-customer relationship. By this time, costs associated with the initial up-front blitz sales effort (selling, prototyping, customization, testing, certification, process work) have been recovered. Eroding loyalty decreases the average number of superior profit years enjoyed per customer.

- Just getting noticed is harder when the number of choices grow. Both sales and marketing expenses are generally increasing as a percentage of profit, driven in part by the energy expenditure required to rise above the noise.

- Many companies fall victim to a downward spiral of product detuning in an effort to combat profit margin erosion. This is a dangerous line of logic that says "If we decrease our quality or capability by only 10 percent, we will yield a cost savings of 25 percent," and the company goes through multiple rounds as competition keeps cutting into the margin: In the long run, these cost savers corner themselves into irrelevance.

Relentless Customers

Simultaneously, the customer environments have become much more complex, stringent, and demanding:

- The balance of power, which is primarily driven by information transparency, has shifted from supplier to customer as information has become free-flowing.

- The expectation of quality has greatly increased as certain firms have used strategies such as Six Sigma to set the quality expectation bar much higher.

- Proprietary products, which often offer greater lifespan and margin for the vendor, are shunned by many customers, who now better understand the benefits of standardization than they did in the past.

- Even in arenas that do endure some level of proprietary content, customers are demanding well-oiled interoperability throughout the enterprise, which opens the door for more competition.

- The standardization pressure has made it more difficult to succeed with a purely proprietary product that enjoys sterling patent protection, yet products that adhere to standards are harder to patent protect and therefore easier to mimic.

- The customer demand for interoperability results in more costs to the vendors, since these "standards" tend to change over time causing rework and retesting, while continually increasing the amount of supported "previous standard" environments.

- Customers are encouraging vendors to compete more often to keep ongoing business—the incumbent is finding that being "on the inside" doesn't save it from having to compete for each purchase order—often against mimic products.

- Customers are holding more supplier auctions, often leveraging business-to-business internet technologies, cutting each vendor's margins ever thinner.

- Customers are consolidating into mega-corporations—vendors must rely on success at fewer but larger customers—making the competition for these "whale" accounts more intense.

- The shift toward fewer, larger mega-corporate customers has brought an increase in the political complexity. Sales that once had five key influencers and one decision maker now often have twenty-five influencers and a final vote in committee.

- Because of past integration dissatisfaction with vendors, some buyers are enabling their own in-house integration capabilities by hiring additional technical and operational resources, then searching for best-of-breed components to assemble into a custom solution. The sheer size of the customers makes the costs of this additional overhead easier to absorb, since there is typically a large number of ongoing projects.

- The more capability customers build in-house, the less likely they are to exhibit loyalty to any one vendor.

- Integrator value-add plays better at first introduction but many customers have a plan to take projects in-house later, contributing to the demise of the typically most profitable years (year 4+) of a vendor-customer relationship.
- Because of the enterprise-wide integration requirement, there is more risk on the buyer's side and therefore more investigation, testing, prototyping, loopholes, driving lower vendor margins.
- Winning a one-stop-shop sale has become tougher.
- The one-stop-shop sale is still preferable but margins for this convenience and transference of integration risk are a small fraction of what they were in the past.
- Genuine innovation is running into the strong headwind of standardization and enterprise-wide integration. Customers weighing the benefits often avoid innovative approaches in favor of not disturbing the delicate balance of an already working "system."

Importance of the Sales Force Is Increasing

In the complex political environments of consolidating mega-corporations, the necessity, effectiveness, and demands for professionalism are dramatically increasing. The greater the lack of differentiation, the more competitors, the tougher the negotiations, the more complex the environments, and the more demanding the customers, the more clever, concise, and professional the sales force and selling approach must become.

The quality of the sales force and sales approach is becoming the single biggest differentiator and catalyst for growth.

Some companies have misread the tea leaves and have started looking at the Internet as a traditional sales replacement. This is a mistake. The only sales force the Internet can replace is one that does not "sell" but rather facilitates the process of ordering, billing, and delivery. While it is true that the writing is on the wall for some types of salespeople—such as those auto salespeople who wait for interested buyers to stroll into the showroom—this trend simply does not apply to the complex corporate solutions environment (CCSE).

In almost any sales environment, and especially in CCSEs, the Internet is simply another tool to build efficiencies in areas such as prospect education, message consistency, order administration, customer confidence, and customer loyalty. If anything, it serves to save valuable salesperson time for higher value-add activities in the selling process.

A company that relies on the Internet for all its customer interface activity is like a military fighting a battle with only fighter jets. It is hard to win the war with only air superiority and no ground strike capabilities.

Contrary to the opinions of some gurus, professional selling is not going away in favor of remote-control marketing and Internet customer interfaces. Increasingly hostile selling environments are putting new demands on sales forces, marketing, and Internet interfaces. Companies that do not change, that do not bulk up their capabilities, that do not invest, that do not strike a balance between the cost of sales development and tangible results such as seizing new market share, improved customer retention, and improved yield per customized solution sold, will find themselves far behind.

The Status Quo and the Sales Force

Professional solution selling is a learned art, not a birthright. While certain talents can speed up the time it takes to achieve "professionalism" in selling, many of the stereotyped skills, such as glib entertaining, are not very predictive of the ultimate success or failure of an individual. There is a clear process for achieving consistent success, yet few companies achieve "best-practices" in their sales operation. I will explore the professional selling process in Chapter 5.

Excluding pockets of excellence and valleys of despair, the following is a status quo snapshot of CCSE selling for the majority of companies.

Complex Corporate Solutions Selling Today

1. **Sales versus Management in Most Environments**

   Executives are isolated from sales managers in regards to strategy, since they often perceive the sales function as a tactical arm of the company. Executives rarely understand how process-based professional selling can be or the years of work that go on behind the scenes of what appears to be an overnight success; therefore, salespeople are often considered to be overpaid prima donnas. Most managers see their mission as a control mechanism for the corporation.

2. **Sales Skills Development**

   The salespeople receive some training on solution selling, but are then expected to incorporate it into their work on their own. The sales leadership does not manage salespeople to a well-defined sales process. Many of the other field personnel, also important to the sale, such as systems engineers, project managers, and customer service reps, receive little or no advanced sales training.

3. **Current Knowledge Capture**

   Knowledge capture efforts are anchored by sales automation software projects. While these efforts are making progress on documenting the basics, most projects are coming up far short of capturing the best nuggets of sales information gold.

4. **Quota Controlled Compensation**

   Salespeople are compensated via a revenue quota-based system, yet quota systems are fatally flawed in most cases. Salespeople's goals are typically focused on revenue not profit, and therefore, are not well-aligned with the shareholders' desire for high-quality earnings.

5. **General Sales Operations**

   Most salespeople remain one-man-show gladiators, not well-coordinated sales teams, even when the company professes that it has a team-selling environment. Where a company focuses on team selling, one usually finds multiple "product specialists" at one prospect account, each with his or her own agenda.

   Company executives focus building competitive advantage efforts on developing superior products or improving operational excellence and execution. Sales forces from opposing companies tend to tie in most cases. It is rare to find a company focused on beating the competition with a superior sales force.

6. **Sales Management**

   The gladiators rarely have a truly open relationship with their sales manager because the quota system prevents total disclosure and honesty, as it is rarely perceived by the salesperson as "in their own best interest," which is usually an accurate assessment.

   First-line managers get little, if any, management training. Often promoted from the gladiator ranks, they tend to want to make gladiators change to their personal modus operandi. Rarely do first-line managers adapt their approach to the individual needs of each of their assigned salespeople.

   Executive management rarely gets involved with new prospects or existing accounts. When executives do get involved, often the salesperson has difficulty in coaching the "play" needed to propel the sale forward.

7. **Recruiting and Retention**

Sales recruiting is stereotyped, centered on sales athleticism, and run by human resources folks without any understanding of solution selling beyond the surface veneer. Salesperson turnover is generally high and assumed normal.

8. **Sales Planning and Use of Time**

Sales planning activities are mostly self-directed. Even the sales people who have succeeded in following proven processes fail to plan when the urgency hurricane swamps them. Without the guiding force of the manager, many previously successful salespeople skip steps and ultimately learn painful lessons in sales losses. Worse yet, many don't learn from the failures.

Headquarters continues to heap administrivia on the salespeople, using the banner of "free labor" that does not show up in the administrative overhead expense line on the financial statements.

Salespeople do not plan their weekly activity and do not update account plans more often than quarterly. Salespeople rarely practice. Salespeople are not required to follow a sales process checklist and management does not manage to a process flowchart.

9. **Current Decision Making**

Most account-level decision making, the most important of which is customer pricing and expense containment, is removed from the individual salesperson. Most first-line decision making lands on the district manager, who often lives in a different city from many of his or her salespeople and prospects. Most pricing decisions, especially for large-scale opportunities, are far removed to a divisional headquarters where MBA-armed financial pricing analysts serve as gatekeepers and influencers at the right hand of far-from-the-action divisional executives.

10. **Careers in Sales**

Promotions tend to lead out of the sales department, at least the "good" career moves, and many first-line promotions to management often decrease immediate earnings potential. Few companies offer high-end career-ending-in-contentment type positions in the field.

11. **The Sales Force and the Rest of the Company**

There is a poor attitude regarding salespeople in other areas of the organization, as salespeople's (and therefore, customer) urgencies produce a stream of unplanned, unwelcome work. Salespeople feel that they are pitted not only against the competition but also against their own organization as well, without enough support to really have excellence in execution once a new customer is landed.

Companies sometimes have out-of-the-sales-mainstream high-profile, highly-complex selling that is led by "VPs of Business Development," in essence high-caliber salespeople / complete business unit owners with reporting structures that allow the delivery personnel to report to him or her directly.

The Marketing / Public Relations / Trade Shows / department(s) tend to have little or poor coordination with the sales force. The public marketing message is often different than the message from the direct sales / customer level.

Development organizations (including product marketing) do not trust the sales team and tend to hide futures for fear of setting unreasonable expectations with customers and jeopardizing current sales. The salespeople often lose customer trust when they are unwittingly torpedoed by their own development, as they sell almost discontinued versions for large projects, only months before a new, far superior, yet secret version is introduced.

12. **Effectiveness Today**

Industry standard "proposal win percentages" of well under fifty percent are accepted as gospel. Companies focus on increasing the number of proposals vs. winning a greater percentage. The result is a downward spiral of sales effort *quality* in favor of proposal and engagement *quantity*. Companies, in an effort to maximize profit, tend to starve coverage and effort at existing long-term clients, resulting in eventual customer turnover. Formal "customer retention" programs are rare.

13. **Morale and Recognition**

Sales recognition programs focus visibility inside the sales hierarchy. Programs are varied but competitive pressures on margins have generally reduced award trips and other expensive contests. Fairness of quota assignment and the ratio of relative bonus to revenue and profit delivered are the chief morale-busters for top sales producers. Mission clarity inconsistencies are common, where sales management tasks salespeople with specific objectives that are not consistent with compensation plan implications, which are often written by finance analysts.

14. **Gathering and Using Intelligence**

Companies do not have dedicated human-driven intelligence management efforts. Companies do not debrief their field operatives in an organized fashion and first-line managers, the most likely debriefing agents, do not have any responsibility to document known activity. Documentation falls on the salespeople who usually make a token effort at best. Failures and losses are not discussed and learned company-wide, but rather quickly swept under a rug and forgotten.

In Summary...

Relentless competition. Relentless customers. Plummeting differentiation. This stark reality of business in the 2000s is clearly elevating the value of a substantially superior sales force.

Few executives have recognized need and potential for serious reform within their sales organization because of all the noise created by the buzz surrounding alternative selling channels, the rapid rise of business partners, the grand unknown of the Internet, the long-lived status quo in selling, and the rarity of top-tier executives or guru-authors that truly understand selling.

Today's sales force is shackled by a business model created in the 1950s which matured over the following three decades. The game has changed. There is extraordinary opportunity for improvement.

Chapter 3: The Vision

Semper Fortis is about having an elite selling force in the field, working as a precision team, bolstered by great leadership and coaching, well-supported by highly-motivated pre-sales and post-sales staff. The Semper Fortis formula extends beyond sales to many departments within the enterprise and has a goal of creating a pro-sales culture throughout the organization.

It is quite clear that products don't sell themselves. It is also clear that extraordinary sales professionals—even working in difficult conditions with dated products, less-than-comprehensive services, and little or no brand power—succeed every day, everywhere. Selling expertise, their "selling value-add," allows them to succeed.

The environment is getting much tougher. Competition is relentless: The number of competitors is increasing due to globalization, trends toward "general contract" service firms, and departmental or business process outsourcing. Customers are increasingly demanding, fueled by consolidation into mega-corporations and improved buying information transparency. The degree of differentiation between products and services has become quite small, product lifespan has been cut in half, and the boundaries between product lines from previously separate industries have blurred.

In this environment, the importance and need for sales competence and professionalism has dramatically increased. Few companies have recognized this reality, fewer still have kept pace, and almost none have seen the change as an opportunity to win market share from their competitors.

Semper Fortis is about tipping the balance of power toward your company. The goal is to have a team so focused, so well prepared, so efficient, that you go into the fourth quarter of most deals leading by five touchdowns, and are not exposed to "Hail-Mary passes" from competitors producing surprise lost deals.

The key words are “professional” and “team.” Today, many companies have a small smattering of “professional” salespeople, usually representing less than ten percent of the company's sales force. The rest are not professional—they do not have the daily discipline of planning, preparation, practice, research, follow-through, documentation, and so forth. These amateurs are “winging it” all the time. Talented amateurs have the ability to succeed from time to time by flying by the seat of their pants, and impromptu creativity is an important sales-*athleticism* quality, but the professionals do so only when left without other choices.

Most company sales forces are not teams; rather, they usually consist of a group of individualists, each doing his or her best Lone Ranger impression. Semper Fortis focuses on making the entire force a professional, well-oiled team.

As highlighted in *The Disciplines of Market Leaders*, market *leadership* is always achieved through superior focus on only one of three disciplines. Specifically, authors Treacy and Wiersema argue that all companies achieve market leadership by picking their discipline:

- customer intimacy,
- innovation, or
- operational efficiency and excellence,

and focusing on that one incessantly. I take this theory one step farther. I firmly believe that unless a company has a natural advantage in the innovation or efficiency arenas, customer intimacy is the one that most should focus on, because it is the most readily achievable through hard work and persistence. Furthermore, companies that have advantages and focus on the latter two areas have much to gain by improving their sales approach, even if customer intimacy is not their core discipline.

In my experience, most company executives agree. Many see their company as having its DNA already in the customer intimacy discipline. Yet few of these companies have focused on the development of a truly superior sales force, the primary interface to the customer that can form intimate relationships! There is one primary reason for this: top executives, having rarely served long, if at all, in the sales force and not having learned the intricacies of the selling trade, don't readily see the enormous potential.

Why aim to be anything but the best? To become the best, jump with both feet into the deep end and never accept the status quo.

The Semper Fortis strategy builds a dominant sales culture and sales force. In this book, I will outline how to make this radical change happen. I have no doubt that many companies can convert their sales minions into true professionals. To do that however, executives must have a clear vision of the future organization.

Semper Fortis sets goals with a vision beyond the present:

1. Build a dominant sales culture and indomitable winning tradition in your company.
2. Convert your salespeople into well-rounded business professionals.
3. Convert your sales force and supporting personnel into a seamless team that trusts one another.
4. Become the dominant sales team, by a wide margin, in your market segments.
5. Leverage your sales dominance to win all "close games," seizing share from your competitors.
6. Once established in a customer account, hold that ground with extraordinary tenacity.
7. Develop and maximize the profit potential of each customer with great urgency.
8. Continue building sales capabilities to ensure lasting competitive advantage in the field.

Semper Fortis will not succeed fully without buy-in and active participation above the top sales manager. Much sales success relies on a pro-sales culture in all departments.

Unless one can first envision the desired result, one cannot create the plan or achieve the goal.

The Semper Fortis Vision:

- Imagine a professional sales team with great salespeople, but with out anti-establishment Lone Rangers.

- Imagine a sales team in which salespeople help each other with brainstorming to help break through roadblocks during engagements, with pricing intelligence, with fresh knowledge about competitors' sales stories, and with practice and preparation assistance for key meetings.

- Imagine a sales team in which *every* salesperson plans account engagements and sales calls in a common sales system free of unnecessary steps and bureaucracy, practices his or her approaches, writes down the results, and learns from them with the help of active coaching.

- Imagine a sales team in which salespeople become true business men and women, negotiating contracts on behalf of their company that offer the best profit and value over a number of years, protecting profitability on behalf of shareholders, managing their expenses to ensure monies are well spent, and building an ever-growing franchise.

- Imagine a sales team, in which most field decisions are made by the salesperson, with non-invasive oversight by management, where the salesperson can ask for decision advice upstream but has final responsibility for decisions and outcome.

- Imagine a sales team that *documents* new information in near real time, and shares information, presentations, and proposals within a week regarding opportunities, product ideas, customer feedback, and competitive changes.

- Imagine a sales team empowered by great external intelligence gathering that identifies opportunities quickly, notices changes in competitor's methods or message, and routes thought-leadership material of interest to a specific customer or prospect efficiently.

- Imagine a sales team where members spend more than ninety percent of their time planning engagements, preparing for sales activities, or reaching out to prospects and clients, drawing on a small pool of specialists when help is required.

- Imagine a sales force that spends very little time "recreating the wheel" or chasing administrative detail, while professional support personnel supply pre-sales materials and another group of post-sales support resources ensure signed contracts flow as planned.

- Imagine a sales team that takes advantage of the unique skills each member has, with hunters hunting new accounts, developers developing iceberg accounts from a small landing success on its tip, farmers efficiently farming existing accounts that are already producing near capacity, and special forces helping to break log jams and launch new product initiatives.

- Imagine sales managers who see themselves as coaches and leaders who adapt their methods to the needs of each salesperson. Imagine specialty coaches who help with the development of specific skills such as planning, presenting, and interviewing.

- Imagine a sales team whose members exude pride and team spirit, believing themselves elite and unstoppable, no matter the challenge, with measurable results of winning a much greater percentage of sales opportunities than in years past.

- Imagine a team that is paid in direct proportion to net profit and profit quality and efficiency. If Julie delivered four million dollars in net profit this year, she can be sure that her take was twice that of George who managed but two million, except for minor adjustments for profit quality.

- Imagine a sales team in which the best-profit homerun hitters are very happy and well-paid, most team members are optimistic because they can see the potential of hitting home runs, and the few that are struggling have great urgency to improve or tend to leave of their own volition because of great disparities in pay found in this profit meritocracy environment.

- Imagine a team that is paid 30 to 50 percent above the industry average as a group, but produces 75 to 200 percent more profit than the industry average per person.

- Imagine a team where the turnover rate of the best salespeople on the team ranges from five percent to zero.

- Imagine a sales team that continues to seize market share from competitors every year.

- Imagine an organization that has an influential departmental sales liaison within every non-sales department, an organization that likes their sales force and looks forward to helping move sales forward whenever possible. Then imagine a sales force that is upbeat and optimistic, rarely complaining, always constructive.

- Imagine a team that rates as one of the most important reasons for their job satisfaction the fact that they feel themselves to be welcome and contributing members of an intimate team that exudes pride and camaraderie.

These visuals help one see the destination for the Semper Fortis enabled organization, the promised land for sales dominance in an environment that is becoming more demanding, one where sales offers perhaps the best opportunity for competitive advantage.

To many executives, this vision seems too good to be true, while to others, the vision can be a bit disconcerting. Empowering street-smart salespeople to make decisions, to manage for profit, and to build their own units can be a substantial departure from the norm. While there is considerable effort required, the end result is well worth the effort.

Chapter 4: The Brief

Eight core foundation pillars support a Semper Fortis Sales Olympian force. The eight pillars include:

I. Integrated Formula Selling
II. Sales Team Aligned with Shareholders
III. Right-Level Decision Making
IV. Pervasive Sales Intelligence
V. Comprehensive Logistics and Support
VI. Selling Readiness Operations
VII. Specialization of Sales Roles
VIII. Elite Sales Team Culture

The program requires the implementation of sixteen key initiatives to cement the eight pillars in place.

All eight pillars rely on each other. When all eight are fully ingrained, sparked by great leadership, the Semper Fortis force reaches a point of fusion, and a tradition of superior effort and winning begins to grow. It's the point where the sales force sees its destiny as a team. All executives start to see the potential, and the company suddenly believes it has the capability to become the best "customer-intimacy" selling firm in its industry.

As with any undertaking, there is up-front investment. But the benefits of building a tradition of seizing share and winning, and growing faster than the norm in an industry arena go well beyond traditional return on investment. On a hard-dollar basis, the additional investment is typically recovered within two or three years. However, investors will note that a trend toward faster growth of earnings, cash flow, and market share has an exponential effect on stock price. Semper Fortis can accelerate the growth curve, and ultimately, the potential return of investment from the shareholder's perspective is significantly higher than most any other capital expenditure on the docket today.

Each of the eight pillars is discussed in great detail in the eight sections of Part Two. Below is an overview.

Semper Fortis Foundation Pillar One

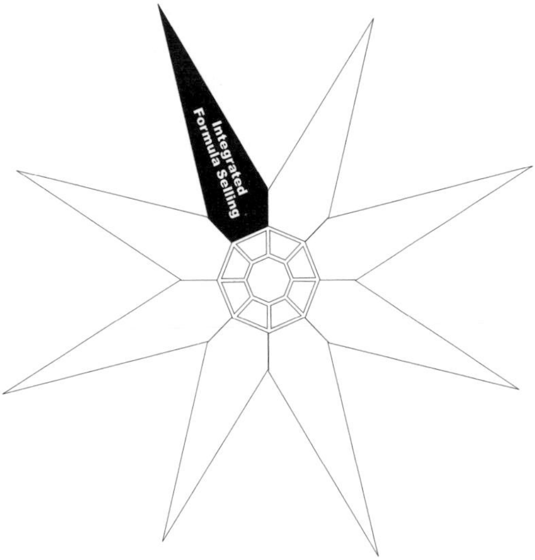

Integrated Formula Selling

Professional solution-selling follows a distinct formula for success. A popular misconception is that selling is a born trait or a black art. True consistent solution-selling success happens when a salesperson follows a proven formula.

Selling in complex political arenas, into the larger prospects, does not adapt well to the gift of gab. (A complete discussion of the selling process and formula is offered in Part Two, Section One).

Excellent training programs that stress the proven formulas exist for professional solution-selling. One of the best is offered by Miller Heiman. Miller Heiman's list of clients looks like the Who's Who of Fortune 1000 vendors. Yet, I find a large gap between the training received and the post-training adoption of the advanced process and planning methods into daily sales and sales management tasks.

Even though salespeople have breakthrough moments of clarity when planning on their own prospect accounts during strategic sales planning training, they immediately revert to their old "reactive" ways when returning to the field:

- The urgency conspiracy keeps piling on more e-mails and voice mails, often on post-sale topics like missing parts or delayed software, issues that should be, but are not, handled by project managers or administrative staff.
- Sales management does not demand that planning become a *daily* activity, a daily habit, after the training.
- Salespeople are not evaluated by how well they plan their activities.
- Demands for other reporting do not go away—the planning documents are quickly seen as additional administrative work.
- As with everything, every new habit meets subconscious resistance, as humans are set in their ways. Unless a person receives management reinforcement, and personal success reinforcement, over an extended length of time nature takes over and the path of least resistance stays the current course.
- Most salespeople are not given clear, concise assignments and a thorough understanding of management's expectations.

In the Semper Fortis force, every burden not related to selling is eliminated from the salesperson's agenda. Sales plans, within the company sales system, become the only required pre-sales documentation. Management uses this integrated system and process daily in all their coaching activity with their salespeople. Salespeople within six months of building the planning-and-writing-it-down habit realize it is a cornerstone of their own success formula and improved financial outlook. Management focuses on coaching salespeople on improving themselves and their approaches, helping move specific sales forward.

Of utmost importance when implementing any new "process" in any company is to only add steps that are well worth the time investment and ultimately deliver profit results to the company and commissions to the sales force. Management must stay vigilant and fight process-elegance creep that adds unnecessary work. Writing down one's plan, what is known about the various contacts, problems, internal politics, and competitors at a customer site is extremely helpful to the salesperson, and secondarily, to his coach. But forecasting profit by week or by month for the next two years is an exercise in futility and does not result in more business won. Keeping it simple, keeping it on target with "winning" deals and delivering results will keep the process helpful instead of a time-wasting burden.

Integration of a sales formula based on planning, preparation, and implementation of a streamlined, focused process within the sales force and sales management is Foundation Pillar One of the Semper Fortis model.

Please refer to Part Two, Section One for an expanded discussion of the proven formula for selling success in complex corporate solution environments, how to integrate management efforts with nimble processes, checklists for implementation, and the numerous benefits of the first Semper Fortis foundation pillar.

Semper Fortis Foundation Pillar Two

Sales Team Aligned with Shareholders

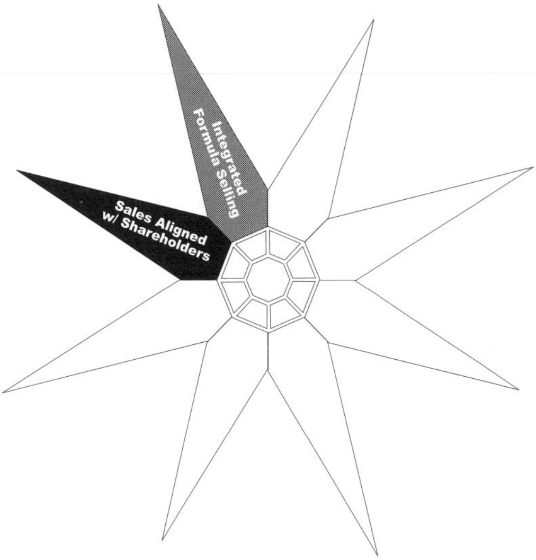

Well over 95 percent of companies use quota-based compensation for their salespeople. Yet quota systems have a large number of flaws which make them a poor choice for most companies that want to maximize sales productivity and salesperson cooperation with company objectives. They are also the key cause of poor morale within a sales force. These systems invariably favor underperforming reps while outstanding reps carry more of the burden for nearly the same compensation. At the heart of the issue is the law of large numbers—it is much easier to blow out your quota if your annual target is $1 million than if it is $10 million—and companies invariably pay bonus based on *percentage* of quota attainment.

The widespread use of quotas is tied to the extraordinary momentum and gravity of existing paradigms and the fact that few top executives focus their full attention on sales pay plan details or think "out of the box" regarding ways to improve. Quota systems have numerous Achilles' heels, and MBA financial analysts have created a complex labyrinth of modifiers to produce the desired results, none of which truly works well.

Management tries to overcome this shortcoming with directions from the top. All employees, and especially sales people, are highly rational and will always choose pay over management's directions. In the best case, sales management direction, shareholder desires, a clear mission from headquarters, and the sales pay plan are in perfect alignment. This never happens in the land of the revenue quota. "*Do as we say and not as we pay*" doesn't work. Ever.

Quotas serve as an earnings valve, trying to prevent a top producer from out-earning second-level management in a company. When the occasional salesperson does hit a home run, many companies adjust quota on the fly to prevent the earnings blowout, or bear down on the individual's quota the following year to average out the earnings.

Nothing is more damaging to morale. Nothing propels more salespeople to leave their companies than heavy-handed quota throttling of the best producers. What shareholder, if he or she thought about the problem for more than a few seconds, would endorse a policy that incites the best, most productive salespeople to leave the company?

The Semper Fortis strategy breaks this flawed thinking—in fact, Semper Fortis throws out the revenue quota system. By changing sales compensation to a model based on net profit, profit quality, profit efficiency, and teamwork, the Semper Fortis force is well aligned with the goals of shareholders and the company overall.

Top Dozen Problems with Quota Systems

Problems with quota systems abound:

1. The quota system favors underperforming reps.

2. Quotas cause gaping conflict-of-interest rifts between salespeople and managers.

3. Favoritism is unavoidable in quota assignment.

4. Quota is the root cause of morale issues in sales forces.

5. Quota parameters often incite poor business decisions in the field.

6. Reps are generally not incited to preserve profitability.

7. Quotas drive fire-sales, which in turn erode long-term profitability by training customers to expect them and ultimately lower the pricing bar.

8. Salespeople waste time and effort with pay plan loophole game play.

9. Data cloaking regarding details about customers makes knowledge capture difficult.

10. Data cloaking results in inaccurate forecasting.

11. Short timeframe deals are favored by reps.

12. Expense controls are weak or cause more audit and oversight work because the rep is not incited to make smart control decisions.

Top Dozen Benefits of Net Profit Compensation

There are numerous benefits to Semper Fortis' net profit / profit quality compensation model:

1. Sales representatives become converted into Customer Unit Business Executives (CUBEs, pronounced "Q-Bees"), learning to evaluate risk versus return and make prudent decisions, more than doubling a company's decision-making bandwidth, and adding nimbleness that highly centralized operations cannot match.

2. The front-line customer contact is aligned for the first time with executive management and shareholder desires for net profit and earnings growth.

3. By managing to the Profit and Loss Statement, CUBEs are empowered to add creative components to deals, often adding outside-the-enterprise pieces to improve a contract's profit.

4. CUBEs, who make many spending decisions, now care deeply about wise use of expenses.

5. CUBEs protect profitability and negotiate from their own company's side for the first time, playing a key role in pricing strategy.

6. CUBEs work hard to sign long-term, multi-year contracts, knowing that they will not be penalized for ongoing business in the following year's quota because there are no quotas.

7. It is in the CUBE's best interest to forecast accurately, ensuring resources are available to match business ramp-up.

8. Successful CUBEs stay in place, managing customer relationships for longer terms, rarely changing employers or territories.

9. CUBEs are empowered to build ever larger franchises.

10. Senior professionals have *field-based* career advancement options that do not compromise earnings.

11. Knowledge capture and management programs can succeed if human intelligence coordinators are added.

12. There is great unity of purpose between the sales CUBEs and management.

The chapters in Part Two, Section Two offer a complete discussion of how compensation changes can change the effectiveness, alignment, and loyalty of the sales force.

Semper Fortis Foundation Pillar Three

Right-Level Field Decision Making

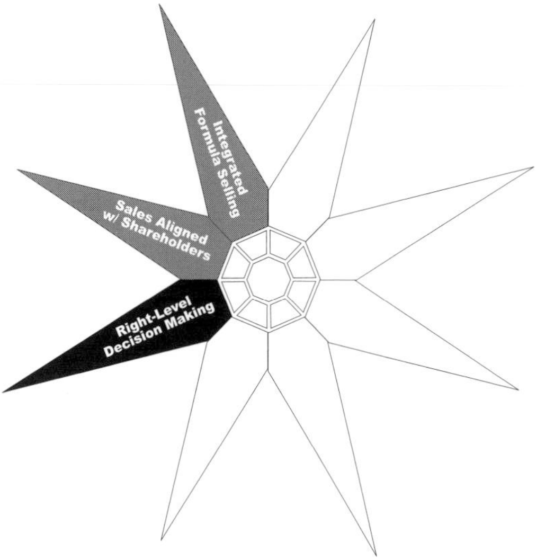

Once a company aligns its sales team with the shareholders via compensation for profit, enabling the sales force to make profitable decisions on the front lines is a must.

No one is in a better position to understand what price and terms will work on a specific deal than the salespeople in the contests. Yet within companies that use revenue quotas, the system sets the salesperson up to negotiate the profit away! The salesperson does whatever is necessary to minimize the risk of losing the deal, which immediately translates to getting the client the lowest possible price. The quota system makes the salespeople agents of the customers, negotiating with considerable insider knowledge of the operations.

In my seven years selling IBM products as a premier business partner, I was never refused "special pricing considerations," gaining superior discounts for my customers and prospects. The IBM sales teams fully endorsed all my special bids, in fact, helping obtain great depth of information from the customers to bolster the case. The pricers at headquarters, without any intimacy regarding the customer, could not refuse a well-developed, well-argued case. I am still astounded that companies feel that centralized, far-removed pricing is smart. Experience after experience illustrated that the sales force in a "revenue and quota is king" system, will negotiate on behalf of the customer better than the customer contacts could themselves.

Many executives unnecessarily fear distributed decision making. There is little to fear because people tend to be very scrappy when their own reputation, career, and, especially, bonus, is on the line.

The Semper Fortis model calls for "right-level" decision making. The person with the closest contact with customers should have the most input on pricing. Region and area leadership are the right levels for resource allocation and support decisions, division leadership is the right level for mission-level decisions, and executive leadership is the right level for strategic ones. Care must be taken that someone who has never made a certain decision does not go alone without advice and oversight.

The financial ramifications of a decision are excellent parameters to parse decisions into tiers. While the salesperson, or in our terminology, the CUBE (Customer Unit Business Executive) is always responsible for a pricing decision, additional concurrence could be required when a deal surpasses a certain dollar amount per year. In this case, the first-line manager, called the sales director in the Semper Fortis model, would also accept full responsibility for a decision. If a deal reaches truly substantial size, yet one more level of leadership may be tapped for concurrence.

Setting up Profit and Loss (P&L) accounting by customer account and by CUBE is critical in making good decisions. Many companies claim they cannot do this because of financial infrastructure shortcomings. I disagree and believe that this is just a case of analysis-and-accuracy paralysis. This system can start out using approximations (for example, creating an internal "cost" on software products that is not actual but estimated) and then transition to real cost in the longer run if the company wants to maximize competitiveness and manage its overall operation efficiently. A firmly stated cost to the CUBE is his or her cost to make decisions, whether true or estimated. However, if costs remain estimated over a number of years, the danger is that approximate cost allows "cost centers" like R&D to inflate costs to the field to retain more profit themselves, increasing their budgets and increasing expenses in the longer run.

Semper Fortis sets up a system of advisors and mentors, allowing, even enticing, CUBEs to bounce their plans off management, other CUBEs, and financial analysts within the company. In many ways, it becomes a microcosm of how a VP of Operations makes decisions. Instead of going to the CFO for advice, the salesperson has an assigned financial analyst. And if that analyst needs to bounce the situation off other financial experts, he or she has a chain of mentors and advisors as well.

On the spending side, the person who pulls the trigger on an expense should also have the final say on how wise it is. By setting up salespeople as businesspeople with P&Ls and income statements to manage, final responsibility for wins or losses, and significant personal pay effect based on how wisely expenses are used, the company gains experience, hands-on understanding, decision-making bandwidth, and in the long run, better control. A manager's role in expenses is reduced to setting guidelines and spot-checking adherence to those guidelines.

This aspect of Semper Fortis will spark entrepreneurship, ownership, and thinking out of the box. Just by basing assessments of sales success on individual P&L statements, sales forces gain the ability to partner with third parties for parts of solutions, innovating new approaches to customer problems. Thoughts like "it's not my job..." and "CYA" go right out the door. Earning profits becomes job one. In many ways, P&L at the account and salesperson levels simplifies and liberates, spurting dormant forces and ideas into furious action. CUBEs are encouraged to grow team members within their unit as long as the business risk is prudent. In the longer run, CUBEs can build their franchises into very substantial, highly-profitable operations without needing promotions by headquarters.

Every salesperson will develop these "overall businessperson" skills at a different pace. The firm is converting the salesperson into a complete, well-rounded franchise business owner. Coaching, adapted to each CUBE's needs by first-line management, is important. Semper Fortis puts a premium on the coaching aspects of management, where sales directors adapt to the individual needs of each employee while serving as leaders of the group, not enforcers of top-down heavy-handed control.

In Part Two, Section Three, we will discuss right-level distributed decision making in great detail and take a look at how a company can and should employ a system of checks and balances to ensure that smart decisions are being made.

Semper Fortis Foundation Pillar Four

Pervasive Sales Intelligence

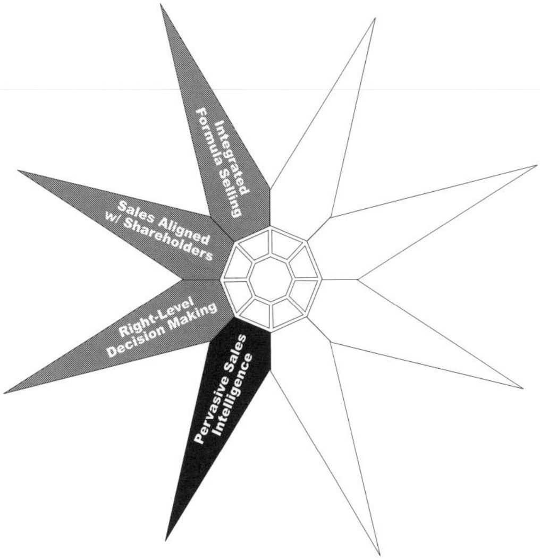

Every company with a substantial sales force has an enormous amount of intelligence about its clients and prospects in the heads of the salespeople but little of it is ever written down, organized, developed, or leveraged.

One of the problems, even to the salesperson who has this store of data in his or her head is that the picture is usually fuzzy. Salespeople are not encouraged and taught how to develop the information, rarely are there systematic checklists of information that should be gathered, there are no processes of distilling and checking data accuracy, and often, there is no effective system for recording it into a database.

Today's trend is toward implementing customer relationship management systems for sales forces, claiming the benefit of capturing this information. Salespeople are street-smart: if compensation is under a quota system (and 95+ percent are), the customer relationship management systems will capture *some* information to keep management at bay, but not the crown jewels, the really important items that make or break sales and relationships.

An evil of quota systems is that quotas provide strong motives not to share client data candidly, because that data is invariably used against the salesperson in the critical-to-compensation quota setting process.

Once Pillar Two (Alignment with Shareholders) and Pillar Three (Right-Level Decision Making) are in place, information is free to flow internally; however, it does not necessarily start flowing on its own. The typical personality characteristics of salespeople do not help with the meticulous task of documentation, so asking them to input everything into the new Oracle sales application is rather fruitless and results in the minimum-to-get-by effort. Therefore, even though the information is ready to flow, human "pumping stations" must be established for at least a few years to start the momentum. In my experience, the benefits and return on investment of having a dedicated intelligence team justify having a permanent intelligence operation, even if it is small.

Semper Fortis sets up a highly motivated Sales Intelligence Group (SIG) to work closely with sales front line management and extract internal information via conversations and frequent, short documentation sessions, categorizing and indexing the data within a corporate intranet system. This same team gets chartered with gathering external information after internal information indexing is well underway.

Certain elements are critical to success:

- The SIG must be anchored by accomplished and respected sales professionals, able to talk the talk and be admired by the field associates.
- The SIG gathering starts with an in-depth territory review, in which each salesperson presents to management his or her own personal state-of-the-union.
- The SIG must have a very proactive round-robin polling schedule to ensure that telephone conversations (too much is lost on e-mail) are short, frequent, and fun, versus long and painful.
- SIG specialists must understand the business issues as well as the best salespeople do, to discern which tidbits are truly important and which tidbits are parts of the background noise.

- SIG specialists must have the ability to document at a rapid pace, usually via prolific administrative assistance.
- The SIG must proactively help in sales situations, setting up a quid pro quo relationship with sales teams.
- The SIG must have budget and computer gurus who enable great gathering and routing of external information.
- SIG specialists must spend quite a bit of time in the field, not only for gathering but to provide help during key customer engagement moments, a key to building relationships with the CUBEs.
- The SIG will also be in a position to spot signs of trouble, such as the imminent departure of a key CUBE, oftentimes better than the CUBE's first-line manager.
- The SIG serves as the guardian of knowledge, keeping track of who is requesting what, looking for signs of trouble as well. SIG information, at least the information rated "sensitive" or above, must always go through a human handler and not just the corporate intranet site.

In sales, the strongest of weapons is better information—about products, prospects, opportunities, competition, industry trends, proposals, and customer concerns. While many companies have lots of investment in sales bodies, few take arming them seriously. Intelligence is the best armament.

Often, a small percentage improvement in net margin pays for the overhead of a SIG department, yet having a SIG usually enables much larger margin and share gains. The hardest part is tracking the hard dollar impact of the SIG. Though it is difficult to place a hard dollar figure on the SIG role, a great soft benefit is having a well-prepared and confident sales team, one that the customer respects for consisting of true professionals. I believe companies should not overanalyze obvious things. If it is clear that SIG is paying for itself by the end of year two, trying to figure out how well seems pointless.

The Semper Fortis company is smarter and more situationally aware than its competitors. Most important, information access has little delay because communications flow quickly via the central SIG clearinghouse. As a result, the Semper Fortis company is an agile organization that listens to and recognizes customer trends, adjusting approaches quickly according to new demands and opportunities.

The SIG can also play an offensive role in helping a company win, but there are serious questions that executives must ponder before launching such an initiative. Warfare and sports both offer many lessons regarding the effectiveness of *disinformation* strategies, where the combatants try to handicap each other with carefully orchestrated leaks.

I advise against such maneuvers, as the potential backlash from customers against what can easily be seen as “questionable corporate ethics” is far too damaging when compared to the possible gains. The SIG, however, must stay vigilant, given that other companies may try such clandestine attacks, and have plans in place to prevent damage to ongoing sales efforts.

Part Two, Section Four discusses the state-of-the-art SIG initiative at a Semper Fortis company, with human operators at the helm. The SIG is a key in building an agile company, with great situational awareness. First-line sales managers play an important role in the SIG scheme, as they are the first line of debrief, alerting the SIG to developing situations.

Semper Fortis Foundation Pillar Five

Comprehensive Logistics & Support

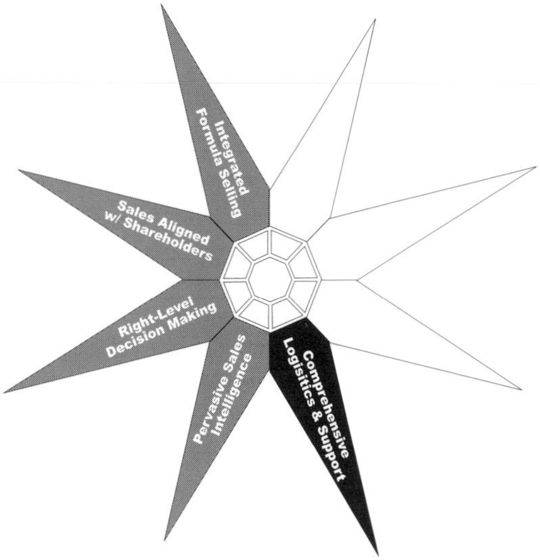

During times of war, the primary mission of the supply and leadership organizations of the military is to ensure that the fighters on the front lines have everything needed to win, to keep morale high, and to have reinforcements ready, if needed, at key battlefields.

Companies are at war with their competitors all the time. Yet, nearly all companies operate as polar opposites to the military model. Headquarters often operates as though field employees exist to serve its needs, and HQ doesn't exist to serve the needs of the field personnel in the contests at the "customer" front lines. This HQ hierarchy may have been effective before the power shifted from seller to buyer, but it is now a whole new ballgame.

The Semper Fortis model strives to achieve a balance. Under Semper Fortis, there are two organization charts, the traditional CEO on down hierarchy for strategic planning and theater-level decision making and adjustments and another upside-down one for winning tactical sales contests. This chart shows how the hierarchy is reversed when a sales effort is underway, with the CUBE and the customer placed at the top.

> **Helpful hint:**
> It helps understanding to review the organization model in Appendix A

The field represents the priorities of the customer and all other functions must stand ready to help however possible, while staying within the company's strategic plan.

Headquarters continues to drive the strategy for new markets, new products, acquisitions, and more. However, when the company is engaged in a sales contest at any particular customer account, the CUBE calls the shots and counts on the company's resources to back him or her up as needed to win the contract.

Semper Fortis places the management and control of account-level administrative support in the hands of the first-line manager, the sales director. Support personnel have centralized "dotted-line" reporting to coordinators at HQ, but serving the customer needs and keeping the logistical details off the CUBE's shoulders is job one.

Field pre-sales support also reports to the sales directors. Additionally, organizations like marketing and centralized sales support coordinate with the Sales Intelligence Group to ensure the company is never wasting time reinventing the wheel. The sales director focuses on keeping support and supply humming while the sales CUBEs focus on job one: winning more business.

Part Two, Section Five offers a complete discussion of how a Semper Fortis company supports CUBEs with comprehensive logistics, keeping the administrative detail out of the salesperson's hands so that he or she can use his or her time to build the business.

Semper Fortis Foundation Pillar Six

Selling Readiness Operations

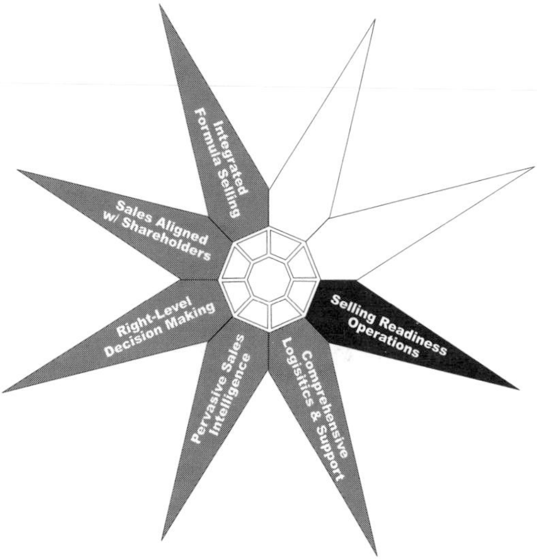

Failure to plan, prepare, and practice is the recipe for failure. Nowhere does corporate America fall farther off the mark in regards to the Semper Fortis best practices.

The sales forces of the Fortune 1000 generally do not plan, prepare, or practice much at all. Surprisingly, most sales forces are considered successful, as success has been *redefined* as proposal win rates at or below 33% on average. These are losing records, achieved by continuous improvisation. It is not surprising, however, that companies do win deals: When every salesperson at every company competing for a given deal fails to plan, prepare, and practice, they all are equally matched. This is, in fact, one of the most important components of the opportunity seized by the Semper Fortis formula.

Typically, planning in most sales organizations occurs once per six months to once per year, usually coinciding with official territory reviews. Upper management drives this trend—they worry about the "sales plan" for the year early in the fiscal year, driving the first review, and then they worry about closing the year out with a strong fourth quarter, which drives a second review during or at the end of the third quarter.

Salespeople naturally know that better planning and prep work would help their sales achievement, but many managers focus on covering more opportunities with less bodies tends to ingrain a belief in a "quantity is better than quality" success formula, which is a fallacy: calling on more customers, superficially, versus calling on fewer customers but more in-depth, to earn more business, is wrong.

Chase two rabbits and they will both escape.

– ancient proverb

A further complication is the continuous addition of non-sales work, like reporting and administrivia, to the job of the sales force. Salespeople wind up not planning and preparing because they are simply out of time.

Because no one in management heads off the supreme confidence that many salespeople have, the ever-confident, ever-improvisational salesperson decides that he or she will win deals without preparation.

A Semper Fortis sales force wins most of the deals it competes for, as it competes for deals that are a good or great fit for the firm's capabilities using a sales approach that is carefully thought out.

When a Semper Fortis team engages, it's like matching an Iraqi army platoon, trained to fire rifles and not much else, against the flawless teamwork of a US Navy SEALs special forces unit, empowered with much better intelligence and communication. The SEAL unit plans, prepares, practices, debriefs, prepares, practices over and over, hundreds of hours for each hour of hostile action. The Semper Fortis sales team rarely loses based on who "sold" better.

In corporate America, one finds little coaching. Most front-line management tries to keep troops moving at a high rate of activity while sometimes lubricating the wheels of bureaucracy. Yet when one looks at examples offered by world-class championship sports teams, coaching is paramount to a team's success. Champion sports teams, just like elite military units, plan, prepare, and practice constantly, for many more hours than they spend in actual contests. Coaches rotate from reviewing fundamentals, to strength training, to drilling plays, to reviewing scouting intelligence and game video, to developing special plays for certain situations, to counseling players to ensure their heads are on straight for the tests ahead.

It has often been said that a good coach's job is basically done *before* the game begins. Yet looking at corporate America, the only "practice" the troops get is during game time, when winning or losing really counts. There is no structured debrief, no preparation, no practice, and no lessons learned, at least not quickly or across the organization. If doctors used the Fortune 500's sales methods, they would have many more dead patients.

The Fortune 500 settle, thinking a specific salesperson's 30% proposal win average is good when in fact it's a losing record. The MBA analysts have a poorly conceived fix—call on more prospects faster—which results in a relentless treadmill that delivers shoddier and shoddier sales work.

Planning and Preparation is the Lifeblood of Semper Fortis Selling

A Semper Fortis company makes planning the life-blood of management. All management processes are based on a daily, continuous planning system, as found in Foundation Pillar One. The Semper Fortis company relieves all non-sales activity from the salespeople through an accurate and comprehensive support logistics structure, found in Pillar Five. This is turn opens up time for continuous practice, coaching, debriefing, planning, and preparation, driven by first-line sales directors, who spend more than half of their time in their "coaching" role.

The chapters of Part Two, Section Six discuss fully the importance of planning, preparation, and practice, and the need to employ these elements daily and not just once every six months.

Semper Fortis Foundation Pillar Seven

Specialization of Sales Roles

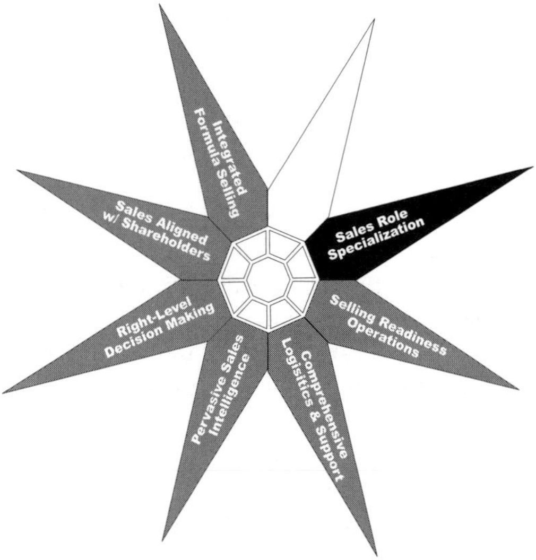

<u>Classified Ad:</u>

XYZ Company Looking to Hire Salesperson!

Our salespeople are all categorized as one type of salesperson; therefore, chances of a long and rewarding career with XYZ are maximized if the new hire can accomplish every one of the following roles in the top tenth percentile of all salespeople in the industry.

- Be an accomplished hunter,
- Be an accomplished major account developer,
- Be an accomplished farmer / guardian,
- Be an accomplished financial analyst,
- Be an accomplished and innovative thought-leader,
- Be an accomplished problem-solving consultant,
- Be an accomplished executive peer to “C” level contacts,
- Be an accomplished project manager,
- Be an accomplished detail-oriented administrator,
- Be an accomplished magnetic personality relationship-builder.

Other Important Notes Regarding the Position at XYZ:

The ability to develop all your own marketing materials is a plus. Territories are typically composed of 20 key major prospects plus 40 or so, smaller enterprises; therefore, personal time management skills are critical. Lastly, XYZ provides little formal training so a self-starter that can learn on-the-job, is required.

The list goes on.

Sounds a bit crazy, doesn't it? The really crazy part is that this list is descriptive of more than half of the sales positions in the Fortune 1000.

Yes, there are a select few individuals who can excel in most of these categories simultaneously, but only a truly select and unusual few. Yet *most companies* classify all salespeople the same way, pay them on the same sales plan, which always has a bias toward rewarding one type of effort, and expect them to transition from excellence in one type of sales work to another in a moment's notice.

Under Semper Fortis, there is specialization that is rooted in common sense. Few genuine thought-leaders can develop thought-leadership material if they spend 96.7% of their time chasing project details on a complex installation schedule. Semper Fortis recognizes that certain skills are rarer than others, pays bonuses differently for different types of work, and constantly re-evaluates the skills of the salespeople on the force. Hunters hunt for new customers, while developers grow the business at existing ones, and farmers harvest sites where the vendor is deeply entrenched. While all are necessary, many companies lose sight of the fact that of the three, the relatively less-glamorous farming role is actually the greatest profit contributor by a significant margin.

Specialties get targeted coaching and training, not unlike football where there are assistant coaches for offense, defense, quarterbacks, defensive backs, running backs, offense line and more. Salespeople get certifications in specialties and specific practice and preparation that are unique to a specialty. This is very helpful in reminding first-line management to prepare coaching for each individual instead of going with a "one-size-fits-all" model.

Semper Fortis builds a special forces group that offers key assistance at critical times during sales campaigns. Complex solution specialists, executive ambassadors, thought-leadership consultants, and more are available to help the CUBE win over prospects.

Specialization also helps support the final Pillar of Semper Fortis—unrelenting teamwork. All specialties work together to maximize the yield from a territory, and often work together on the overlaps, of which there are usually plenty.

Part Two, Section Seven is a complete discussion of why a sales team with specialization and special force operators makes great sense.

Implementing Semper Fortis on a Tight Budget

Semper Fortis can be implemented on a tight budget. Throughout the book, suggestions for such an implementation will be noted in sidebars.

While the nature of sales makes it difficult to track the precise dollar impact of certain types of activities, the commander-in-chief of sales must pay attention to the big picture and track which facets are financially justified through improved sales force competitiveness and new wins.

While some of the facets of the model may start out as part-time duties for existing managers, in the longer run, I feel strongly that all of the functions found within the Semper Fortis model will grow into full-time positions, even in relatively small organizations.

Semper Fortis Foundation Pillar Eight

Teamwork Is Job One—Elite Sales Team Culture

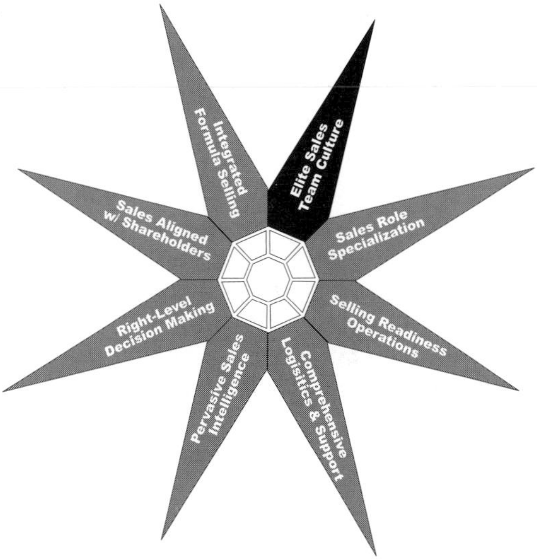

Many corporations have given lip service to teamwork but few companies have created a culture of truly gung-ho teamwork, especially within the sales force. More often than not, team-based bonuses have caused as much harm as good.

With most team pay approaches, the top producers feel that they are suddenly in a socialistic corporate society, where their individual superhuman effort and performance is not adequately rewarded. Conversely, slackers wind up earning undeserved bonuses on the tailwind of a good team, causing many performing team members to be frustrated.

Rarer yet is a company where sales teams well with other departments to win new sales.

Semper Fortis approaches teamwork through culture, focusing on recognition and opportunity management. Compensation components exist in the plan, but only as last-ditch negative reinforcement measures and psychological deterrents, never as key components of mainstream achievement. This allows top profit producers to still make top bonuses, slackers to remain unhappy, and teaming bonuses to be discretionary and unexpected.

While culture starts at the very top of the company, an organization must still be “sold” on the value of teamwork. In the first year of the effort to change the culture, feedback must be clear and precise. Salespeople who are not willing to accept the new culture will find that they may not get quite as much “team” support as others who play ball. While the company is careful not to affect customer activity, the uncooperative salesperson’s life can become more difficult quickly. There are various escalations that help illustrate a company's resolve. Ultimately, one or more hot shot Lone Rangers, even (perhaps especially) if they are top producers, may have to be publicly called out for lack of teamwork. This may or may not mean firing a salesperson, but it could certainly mean the reduction of territory opportunity and other financially painful measures. Hitting the wallet is a great attention-getter!

Nowhere is the requirement of teamwork more paramount than in the military. Unfortunately, all too many professional sport programs are seduced by the “top gun” player and wind up exhibiting less teamwork and more one-man showmanship. But in the military, lack of teamwork gets people killed, so expert sharpshooters don't get the “get out of teamwork jail free” pass that the Deion Sanders's of the NFL count on.

Part Two, Section Eight explores the various tactics within the Semper Fortis model to forge a culture of extraordinary teamwork within the sales ranks, and between sales and other departments like R&D, product marketing, product management, customer service and support, and others.

Achieving Fusion

Sparking and Sustaining Fusion: Fair, Crystal-Clear Leadership

Semper Fortis offers a clear, repeatable strategy to convert a company's sales force into an extraordinary asset that enjoys competitive advantage over others in a market segment.

The vision is clear. Highly trained, highly motivated Sales Olympians engage key customers and prospects, building relationships, winning trust and confidence, and seizing share from competitors. Once in, customer ground is carefully held.

None of this is possible without clear, focused leadership. There is a tremendous difference between management and leadership. Imagine a large group of firefighters, battling a hungry forest fire. Managers are in the middle of the effort, directing operations as the crew cuts down trees and plows land to build a new firebreak, keeping machinery running and chain saws sharp, as specially-converted cargo airplanes dump thousands of gallons of water on the area with each pass. The leader, however, is one who climbs the tallest mountain, senses a shift in the wind, and radios the managers to scramble the group to the next mesa north to prevent a new breakout as the blaze changes direction.

Perhaps another way to look at is that many company presidents see their role as piloting the airplane instead of designing it. At least fifty percent of their effort must be on design for the company to continue to blossom once size and scope grow past the abilities of the current team. As the "airplane" design changes, the executives must also focus on implementing new, forward-looking measurements to ensure that the company stays on course and performs beyond expectations.

Warfare, no matter if corporate or military or team sport, requires leaders. Semper Fortis converts the salespeople into CUBEs or Customer Unit Business Executives—a model in which they can develop and grow as leaders themselves. This responsibility greatly diminishes the need for traditional managers, but increases the need for respected leaders. It also permits a flatter organization, as first-line sales directors tend to wield considerable influence and authority without requiring upstream approval.

Implementation of Semper Fortis requires doing a number of things differently, starting with a belief in teamwork, an openness not normally found among corporate workers, a tradition of best effort, winning, and helping one's comrade, a culture of planning, practice, preparation, coaching, and trust within sales and within the entire company. This environment will not flourish in the Petri dish of corporate politics, double-talk, backstabbing, and office secrets. Leadership must be crystal clear regarding expectations, corrections of behavior, and decisions, striving for unbiased fairness. Leadership must instill a sense of complete commitment, reverence for the front-line fighter, a belief that failure is not an option. Leaders must lead by example.

Upper management must not only support and endorse the initiative but they must also be willing to see the sales executive in a key tactical decision-making role, coordinating support and resources as the ultimate decision maker on customer front-lines. As salespeople are converted into CUBEs, they will ask and rely on leadership / management for opinions and advice, ultimately seeing themselves as franchise owners and micro-empire builders, wholly responsible for success and failure in their world.

The key link in the chain of leadership is the first-line manager, the sales director. Close enough to the action to make an immediate impact, yet experienced enough to command attention from upper management when reinforcements or special tactics are needed in a particular engagement, these platoon leaders form the core of the team, splitting their time between teaching and coaching and "directing the daily operations" of the base.

The Semper Fortis model, with its eight foundation pillars and sixteen base implementation facets (covered in great detail in the sections of Part Two) will not achieve fusion by skipping any one area. For example, excellent intelligence simply does not happen while keeping salespeople on a revenue quota system. The final component, the catalyst of the entire program, fusion leadership, is perhaps needed the most.

This book outlines the basics to achieve competitive advantage "fusion." I fully anticipate progressive companies will eventually add their own innovations to the model, giving themselves unique advantages. The one thing so true about this ever-accelerating, ever-changing business world is that standing still is as good as being dead.

Many companies will not have the will to pull off Semper Fortis. But then, many companies do not have the will to do what it takes to achieve leadership in their market segment either.

Opportunities are usually disguised as hard work,
so most people don't recognize them.

- Ann Landers

Semper Fortis in many ways is a race for dominance. I believe a gung-ho firm can make great progress in one year, achieve cultural fusion in two years, and start harvesting the fruits of its program in earnest within three years.

Part Two

~ ~ ~ ~ ~ ~ ~ ~ ~

Detailed Discussion

"The journey of a thousand miles begins with one step."
- Lao-Tzu

Section One

~ ~ ~ ~ ~ ~ ~ ~ ~

Integrated Formula Selling

Successful selling in complex corporate arenas follows a distinct process and is not the black art many imagine. Professional salespeople are taught, not born.

To achieve true success, management must align all work around the defined process and a company's process must be fine-tuned to perfection, something few firms do today.

"The pessimist sees difficulty in every opportunity.
The optimist sees the opportunity in every difficulty."
- Winston Churchill

Chapter 5: Understanding the Professional's Selling Process

Professional selling is perhaps one of the most misunderstood occupations by those outside its ranks. Even among those who have served for some time in sales, many can be found who have not fully grasped the formula that makes a truly successful and certified professional salesperson, just as many people have played chess and even won a number of matches, without seeing more than just a few moves ahead.

So that there would be no confusion, a proven, "certified professional" salesperson has succeeded in winning *multiple* large-scale projects with *multiple* product lines and services, within *multiple* geographic territories, while often working for *multiple* companies and *multiple* managers. The professional is realistic and aware of the process and subtleties of selling. When asked about succeeding in sales, the professional immediately discusses his or her personal process and formula that he or she has repeated from one engagement to the next.

While it may be possible that there are truly learned salespeople who have experienced selling in just one territory, until they have repeated the success of their process, there remains a question of proven certification. There are many cases where the successful salesperson has been unconscious of the distinct process steps, and loses his or her way when faced with new situations and adversity.

Many people, including a great number of salespeople, believe that selling ability is a genetic trait, often referring to a positive, outgoing personality or outspoken leadership as evidence. This is no more true than saying that being blessed with a 36" vertical leaping ability immediately makes one a great basketball player or having 4.3 second speed in the 40 yard dash instantly makes one a great football receiver. While genetic hang-time or lightning quickness helps, a multitude of skills must come together to make it in the NBA or the NFL. I can't remember the last time I saw Olympic class high-jumpers signing megabuck contracts with the L.A. Lakers.

Most top-tier executives within the Fortune 1000 did not work in the sales force. Most of the ones who did serve, did so only briefly, many times starting in regional management to "get some experience in the field." Many executives, therefore, perceive the sales force as almost renegade gladiators with genetic traits of survival, persuasion, and greed, focused on "what's in it for me," not concerned about the nuances of the company's vision. While this isn't the only reason so few salespeople rise through the ranks to the top-tiers, these perceptions do close some doors on the road to the top, making it harder, and therefore, rarer to find a ten-year sales veteran in the top ring. Most do not rise beyond VP of Sales and Marketing, a position often found on second tier of the corporate hierarchy.

The gladiators do exist, and in fact dominate the landscape, but these one-man-shows exist as a *result* of the system they work within. The current dark-age sales system was created by the executives of companies many decades ago and it has changed little as it has slowly evolved into its current state.

We will soon discuss how to convert the sales force of one-man-show gladiators into highly-coordinated and elite teams that can achieve and maintain competitive advantage for decades. But first, it is crucially important to set the record straight:

Consistent, multi-year, multi-territory, multi-product success in professional selling comes from learning and executing a clear process, not inheriting the gift of gab.

It can be taught. It can be learned. Certain genetic traits might make the transformation quicker and easier, just as great vertical leap helps one rebound in basketball, but, many people with focus, dedication, and commitment can become professional salespeople, just as Kevin McHale of the Boston Celtics and Bill Laimbeer of the Detroit Pistons proved that skill, dedication, and a formula can even overcome poor leaping traits in the NBA.

The intricacy of the sales process is directly aligned with the nature of the company and the products a salesperson represents. The sales spectrum covers a broad range of intricacy.

At its simplest, a salesperson can represent one commodity at a one-commodity company, where all sales flow through a single purchasing decision maker at the prospect company. That's not to say selling in this environment is simple or easy. One-path selling can be extremely difficult, but follows a different success path from the complex solution selling environment discussed here.

At its most intricate, the salesperson can represent a company like IBM Global Services, for example, bidding for a ten-year outsourcing agreement of a prospect company's entire Information Services department. Such opportunities often encompass taking over personnel, anticipating service levels, measurements, and reporting requirements, assuming and operating existing data centers and processes, integrating new and existing product platforms from IBM and from third parties, creating highly detailed financial models, while anticipating and forecasting future needs. In such a sale, hundreds of players must be touched and there are often more than a dozen key decision makers with several dozen recommenders and influencers.

The Semper Fortis strategy leans toward addressing the more intricate end of selling. The delineation concerns whether or not a sale involves the complex politics of many people serving as decision makers, recommenders, and influencers on the buying side.

The more intricate a sales environment is, the greater the contribution by the salespeople in terms of winning and losing. Many executives have a misconception that deep, indulgent, feature-full products sell themselves. Even a single product with these attributes becomes more complex to sell because prospects rarely have the time to spend hours learning the details of an offering. Integration of any product, even a relatively simple one, is often a daunting task. Apple's Newton, which was years ahead of the Palm Pilot, is an example of a complex, highly-capable product that required too much effort, too much learning to sell via retailer shelves. The Palm Pilot sold on sheer simplicity.

Consistent success in selling comes down to following a proven process. True artistry and professionalism in selling is achieved when the steps become second nature: the salesperson reads the tea leaves and can adjust the process to finely match the progress of the sale, not missing fundamental important steps while little time and effort is wasted on the way to a successful win / win (both the seller and buyer get a good deal) transaction. Win / win selling is crucial if a company wants to build a long-term supplier relationship with the buyer.

The Professional's Selling Process

I will briefly describe the professional's selling process. Understanding the right way to sell is a crucial building block in understanding the Semper Fortis formula, as the first step of Semper Fortis is to integrate world-class process into the daily workflow.

At a high-level, the steps in the process start long before the first sales call on a new prospect.

> For greater detail on the professional selling process, see link at www.SeizingShare.com/process

Step 1: Defining Great-Match prospect profiles for your company.

Certain environments and types of prospects are a better match with the selling company's products and services than others. Defining Great-Match profiles helps the sales force know what key clues to look for to spot the crème-de-la-crème opportunities in each territory. They are not always the largest.

Step 2: Finding prospects that fit your Great-Match profiles.

Once you know what a great match for your products and capabilities is, smart, efficient territory intelligence gathering and analysis helps speed the organization in building a sales-radar opportunity screen, ranking prospects by suspected potential.

Step 3: Gather pre-approach intelligence about the prospect, specific executives, and specific initiatives at the targeted company.

By learning as much as possible about a company and its executives before the approach, the sales professional improves his or her chances of making the right contact and positive first-impression, building credibility.

Step 4: Opening calls, as high in the organization structure as feasible.

The goals of the first sales calls are the following:

- Gather clues that will bring the components of Great-Match, opportunity validity, and opportunity size into clearer focus.
- Build credibility for the salesperson and the vendor company.
- Understand the problems and challenges most on the mind of key executives at the company.
- Gather clues regarding other opportunities that may exist but have not been anticipated.
- Start establishing lasting relationships with one or more high-ranking company executives, preferably in operations and finance.
- Position the vendor as a consultant with custom solutions, not a one-product seller. This is accomplished by not leading with product information, but rather, thoughtful questions.

Step 5: Building credibility as "consultative" beacon of light: Conduct interviews full of well-prepared questions and concentrated listening while introducing your company in general terms, steering clear of specific solutions whenever possible.

Each meeting must build the credibility momentum and never waste a contact's valuable time. Questions designed to check credibility perceptions should be asked often, as well as questions that are designed to build credibility.

The sales professional must have excellent knowledge of the industry and competitive offerings. A salesperson with awareness of only his or her own company loses a tremendous amount of consultative positioning in the eyes of contacts.

Step 6: Expand contacts at prospect accounts, forging each relationship with same principles of credibility building and intelligence gathering.

A successful professional will leverage his or her executive contact to be introduced in a highly-positive (consultative) light to a number of important influencers and recommenders within the prospect organization, while not losing the connection with the top-tier executive.

By asking well-prepared questions, the salesperson flushes out the problem-to-be-solved, as well as the politics that may influence success or failure of a proposed solution.

Step 7: Develop special "coaches" within the organization.

Few intricate sales are manageable without a tremendous amount of time investment unless special pro-vendor contacts can be developed into true coaches.

Coaches must have the following qualities:

- Good political operators.
- Broad informal connections throughout the organization (an ear to the ground).
- A desire for change and improvement while they stay in the background and (usually) don't require (much) fame in the effort.
- A good understanding of the problems.
- A sense of history at the company.
- A preference for your solution and company.
- An unbiased, realistic lens through which they see the situation.

The situational awareness of a vendor's internal coach can either improve or diminish the odds of success significantly.

Step 8: Form initial sale hypothesis and develop tactical plans to prove or disprove it without jeopardizing other possible opportunities.

Throughout the first half of the engagement, a hypothesis forms regarding what problem can be tackled in what way, by what combination of products and services. As soon as confidence reaches a high level through several rounds of verification, it is important to specify the sales hypothesis in written form. This hypothesis not only includes the solution but also discusses how to best position against competition, how to best justify the budget, how to highlight the urgency of the project, and how to deliver the positive vote of all key influencers, recommenders and decision maker.

Step 9: Personal meetings to see if hypothesis holds water—deliver thought-leadership, build credibility momentum, steer questions to test and flesh-out sales hypothesis.

During this stage, the sales team starts outlining the vendor's view of the problem to be solved and their solution vision to key players. It will be important to gently test and adjust the solution based on feedback. As a secondary goal, the salesperson should begin watering the seeds of urgency.

Step 10: Internally adjust hypothesis and form a clear plan for the sales effort.

After the fine-tuning is complete, the sales team defines the clear steps to get from point A to point B and win approval of the project. The missing link is usually a hard data financial justification of the project.

Step 11: Present the hypothesis and going for a "close" to get an official survey approved.

The sales team, with a solid definition of the problem and solution, goes for the first important hard-stop win: the green light to conduct a detailed "survey" of field operations under the sponsorship of a key executive, specifically to gather detailed data elements to build a financial justification model.

A common mistake is to conduct a survey too early in the process. The dangers lie in not having built relationships and intelligence with some of the key influencers and recommenders, becoming too focused on the "perceived" problem and missing other, often political, factors. Without a good "lay of the land" and without establishing credibility, the sales team is then faced with presenting findings from an unfocused survey effort in the field.

Step 12: Bring in more / specialized troops to help with the survey effort.

Before any first sale, it is difficult to show organizational competence in action. The "survey" offers a golden moment to bring in "wow" operational troops. Up to this point, much of the impression regarding the vendor is formed only through interactions with the salesperson. The prospect will be hungry to see if your company is as good as the "demo."

Step 13: Internally develop the proposal / presentation, including specifics regarding the problem, solution, justification, and "*why we are the best vendor to accomplish the project.*"

The sales professional spearheads the development of the written proposal and accompanying presentation, in customer-ready form. The team then practices presenting the material in a complete "customer-level" simulation, to a small group of experienced salespeople and technicians that have no knowledge of the project, as well as the first-line sales director who has read all the debrief documentation and can simulate some understanding the problem and financials of the situation.

Step 14: Educate and soft-sell the proposed solution to the problem one-on-one with key contacts, using special care to continue to ask questions to validate the sales theory on personal wins, business wins, and political wins associated for each.

A successful team wants to limit exposure to a hard "no" answer at the end of the big meeting or, for that matter, at any time in the process. The best way to anticipate issues is to test sell or preview the now razor-sharp proposal, first with allies and coaches, then with key influencers, then with key recommenders, and finally with the decision maker before arranging the "big pitch meeting." At each meeting, the sales team targets winning the contact's commitment to support the proposal, while finding out if there is anything else that could make the person's support truly enthusiastic.

Step 15: Create perfect meeting atmosphere for the final presentation and decision moment.

Once the personal soft sell phase is complete, many sales require a "big meeting" to bring the effort to a decision. A limited window of time exists to call the big meeting, when allies are enthused, when the problem is defined and urgent, when other projects are not dominating the "thought-share," and when many of the potential enemies have been neutralized.

Step 16: Once the vendor receives the green light, a rapid deployment plan must be set into motion immediately.

Many "in the bank" sales have been lost because the winning vendor hasn't put the implementation on the fast track. Buyer's remorse and last ditch efforts by displaced incumbent vendors and other losing competitors are always dangers.

Selling Process can be Taught

For those who thrive in the depths of the complex selling environments, it is clear that consistent selling success starts with process.

Most of the skills required to succeed are teachable. In reality, extraordinary sales professionals come in all shapes, sizes, and varying degrees of outgoingness. There are five common, almost genetic traits that are difficult to teach, yet allow certain individuals to outsell their counterparts:

- High personal integrity.
- Initiative.
- The willingness and dedication to follow a proven process.
- Logical problem solving.
- Emotional intelligence, listening well, empathy, and being a quick, accurate "reader" of people.

Virtually everything else, including planning, forming, and asking excellent questions; listening and learning well; asking questions that walk the prospect down a path toward urgency, a decision, and ultimately, implementation; intelligence gathering; credibility building, problem analysis; networking; and basic communication skills *are all teachable items.*

Within a range of tolerance, the "outgoing personality" trait many people think marks a good salesperson does not make a dramatic impact on the proven process for solution selling success. Note that the stereotype of glib entertainer is not well represented on this list of needed skills. Slickness and entertainment can help once in a while, but often hurt the sale, especially in the critically important task of building credibility and trust. Many prospects tire of the ever-talking entertainer who often does not focus on listening and problem-solving value-add.

The purpose of this book is not to deliver a dissertation on the processes of strategic selling; however, executives must understand what makes salespeople professionals versus amateurs. Most of the salespeople in the world, no matter where they work, remain amateurs. For those readers who want more depth on the basics for solution / consultative selling success, I would suggest reading *Strategic Selling* by professional sales training firm Miller Heiman for a more complete discussion of the process aspects of professional selling.

We have discussed the basic process in its easiest terms: one opportunity at one prospect account. In future chapters, I will address one of the most important roles of first- and second-level sales management: Coaching, management, coordination, and balance of first-line and backup presales resources across many ongoing opportunities and engagements become a symphony of scarcity. Too small an allocation of resources at one sales contest becomes a total waste, as the sales effort is starved and the opportunity withers. Too many resources and too much effort deployed at another is also a waste, hopefully ensuring a win at that one sale, but perhaps at the price of not competing for another that could have been successfully engaged.

Professional sales activity at one complex account is political chess. Successful selling across a great number of large corporation prospects is three-dimensional, multi-level political chess with not quite enough pieces to win every contest, or even the majority of the front-line sales contests at the same time. When one starts digging into the specifics of many sales forces, often one finds pockets of sales strength and weakness, a possible sign that sales management is too focused on "control" and not on strategy and tactics.

In Summary…

Sales professionals follow a well-defined process to achieve repeatable success, no matter which company or which product or services offering they represent.

Contrary to popular misconception, sales professionals are not born—almost all the necessary skills can be taught. One of the reasons that this fact is not always recognized is that many of those in the profession, as well as many of the managers driving the sales force forward, do not understand what it truly takes to be a professional. Many salespeople remain amateurs even though they have spent decades in the sales ranks.

Chapter 6: Integrating Process and Management

Many companies in the Fortune 1000 train their sales forces on the professional selling process. More than $500 million is spent annually on sales training. While most of this amount targets entry-level block-and-tackling sales skills for the newly hired, a considerable portion is invested in strategic sales planning process training. Yet extraordinarily few companies put this proven formula for success into their daily activities and management operations. Most of the advanced training money might as well be thrown into a fireplace.

Salespeople often have breakthrough moments of clarity during the advanced training sessions, as they typically develop selling plans for one of their current opportunities. They suddenly see that they are missing key pieces of intelligence or relationships, they understand that they have not completed all the steps with several important contacts, they find new ways to bring in other resources from their company to mend relationships that got off to a rocky start, and much more.

Sales managers generally understand that process focused on planning is key to strategic selling success, yet few have insisted that the process be linked into the daily management of the sales force.

Unfortunately, the formula rarely makes the transition from the classroom to the field. The value of the advanced training is lost because it is not put to use. When the salesperson returns to the territory, he or she quickly finds that management still has all the same reporting demands, all the "urgency" noise of phone calls, conference calls, meetings, and e-mails fill the day, and managers do not appreciate or require daily, weekly, or even monthly planning. Continuous planning is definitely not added to the salesperson's personal evaluation criteria.

Falling back into the same habits of old is not only easy, but nearly everything around the salesperson is pulling him or her back to reactive selling habits. Salespeople are much like any other type of employee. Unless the organization makes it a priority to implement new methods of operation, the path of least resistance will prevail.

Interestingly, most salespeople interviewed in the first months after strategic selling process training will admit that planning their sales and doing the "homework" would lead to improved success. But given that it would take a year to see the fruits of the process, and that most sales cycles in this complex sphere of selling are long, they default to the path of least resistance.

Old habits die hard.
And daily urgencies and noise conspire against doing things "right."

Today, many companies wait to train salespeople on process-based solution selling until they have a minimum of three to five years of field experience. Some of the more senior players see the value and take the initiative to apply the advanced techniques to their activities. These companies have found that advanced sales process training does not strike home with new salespeople, as they are struggling with the basics and can't see the value of following a stringent process in their first years because the two—process and management—are disconnected.

Humans are habitual. Learning new habits requires breaking old ones. Rarely are individuals so driven and self-aware that they learn and apply what they know if it goes against the grain of the rest of the organization. Unfortunately, the more senior the salesperson is, the more he or she tends to be set in his or her ways. Without a focused effort by management to change daily sales activities, old habits, like improvisation at meetings and throughout an engagement, die hard.

The Semper Fortis strategy demands integration of the strategic selling planning process with all management activity, reporting, training, and evaluation.

Today, the daily interaction between management and the sales force at most companies resembles a fundamentally flawed golf swing. Imagine a golfer who stands too far off the ball, has a poor grip, Zorros his back swing like Indiana Jones's whip, dips his shoulder a bit while the club head travels from outside back in and across the poor unsuspecting Titlest, and does not finish on the follow-through. When the professional selling process becomes the only formalized management formula, when required reporting only concerns itself with winning more business, and when salespeople are supported by the rest of the company so that most of their time can be spent selling, planning sales, researching, or practicing, it's as if the golfer suddenly inherits Tiger Woods's stroke: effortless, accurate, consistent and too long for most casual golfers to imagine.

In a Semper Fortis organization, process training does not wait until salespeople are seasoned enough to see the value; rather, the process is embodied in everything a salesperson does, everything a sales manager does—and the process becomes second nature to all.

Salespeople should be focused on their primary directive: selling. Over and over when I talk to salespeople in technology and elsewhere, I hear that nearly all of them spend less than half—and sometimes as little as a third—of their time on activities directly related to gaining more business.

Where is the time going? Admino-noise. Chasing missed shipments, configuring repetitive orders, following up on software development progress or lack thereof, producing activity reports, filing expense statements, sitting in on internal conference calls, auditing commission statements, forecasting future sales, and filling out reports for everyone from marketing to finance are the activities that dominate most salespeople's days.

First-line management is not focused on selling for the majority of their time, either. More reports, more forecasts, a great number of internal calls and meetings, control activities and other things keep the sales manager out of view of the salespeople and the customers.

More important, first-line management is typically placed in a difficult fence-straddling position, caught between serving the desires of upper management and the need to exceed their sales productivity goals with their team of salespeople. Most sales managers tend to side with their superiors and an endless number of reporting requests, as siding with the needs of salespeople rarely results in a skyrocketing career, and if anything, more often torpedoes one's upward progress.

In most organizations, first-line sales managers have few reasons to rock the boat.

First-line managers have little reason to change. Just as salespeople are not evaluated by their strategic planning prowess, neither are their managers. Managers' pay packages are usually tied closely to following upper management's initiatives, with a greater component of bonus tied to qualitative versus quantitative measures as compared to those of salespeople.

As discussed throughout Part One, upper management generally does not have an in-depth understanding of the sales function. It's no great surprise that the majority of headquarters' requests have little to do with information integral to selling more product or service.

Integration of Process and Workflow

Semper Fortis changes everything. Not only do well-designed processes become the focus of the sales force, they become the primary basis for management. Process is taught from day one, not just in the classroom but on a daily basis by managers, mentors, and peers.

Management's centerpiece of a process-based system is a comprehensive, usually computerized opportunity management system.

Prospective sales opportunities are put in the system, and the system guides salespeople through completing the required process steps, fleshing out buying interrelationships, identifying influencers and recommenders on projects, documenting possible roadblocks and issues, and so forth. First-line management uses the system as the basis for all understanding, questioning, coaching, and providing additional resources for the salespeople on various opportunities. Upper management uses the opportunity management system for all consolidated views of the enterprise's prospects and customers.

The better systems on the market allow a great number of reports to be generated from an opportunity management system, often providing much of the data the financial types are seeking. Information rolls up from a district, to a region, regions roll up to areas, and areas up to country views. Upper management enjoys the ability to "see" the big picture, while retaining the option of drilling into the detail when required.

In the last decade, a new breed of software applications that include opportunity management have emerged, led by Seibel Systems. Seibel continues to enjoy the greatest breadth of state-of-the-art components in the various areas of customer relationship management (often referred to as CRM) software, but other key players are striving to close the lead, including Oracle, SAP, Peoplesoft, and other newer vendors.

The difference between excellent implementations and poor ones always comes down to the data deemed important by management. For the sales force to succeed, and for sales management to support and motivate the troops, the system must focus on the data that helps a salesperson understand his or her positioning and win sales. In a Semper Fortis world, the system focuses on:

- Profiles of key contacts (and related information gathering),
- Inter-relationships between decision makers, recommenders, and influencers at the prospect,
- Inter-relationships between various projects, some already sold and some being sold, at a client company,

- Information regarding business motivators by company, functional area, department, and key contact,
- Information regarding personal motivators by company, functional area, department, and key contact,
- Each contact's personal perceptions of reality,
- Return of investment survey and analysis data,
- Roadblocks preventing success, and more.

Good or poor implementations can be had using the exact same vendor's software. The design is often flexible, allowing the wrong influences, such as finance rocket scientists or operations executives, to design the system to better accommodate their wants and desires, while making the system miss the mark of helping salespeople and sales managers succeed.

Let me be clear. An enterprise does not necessarily need state-of-the-art software. The software by itself doesn't make best practices opportunity management happen, it only makes it easier and more comprehensive. Without a doubt, formalized software makes it exponentially easier to accomplish roll-ups of data to the commander-in-chief of sales as the sales organization gets larger. But I have seen great complex sales process integration using pen and paper worksheets and relatively simple Microsoft Excel spreadsheets. The key is to align process, management, data collection, and reporting to show salespeople the light—follow the formula and find a path to an earlier retirement and that 42-foot sailboat moored in the Caymans.

In all, the benefits of investing in software focused on the organized documentation of the selling process, capture of sales information, and an accessible pervasive awareness of who within the company is talking to whom at the customer company about what far outweigh the cost of the implementation. The complexity is increasing daily, and every year lost makes the job harder to wrestle to the ground later.

With the goal of salesperson effectiveness at the fore, management focuses on documenting only what is necessary, only what truly helps the salesperson's success, and concentrates on eliminating all "busy" work for other departments or sometimes, for reports that no one really uses anymore. There must be continuous questioning to contain "process documentation elegance creep" as corporate America tends to favor too much analysis. As long as the salesperson's goals remain paramount, integration of management and sales process produces a great impact on the bottom-line results of the corporation.

In Summary...

While many firms recognize that professionalism in selling starts with teaching and following a well-defined selling formula, few companies ensure that managers manage their troops to the process.

Putting CRM systems in place can help, as they simplify consolidation of sales and customer data. So can eliminating all the reporting requirements and other time consuming work that have little to do with landing more business. However, these initiatives will not accomplish the ultimate goal until first-line managers insist that all work activity, all reporting, and all conversation stays in perfect alignment with the company's defined sales processes.

By the end of this book, we will have built the Semper Fortis model in its entirety. We have now added the first of sixteen facets that attach to the eight Pillars of the model that was outlined in Part One:

The Semper Fortis Model, including Facet 1 of 16:

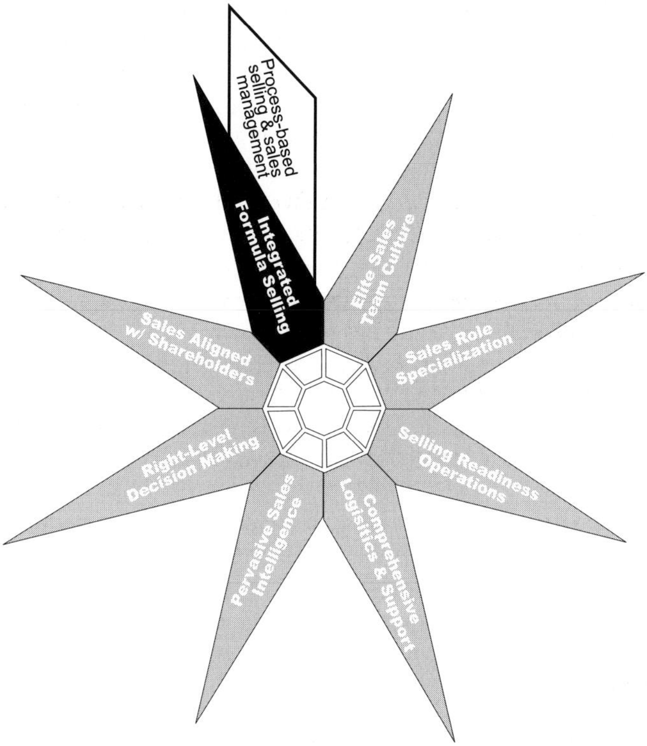

Chapter 7: Recruiting and Keeping Professionals

Companies often forget that the quality of individuals matters a lot. In certain “knowledge-based” professions, such as software development, executive leadership, or professional selling, the difference in recruiting an “A” player versus a “C” player can be dramatic – the “A” players often deliver twice, three times, or even ten times the business impact of a “C” player. If Rochester Software has all “C” players on their sales force while Buffalo Software has all “A” players on theirs, my bet will always go with Buffalo, even if Rochester might have a better approach and methodology. The quality of players is that important.

Any company committed to seizing share with a Semper Fortis approach will quickly gravitate toward recruiting and retaining the best possible candidates for field positions. Typically in the complex major account selling environment, one additional sales win per year easily pays for a 30% cost premium associated with top rung talent.

The caveat is that Semper Fortis is a system that, in addition to focusing on success, concentrates on adhering to a professional process and whole-hearted teamwork among peers. Lone Ranger hotshots who do not participate as helpful team members have no place in the system. Yet, in today's status quo of the sales universe, salespeople do not typically appreciate the value of teamwork and process.

Recruiting “A” Players That Fit

Semper Fortis thrives on an indomitable, winning-by-formula, disciplined professional culture. The younger and less experienced the new hire, the more likely he or she is to accept the culture. The more experience a new hire has, the more likely that he or she will have habits and baggage that must be overcome. With the former, the company suffers through “basic training” delays, while with the latter, a lot of effort and attention must be paid in the first year to ensure that expectations are crystal clear and that the new hire becomes indoctrinated in the Semper Fortis discipline.

Of the two, both have pluses and minuses, but more success is typically seen with experienced hires. They tend to bring a plethora of ideas and thoughts from previous experiences that make the entire whole stronger. In my experience, the best bet is to hire those with the most "upside"—true "A" players—even if the molding sometimes takes a bit longer before they are completely indoctrinated in the Semper Fortis disciplines.

In Semper Fortis, the sales organization has one or more dedicated recruiting and retention specialists who focus on this crucial human resources objective. On the recruitment side, the specialists must accomplish a number of objectives:

- Begin explaining the culture and the tremendous potential of working in a true meritocracy, long before extending an offer,
- Evaluate the willingness and level of ability of the recruit to follow logic and process,
- Ascertain the willingness and level of ability of the recruit to work in a generous teamwork manner,
- Determine each recruit's personal drive for excellence and desire to become an "A" player in the field,
- Clearly communicate that the recruit will fail quickly if they are unwilling to learn the Semper Fortis formula,
- Narrow the field to the best players with the right characteristics for the gung-ho, yet disciplined Semper Fortis culture,
- Research the best candidates more thoroughly than other companies do, and then
- Hand pre-qualified recruits to experienced sales people on their recruiting "tour-of-duty" for a second opinion and ultimately, a full-court "sell" on working for your company.

When it comes to successful recruitment, corporations have so much to learn from college athletics and the U.S. military, especially the U.S. Marine Corps. When a prospective Marine meets with recruiters, he or she is meeting with model soldiers, individuals with the extraordinary experience, bearing, and confidence who inspire the recruit to want to become one of them.

In corporations, recruiting is typically run by lower or mid-tier human resources (HR) specialists for most, if not all, of the engagement. During the first interviews, the recruit rarely talks to a salesperson or sales manager, and never sees a top gun. HR specialists, no matter how good they are at HR, are generally not looked up to by prospective salespeople, and the HR person in turn, doesn't necessarily appreciate the good, the bad, and the ugly of sales personality traits either.

With recruitment run by "non-sales," new hires tend to follow stereotyped images of what makes a good salesperson, those entertainer traits that may not be best in the long run.

Conversely, the best recruits tend to have more employment options than the mediocre ones and are harder to land. They look to the quality of the people they meet, and the quality and care of the recruitment process, as clues to whether or not your company would be the best choice for them.

In a Semper Fortis organization, the best salespeople and sales managers pull short-duration assignments in the recruiting effort. Recruiting teams are pulled together, thoroughly and professionally briefed, re-emphasizing the importance of recruiting the best and putting the company's best foot forward, and models are developed to help weed out characteristics that do not work well in the environment.

In the upcoming Section Seven, we will discuss that there is no such thing as a one-size-or-type-fits-all salesperson. Different traits and skills are needed for the different roles found within sales: hunters, developers, farmers, and specialists. Recruiting must be done with an eye toward identifying how the recruit would naturally fit in one or more of the areas, making sure to balance this assessment with the needs the company is anticipating in the next few years. Not unlike selling prospective customers, "best-fit" models are developed, helping the recruiter spot diamonds-in-the-rough within the group.

By using successful salespeople in the recruiting process, the Semper Fortis company has a much greater ability to pre-sell the recruit on the value of joining, on the cultural differences (for example, teamwork), and on the attitude, the tradition of success, and the reputation of the firm. Peers are often quick to spot troubling clues that may indicate a recruit is not all that he or she has claimed to be.

Once a recruit is targeted, the organization must show special attention and empathy to land him or her. Unlike the well-known efforts of leading consultancies to land Ivy League MBAs, recruiting of salespeople, even top-notch candidates, tends to be casual and at a distance. Any company that makes it the norm to spend a bit more effort, to try a little harder, to show great courtesy, to pay attention to details, can easily move up to a top candidate in the mind of the recruit. Little things make a big difference. Examples include a phone call from the CEO or president of the firm, joining a senior executive for lunch, a genuinely entertaining golf outing (many are not), or a visit to headquarters to meet some key managers.

Above all, the professionalism of the interview process sends a clear message as well. A prospective employee looks to the subtle details in forming his or her opinion about the firm, not just the interview itself.

The importance of your company's reputation cannot be overstated in helping recruit the best personnel.

One of the most important assets of a company is a reputation for providing a great training ground and work environment for the best salespeople. If a company can position itself as the corporate sales force equivalent of the U.S. Navy's "Top Gun" aviator program, recruiting the best "A" player salespeople becomes so much easier.

In Chapter One, I discussed the extraordinary success certain athletic programs such as Miami, Nebraska, Florida State, Notre Dame, and others have in NCAA Division I-A football. Recruitment plays a large role to ensure that each of these teams is filled to capacity with "A" players. The players who make the team and the starting lineup know that they have a better chance of making it in professional football than they would have had they attended Northwest Texas State. While I don't mean to belittle the proactive scouting and recruiting efforts of these schools, I don't think any one of them would deny the value of sterling reputations when signing sought-after recruits.

Corporations can also learn from athletics in the realm of scouting. Most companies today cast a wide net into the sea and then select the best few candidates who happen to swim into the net. There is little organized activity to identify and target potential star-quality recruits. Semper Fortis tasks the recruiting and retention specialists to identify stars through continuous polling of sales reps, sales managers, executives, and customers regarding sharp salespeople from other firms. Then, the firm proactively contacts such professionals to find out if any have an interest in making a change.

Lastly, while a number of companies have the goal to attract "A" players, Semper Fortis has additional requirements. The most successful players must have characteristics of genuine whole-hearted teamwork, superior logic that enables them to be consultative problem-solvers and to flourish in a process-based environment that fuses logic, emotional intelligence, and creativity into a rarified art form.

Retention Is More Important than Recruiting

Frederick F. Reichheld, author of the bestseller *Loyalty Effect* and a director at consulting house Bain and Company, argues that productivity gains between competitors are closely linked to employee turnover. Many companies in the U.S. have turnover rates near 20% per year, resulting in a nearly complete turnover and wash-out of knowledge workers and their knowledge and experience every five to ten years.

Considering the long ramp-up time for a professional salesperson in a complex environment, and the rarity of finding a top one-percent performer, the cost of losing an experienced top gun is often more than a decade of salary and bonus expense. Most top guns outperform the average salesperson by triple, and typically lead the pack in terms of creative selling solutions that can propel overall organization productivity in the future.

Yet few companies focus on near-zero defection of the top half of their force. They should; it is well-worth the effort. The same is true for the value of the top half of customers.

There are three key issues in retention, especially in retention of top-echelon professionals, which many companies choose to not face. First, employees must trust that their leaders have their best interests at heart. Trust takes years to build and one event to lose. The leaders must have unwavering personal integrity. Second, they must see, feel, and taste the meritocracy. The environment has to be fair and must offer everyone an opportunity to take the bull by the horns and strive to become the best. The best talent, the great producers, the idea guys with genuine commercial impact, should greatly out-earn the weakest, making more than they would at any of the company's competitors by a generous margin. In the same vein, the best must have promotion opportunities and challenges worthy of their talent. Lastly, retention starts with highly selective recruiting and a whole-hearted, highly orchestrated indoctrination into the corporate culture and values immediately after starting employment.

Semper Fortis makes retention an active concern and process within the sales force. One of the key steps is to clearly identify the best sales professionals, not just in terms of current and historical sales results but in qualitative perspectives as well. Sales directors submit a candid ranking and review of their direct reports every six months. Area vice-presidents do the same with their sales directors and so forth. Within a region of sales professionals, the manager ranks each one every six months from the strongest to the weakest and writes a one-page discussion regarding each person's ability and potential, as well as the advice he or she has been given to improve their ranking.

The company then makes it a *proactive* priority to not lose personnel who are consistently in the upper half of the population. Unexpected awards and bonuses are awarded, heart-to-heart sessions are scheduled with executive mentors, recruiting and retention specialists look for warning signs that a top gun might be losing interest, and sales directors are incited to keep their fingers on the pulse of their areas and especially on the top pros. By making retention a monitored program with distinct goals, everyone keeps their eyes open, spotting issues when they are small, and heading off departures long before the issues become serious festering wounds.

Planned Upgrade of the Force

The U.S. Armed Forces have a healthy view of keeping the weak out of the game. Using a well-known "moving up or moving out" plan, soldiers that do not have the willingness to improve, to expand responsibility, to grow, are pushed into civilian life.

Under Semper Fortis, salespeople who consistently rate below average are systematically warned of their low ranking status and coached on ways that they can improve their outlook with the company. Depending on the availability of fresh, high-potential candidates and resourcing levels needed, the company designs turnover targets to match, rarely falling below 5%. Salespeople who do not show significant improvement within six months of falling to the bottom rung of the qualitative warning system are reviewed for account reassignment, even if they are producing numerically, transferred to another sales director under a two-strikes-and-you-are-out guideline, or simply let go for lack of willingness to change.

While it may sound a bit harsh, the willingness to reward those who excel and shed the ones who bring down the professionalism and the production averages of the group sends a loud and clear message to all. Be a professional, deliver results, be enthusiastic about the company and your work, and you will be noticed and recognized, your financial fortune will swell, and money, time, and resources will not be wasted, at least not for long, on underperforming members of the team. Over time, the "strong survive and prosper" program helps bring up the quality and average of the entire force.

A word of caution—for this program to succeed and not become a source of discouragement, everyone must be briefed and must understand the necessity of such a system to drive a true meritocracy. As long as favoritism is avoided at all costs, the best employees will become enthused, the worst will start interviewing, and that's just what makes a good company great.

The final area that truly helps with retention is recognition and access. Semper Fortis targets "recognition" well beyond the norm of plaques for the wall. Important recognition for top producers means being acknowledged as important contributors to the health of the company by the executives and being celebrated in front of their peers. Yet often, a top 5% profit contributor hasn't met any of the executives in his or her firm, nor had any of his or her ideas listened to and put into effect. People must be treated as though they are the spark plugs that make the whole machine run. When people feel they are seen as key ingredients and not as replaceable, faceless employee numbers, they will be much more successful and loyal over their careers.

A proactive retention program is possible with only one or two dedicated recruiting and retention specialists, as much of the work is coordinated with first-line managers. By having these few dedicated specialists, the company can keep a continuing focus year in and year out. The specialists work in conjunction with local management to monitor developing situations, spot early warning signs, and react quickly to head off a separation event. Additional information regarding recognition is found in the upcoming Section Eight.

In Summary…

Few items make as large an impact on an organization as fielding "A" players in all customer-facing roles. In the Semper Fortis model, the firm is focused on proactively scouting and recruiting top candidates, much as professional athletic teams search for the best college, high-school, and overseas talent.

Simultaneously, the company places a priority on keeping the most talented sales professionals on-board and happy, while facilitating a healthy turnover rate of employees that rank near the bottom of the sales force.

We have now added the second of sixteen facets that attach to the eight pillars of the model that was outlined in Part One.

Semper Fortis Model, including Facet 2 of 16:

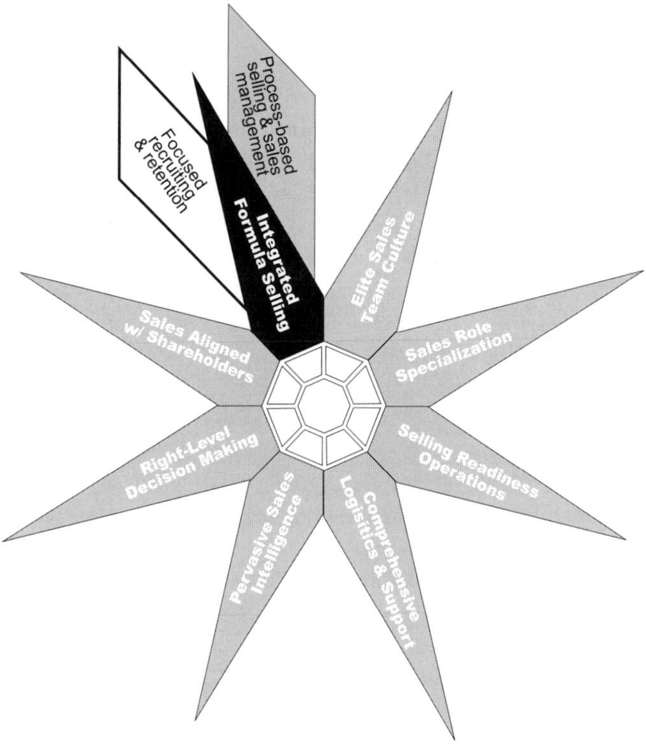

Section Two

~ ~ ~ ~ ~ ~ ~ ~ ~ ~

Sales Aligned with Shareholders

There has been much discussion in recent years about the importance of aligning senior executives' interests with that of the shareholders.

For all the same reasons, and because the sales professional is the single most important contact in negotiations with the customer, companies must align the sales force's interests with the shareholders as well.

"Singleness of purpose is one of the chief essentials for success in life, no matter what may be one's aim."
- John D. Rockefeller

Chapter 8: Aligning Salespeople with Shareholders

What do shareholders want? In its simplest form, shareholders want appreciation and total returns that meet or exceed their minimum acceptable return in relation to risk. However, the factors that drive market pricing of any particular equity investment at any particular moment in time can be quite complex.

Fair, rational pricing for a stock tends to work itself out over a long-term (ten or more years) trend but prices tend to fluctuate above and below the trend line, influenced by investor perceptions. Paraphrasing investor Warren Buffet, "*In the short run, the stock market is a voting or popularity machine, but in the long run, it is a weighing machine.*"

But what is the primary item weighed? Even though other elements may become fashionable from time to time, earnings remain king. Keeping the longer-term "weighing" dynamic in mind, the value of a company is primarily driven by five improving (or degrading) factors:

- earnings (and dividends) per share,
- revenue per share,
- cash flow per share,
- tangible book value per share, and
- the safety/risk of the company.

Shareholders ultimately benefit the most from increasing earnings. The sales force is arguably the second most powerful group after the top-tier of executives in making a large impact on net profit, which directly affects earnings. Salespeople are at the forefront of every customer interaction and contract negotiation. When they are aligned with shareholder desires, they seek to maximize profitability, reduce risk, increase contract life spans, and minimize expenses.

Yet few—very few—companies align sales professionals with shareholder goals.

> A great number of intertwined factors lead to equity appreciation complications.
>
> For an in-depth look at shareholder concerns and the need for better corporate measurement than current GAAP accounting, please download my brief at www.SeizingShare.com/sh

Today, most companies strive to align only the top managers with shareholders, usually by linking bonus potential of their top executives to stock valuation metrics. The simplest and most common way is to award options that only gain worth if the stock appreciates past a certain point. There are numerous difficult issues with options, given volatile stock prices, the emotions of the market in the short-term, adjustments to option prices based on market activity, and new rules under consideration by the government that may change accounting treatment for option expenses. Even so, any link between equity appreciation and employee bonuses is seen as a positive by most investors.

While executive bonuses are often linked to stock appreciation, salespeople are rarely incited to make smart business decisions from a shareholder perspective.

Making the Next Logical Step

Due to the existing, deeply entrenched but flawed pay plan paradigms, most large corporate sales forces are not aligned with shareholder goals and desires. Semper Fortis changes that. In my model, salespeople are offered greater compensation for great profitability, lower expenses, and longer-term contracts. Under Semper Fortis, the sales force is empowered to have a much greater impact on the ultimate value of the company.

In Chapter 8, I discussed the importance of keeping top salespeople in the sales force longer. One of the most important factors in their decision to stay or go is how they are compensated. In business, people are all too rational and a company's pay plan is a critical spot where the rubber hits the road. Even though the overwhelming majority of companies use quotas—and specifically revenue quotas—as the basis of sales compensation, it is the wrong model if one wants to build a dominant Semper Fortis force.

Quota Systems Have Too Many Achilles' Heels

All executives agree that a company is much better off if its top sales performers are happy and satisfied in their jobs while the poor performers are less than satisfied. Yet most companies use revenue-based quota as their sales compensation system, a paradigm with many flaws, most often favoring the underperforming salespeople rather than the overachievers.

As you will soon see, systems based on revenue quota models favor the lower quota salespeople, who deliver less business, profit, and value for their company. The law of large numbers makes it easier to attain 250% of a $3 million objective rather than a $20 million objective, yet most companies compensate based on *percentage* of quota. Often, a company's best salespeople watch others with one tenth their business volume earn more and/or receive more recognition, leading to morale and retention problems.

Quota systems can work, but to succeed, management must set objectives that are consistent and highly accurate in relation to individual territory potential. In practice, many real-world dynamics conspire to make this mission nearly impossible.

Only in rare circumstances are the markets so transparent that quota setting becomes highly accurate. Sales managers at Schindler, one of the largest elevator and escalator companies in the world, enjoy this kind of anomaly, as industry contractor bidding systems permit excellent visibility of all major construction projects in all metropolitan markets well in advance of bidding deadlines.

Assigning quota in perfect synchronization with individual territory potential is a financial Rubik's Cube.

Because the salesperson is the closest link to the customer, most companies use a bottom-up process to develop first-pass objectives. Predictably, every salesperson intentionally understates the numbers as the starting point in their effort to negotiate for a lower quota. The low-ball effect continues upstream, as district sales managers, regional directors, and area vice-presidents all lobby for lower numbers as well.

Executives and their financial analysts look at corporate objectives and develop top-down numbers that are then distributed to the field branches of the organization, somewhat based on the bottom-up potential estimates. Too often, the bottom-up figures are ignored completely. Given the complex multi-layered low-balling in the bottom-up processes, the fact that everyone in the field hides critical sales opportunity data elements to improve their argument, and because all opportunities are not visible six months or a year in advance, it is not surprising that quotas are usually misaligned with actual potential in a given sales territory.

A further complication is that top-down numbers are often more aggressive than bottom-up estimates, even when the fudge factor is removed. In this classic clash between executives and salespeople, management always wins. However, there is no greater impetus for a salesperson to polish and send out his or her resume than the day he or she receives a $12 million objective in a territory that will have to stretch to deliver $5 million in the current year. Why stay if given Mission Impossible?

Unable to fairly allocate quota, some outfits, such as IBM, simply fall back to a relatively consistent setting: without major contortions, a salesperson's current year quota is set at 130% of last year's attainment. Fairness and setting objectives that are in line with potential are mostly ignored.

There are other deficiencies in the revenue quota model systems. A key few ones include:

> Intentional inaccuracies in forecasts: Strategic and tactical plans for production, human resources hiring and training, and working capital are driven by sales forecasts that will be inconsistent and inaccurate because of quota-induced secrecy.
>
> Loop-hole searching: Quotas invariably result in complex matrix pay, causing salespeople to search for loop-holes, such as keeping orders "in the drawer" until next year when their current numbers are unattainable, or alternating years of feast or famine to manipulate the system.

Summarized Problems with Quota Systems

- Favor underperforming salespeople
- Cause conflict-of-interest rift between salesperson and management
- Favoritism in quota assignment is never completely avoided
- Key cause of morale issues
- Root of poor decisions in field
- Sales representatives are not incited to preserve profitability
- Quota deadlines drive fire-sale profit erosion
- Customers get accustomed to waiting for the next fire-sale
- Loop-hole game-play
- Data cloaking about customers
- Inaccurate forecasting
- Short timeframe deal horizon is preferred
- Expense controls weak or cause more work, because rep is not incited to make good control decisions

Quota and bonus-driven fire-sales: Quarterly and annual extra bonuses result in salespeople driven to sign business contracts by certain dates, training customers to wait for these "special mark downs," eroding profitability with ever-lower price points over the years.

Quick deals vs. multi-year contracts: Self-preserving salespeople refrain from selling many multi-year contracts, knowing that the long-term business will be assumed and factored into their quotas.

Because of the game play on both sides, management's financial analysts typically adjust the plan annually and the sales force finds new loop-holes to replace the ones that worked last year. The result is typically a complex, spaghetti-like pay plan that is not well aligned with the strategic objectives of shareholders or executive management.

The Case for Net Profit Compensation

In many cases, net profit-based compensation models make more sense. In a Net Profit Model (NPM), the salesperson is compensated based on the remaining profit in his or her territory, after revenue less cost of goods and selling expenses is calculated. When a salesperson must manage to his or her Profit and Loss Statement (P&L) and is paid a percentage of net profit, he or she is magically converted into a scrapping and complete businessperson, negotiating pricing that preserves profitability, closely controlling expenses, planning resource use with care, and seeking ways to grow business for the long term.

Once a company decides on the NPM course, danger lurks in the form of continued fine-tuning of the sales plans. Plan consistency, year after year, is critical to a focused sales force. Great care must be taken to ensure that the sales force believes that the NPM plan will stay in place for years. Confidence can be lost, resulting in a loss of the "ownership of franchise" belief which is the cornerstone to the program's success.

The impulse to modify plans must be avoided: the only pay modifiers that can be used effectively must be in the formula when first announced and must be congruent with running the business for net profit. Effective modifiers that can be used include bonuses for profit quality and targeted sale type rewards. Semper Fortis believes in specialization of the force, which will be discussed in the upcoming Section Seven. Slightly different pay rates and specifics can be feasible by type of sales person, but the company must ensure that the discrepancies are not too great.

Consider the following table of key differences between the models:

Issue	**Revenue Quota**	**Net Profit**
Who protects profit?	Analysts or managers far from customer.	Salesperson, who is intimate with the deal.
Who negotiates the pricing and terms?	Salesperson is often on the buyer's side.	Customer.
Year-end markdown activity.	Salesperson motivated by revenue / deal bonus.	Salesperson protects profitability and terms.
Are the prolific sales producers happy?	No – feel small quota guys are subsidized.	Yes – true meritocracy.
Is organization in sync internally?	Quota causes sales vs. management rift.	Sales perfectly in line with management.
Can company capture sales knowledge?	Difficult. Not in best interest of salesperson.	Easier. Salesperson has no quota to posture for.
Is forecasting accurate?	No. Not in the best interest of salesperson.	Motivated to ensure resources are ready.
Salesperson longevity with company.	Every year and quota is evaluated discretely.	Salesperson is building a growing business.

Under the NPM, the salesperson's best interest is in sync with the shareholder and executive management. At this upper tier, the interests of most companies are consistently centered on profits, earnings growth, and profit quality. The results can be stunning when a company's closest contact to the customer is in line with shareholder goals and desires.

Benefits Summary of Net Profit–Based Sales Compensation Models:

- The front-line customer contact is aligned with management and shareholder desires for net profit and earnings growth.
- Salespeople, who make many spending decisions, care deeply about wise use of expenses.
- Salespeople protect profitability, playing a key role in pricing strategy.
- Salespeople prefer signing long-term multi-year contracts.
- It is in the salespeople's best interests to forecast accurately, ensuring that resourcing activity matches business potential.
- Successful salespeople stay in place, managing customer relationships for longer terms; they rarely change employers.
- Senior professionals have field options that do not compromise career or earnings capability.

Not a Prefect World

There are always compromises with any compensation program. Net profit pay has certain short-comings, but in general, these shortcomings are much easier to overcome than the fatal flaws of revenue-based quota or profit-based quota compensation systems.

Some companies make "strategic" decisions to "buy" market share and momentum through lost-leader pricing on certain, often new, products and services. Salespeople would starve to death on a NPM plan, as deals simply are not profitable.

The simplest fix is to add "landing" bonuses on the target product lines or customer types as fixed dollar amounts or as a percentage of the revenue of the initial deal. The amount should be paid as straight bonus, keeping the salespeople motivated while maintaining accuracy and focus in the overall P&L by customer system.

- Knowledge capture and management programs have a decent chance of success.

- There is great unity of purpose between sales, management, and shareholders.

In Summary…

The benefits of converting the generally crafty and resourceful sales force into independent business franchisees are enormous. The simplicity of compensation based on net profit is the cornerstone to renewed vigor and growth for many companies stuck in the quota paradigm. Net profit–based compensation is the cornerstone for a true meritocracy and renewed vigor and growth in a company.

We continue to add key implementation facets to the Semper Fortis Model:

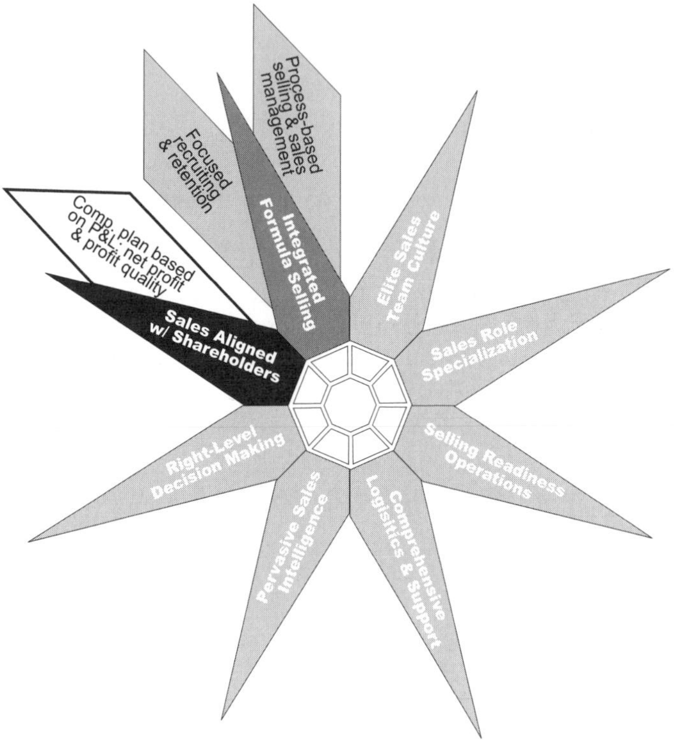

Chapter 9: Implementing the Compensation Model

The power of the Net Profit Model used within Semper Fortis is extraordinary. Its secret is simplicity and clarity. Once the model is in place, the momentum grows as each salesperson begins to envision building his or her own franchise, with growth in revenue, profit, additional employees, and consistent, larger bonuses, instead of an annual quota hurdle artificially controlling and limiting his or her potential success.

One very important word of caution: once the model is set, companies should do everything possible to not change it year to year, except perhaps in a more lenient direction and even then, only if clearly necessary. For salespeople to begin the conversion to Customer Unit Business Executives (CUBEs) planning their unit's future with a multi-year horizon, they must have a *stable foundation* from which to make assumptions, plans, and decisions. Unfortunately, a company will add more criteria, change a pay rate somewhat, and the field force will often see the model as a disguised quota system and immediately lose the two magic motivators: sense of ownership and entrepreneurship.

While simple to visualize, implementing the Net Profit Model (NPM) well can sometimes be tricky, as designing the targeted compensation range is difficult. The primary reason is that sales productivity per CUBE will rise considerably in the first few years under the system. Management tries to guess at this change, but it is quite difficult to predict from one company to the next. Simultaneously, too strict a plan could crush all motivation immediately, driving an incorrect perception that this is a tougher way to "quota" the team.

Some senior managers' egos also become an obstacle. A number have difficulty accepting that a few super performances should and will happen under the NPM system each year, resulting in a few CUBEs out-earning top-tier execs. The cry is familiar: *"Hey, wait a minute! I've been slaving away here for 32 long years and I still don't make that kind of money. Why are we letting a person with only 6 years of experience knock it out of the park?"*

The leader of the company must prevent all attempts to dampen the meritocracy. If a salesperson delivers five times the profit, he or she deserves five times the pay of the average salesperson. Meritocracy at its finest will motivate everybody and people need heroes to look up to so that they will get up two hours earlier in the morning and strive valiantly throughout the day.

The second major area of complication is that management invariably wants to modify CUBE behavior beyond delivering more profit, and problematically, often in ways not congruent with the salesperson's primary mission. Some modifiers can be helpful but they should also stay constant from year to year. Management must give extensive deliberation to modifiers, always remembering that the goal is simplicity and focus on sales and profits.

It is important to renew the focus on profitability. In this day and age of highly evolved business theory, many business "gurus" seem to have forgotten that a company's mission is to deliver economic value-add for their clients, in other words, value at a profit. There seems to be almost a sense of shame at some of the companies I visit about earning better-than-average profits. This is a mistake. A company exists to earn as much profit as it can for its owners. If it creates a better widget that solves customer problems better than any competitor's product, boasts phenomenal financial payback metrics for the customer, and is clearly differentiated against its competitors, it deserves as much profit as it can get and the market will bear.

Paying personnel, especially offense players like CUBEs based primarily on profit, is sane and rational.

Establish Trust

The first step is to establish trust between sales representatives and management. Today, most companies go to market daily without trust between their primary contact points, salespeople, and their managers. While most people can't imagine these operating conditions in a NASA space shuttle program or within an NCAA football team, the status quo in sales has conditioned business leaders to believe that this is a normal and acceptable state of affairs. It is not.

Trust is mission-critical for world-class results.

Salespeople have been taught to not trust management after a great number of years of haggling and secrecy surrounding the personally all-important quota. On a company level, management traditionally changed the parameters of the quota system annually, trying to eke out more effort and productivity while factoring bonus stinginess against the potential loss of motivation or above average turnover. At the individual level, whenever a salesperson had a big year, the quota rose dramatically as a throttle on his or her earnings in following years to average earnings down over three years. It is not surprising that trust was lost quickly.

When moving to the NPM, it is very important to not adjust the model annually—if ever—given the objective of building trust. Salespeople are being transformed into business franchisees or CUBEs. Lack of adjustment will bring confidence to the sales force that this time, the change is truly different and remarkable.

A Net Profit Model clearly uses net profit as its primary pay determination factor. However, pay based on pure profit sometimes drives potentially unhealthy short-term profit decisions that are not constructive to long-term customer satisfaction.

While the Semper Fortis strategy advises keeping the plan as simple and focused as possible, it does make sense to add just a few compensation modifiers / controls to bias decisions toward long-term customer retention and satisfaction. Management must balance the power of simplicity and focus against the reality of other needs of the company. Acceptable modifiers include:

1. Customer retention,
2. Profit quality (best-fit and profit percent),
3. Longevity of the sales contract,
4. Customer satisfaction and economic value-add, and
5. Teamwork, with the side-benefit of knowledge capture.

Modifiers should concentrate on making sure deals are long-term win / win for both the vendor and the customer. Semper Fortis sets up the first four modifiers to measure key aspects of the selling relationship beyond pure present-day profit.

The final modifier, teamwork, is in place more for emphasis than practical use, unless wide-spread problems occur. Semper Fortis requires teamwork in a day and age in which salespeople have been conditioned to not work as members of a team. Within Semper Fortis, teamwork motivation is accomplished first through culture, secondarily through active management and territory control. However, if teamwork is not included in the pay system, employees get the wrong impression that a company is not nearly as serious about teaming as it is about profit. Therefore, teamwork and its very important side-benefit, organizational knowledge capture and growth, must be included in the compensation formula.

The Path to Net Profit Compensation

Step 1: Profit and Loss and Income Statements by Account

The key building block of NPM compensation is reporting a Profit and Loss Statement by customer (Level One P&L). Yet many companies do not have accounting systems that can produce this level of detail easily. Cost data is not available or not developed for many products, especially for internally developed items like software. Financial tracking systems are simply not in place. Surprisingly, in our capitalist society, many companies can't determine the profitability of any given customer relationship.

These hurdles should not get in the way of implementation. If necessary, creating approximate cost figures and plugging deals into PC spreadsheets is still healthier, and well worth the financial administration time, than staying on the quota bandwagon. All expenses related to any specific account are also added into the overhead surrounding each account.

The few companies that enjoy healthy gross margins argue that tracking profit by account and by salesperson is not necessary. Nothing could be farther from the truth. When one of these "fat and happy" firms changes to profit tracking by customer, executives suddenly discover that several percentage points of profit, if not more, have been dropping off the table. Every percentage point that can be delivered to the shareholders must be delivered, if the firm's management is serious about their duty. Tracking profit is an important step.

If estimated cost is used initially, the company will discover natural reasons to improve the accuracy of these figures over time. The better the cost data, the more competitive a company can become, able to make better project and negotiation decisions. Most companies find a way to develop costing that makes sense within two years of adopting a net profit by customer system. The smartest enterprises don't allow the improvements to be driven exclusively by finance, but rather, poll the sales department to focus on improving items that will truly impact results and improve process, while minimizing bureaucracy.

Step 2: Profit and Loss and Income Statements by CUBE

Account P&Ls and Income Statements are then consolidated into CUBE-level P&Ls (Level Two P&Ls). All expenses related to the territory that are not specific to any one customer account are added as overhead, including salaries, draws, and expenses.

The salesperson is then paid a percentage of net profit. For some enterprises, the right number might be as high as 40% while for others it might be as low as 10%. The percentage picked is a result of estimating productivity and the percentage that will result in a slightly-higher-than-industry-average total compensation package for the slightly-better-than-average salesperson.

If the company hits the mark properly, the below-industry-average salesperson will be making considerably less at the company than they would at another with the standard quota system and will therefore be motivated to depart. The average salesperson will be at par with the industry, the more productive salesperson will be 25% above average and the super producers will be very happy, typically out-earning top-tier individuals at other companies by 75% or more.

Net profit, after salesperson salary and commissions, is then rolled up to the sales director-level P&L statements. The sales director then adds in his or her travel, salary, and bonus as expenses, and rolls the profit upward to his or her area vice-president and so forth.

Corporate overhead does not belong in sales and marketing investment P&Ls.

There is a distinct difference between the investments companies make in bringing their products to market and the costs of producing the products, services, and simply being "in business." A sales and marketing investment is a strategic expense: wise investments in areas like sales, marketing, telesales, etc., result in additional profit per dollar invested. Everything else is a tactical operations cost, which management should continually question and cut wherever possible while preserving the core value that the customer is purchasing.

Companies that outspend their competitors as a percentage of revenues on sales and marketing investment while saving more per revenue dollar on tactical operations costs, tend to succeed in the long run. Corporate management's job is to ensure that sales and marketing investment is not only fully-funded but sales leaders are challenged to put more funds to work while keeping each dollar invested returning the minimum hurdle return rate. Simultaneously, management must bear down on all tactical operations cost expenses while preserving the value-add that the customer is willing to pay for.

Allocating overhead or tactical operations cost out to sales and marketing investment P&Ls is a mistake. The tendency of these overhead departments is to grow in size and expense. Allocation is a red carpet for growing overhead. For example, if financial administration adds head-count and the cost is allocated, the cost gets absorbed by the sales groups. In this scenario, why wouldn't the financial department head want four more number crunchers?

By not mixing the sales and marketing investment side of the house with the tactical operations cost side, executives maintain a clear picture of investment return on both the offensive and defensive sides of the corporate game. The recommended implementation of the NPM within Semper Fortis is to keep sales-related revenue, expense, and net profit "clean" all the way to the commander-in-chief of sales. Then the remaining profit is used to fund the tactical operations cost side of the business. Management, in this sort of arrangement, is motivated to ensure the overhead number stays below what sales is delivering, as the remainder represents shareholder earnings.

Semper Fortis keeps church and state separate, preventing the allocation of expenses unrelated to winning more business to sales profit centers.

Step 3: Accommodating and Accounting for Solution Sales Specialists

So far, the discussion has been relatively straight forward, assuming one CUBE has responsibility for each customer account. When a business needs solution sales specialists that represent complex product lines or intricate services, too detailed to be handled by the CUBE alone, the P&L system must accommodate the revenue and profit generated through sales specialists.

Solution sales specialists are typically advanced technical personnel that have received comprehensive sales and product solution training. Organizationally, they are part of the special forces group (discussed in Part Two, Section Seven) and have a dotted-line reporting relationship to CUBEs when assigned to specific opportunities. Specialist sales are reported first on the Level One (customer / account) P&L, just like any other sale. It is critical the company retain visibility of the value of the customer account, first and foremost.

When the "project" rolls up to the Level Two CUBE P&L, the project is also consolidated to the specialist P&L. The specialist P&L is used for management purposes and for calculating any commissions due the specialist, while the CUBE P&L consolidates and rolls the sales upward. The only difference is that the project takes one additional cost line item, the cost of the commission due the specialist on the sale.

The specialist P&L must accommodate the cost of his or her fully-burdened salary and expenses over the year; in other words, a specialist's commissions in the end are net of his or her own salary and expense. Any imbalances at the end of the year, such as the departure of a specialist after six months of a losing P&L and therefore a negative total on salary and travel expense, are allocated into the VP of Special Forces overhead cost.

The company, as part of the decision to invest in solution specialists winds up paying out greater commissions, as both the CUBE and specialist get bonuses on the project, albeit at different rates. This reality ensures that specialists are only used in areas that are critically important and offer potential higher profit to the company. The VP of Special Forces is challenged to balance the number of specialists to add and still maintain an acceptable return for the investment in sales capability.

Step 4: Implementing Suggested Modifiers to the Pay Plan

The injection of pay modifiers in a Net Profit plan, intended to create a genesis of entrepreneurial activity, creativity, and franchise-building, is difficult. If there is any question whether a modifier should be used or not, the best course is to avoid it and let net profit run its magical course.

When modifiers are applied, the following guidelines are important:

1. Keep the modifiers to a minimum—any scheme with more than 5 or 6 begins to look like the Internal Revenue Service's tax code.

2. Change modifiers rarely, or better yet, never—if a change is needed, go far out of the way to explain the business reasons, the reasons this change will result in more business or the reasons this is absolutely necessary, to the CUBEs.

3. Modifiers should be short, simple, concise, and clear.

4. Modifiers must be helpful to building the franchise model—if a modifier clearly exists only to keep pay levels down, it will have a negative effect on building the competitive advantage Sales Olympian force.

The Semper Fortis formula acknowledges value in five modifiers:

1. **Key customer retention.**

   With the lion's share of profit earned *after* the first three years of winning a customer account, it is crucial that expectations are set reasonably and that the firm exceeds those expectations. A number of customer retention and

> For ideas and detailed pay plan modifier discussion, download my brief at www.SeizingShare.com/mod

customer satisfaction strategies, combined with time-vested bonuses, help ensure the sales force is focused on keeping and growing existing customer business volumes.

2. **Profit quality.**

   Profit quality is a rating combining how well a customer project matches the company's best-fit rating system and if the project is at, above, or below average gross profit percent in comparison to other similar projects sold by the company.

3. **Longevity of the sale contract** (consider).

   Longer term contracts help companies forecast finances, resources required, production levels, inventory requirements, and more. Financially inciting the sales force to sign longer term contracts usually helps the firm run more profitably and efficiently.

4. **Innovation** (consider).

   Sales professionals often have the ability to work closely with customers to develop new offerings that are applicable to similar customers; however, such business is often less profitable and more difficult for the salespeople involved in the early development. A company that makes such business more attractive tends to grow its product portfolio quickly. The salespeople must work closely with product marketing and development staffs to ensure new solutions have broad applicability in the marketplace.

5. **Teamwork** (consider).

   The final modifier is one of the most difficult to implement. Many team pay scenarios do not result in teamwork but rather socialistic bonuses where non-producing team members draft on the coat tails of successful ones. Teamwork with a Semper

Fortis organization is achieved through culture and management, but there is an important "send a clear message" reason to include it within the pay plan structure. Unless the modifier exists, the sales force might misinterpret the importance of the teamwork culture.

There is no perfect way to implement modifiers. I have seen different methods, and each implementation technique has pluses and minuses. An overriding factor must be resistance to over-complication. Of the modifiers, the first two are critical while the remaining three are optional.

The most common ways to apply modifiers are:

- Positive Accelerators – If a salesperson rates high in a category, he or she receives an accelerator percentage on commissions, often after surpassing a certain base level.

- Negative Commission Filters – If a salesperson rates high, he or she receives all the commission earned; otherwise, the lower the rating, the more is withheld by the company.

- Vesting Commission Strategies—Commissions are accrued and delayed, pending a rating in certain time-sensitive categories.

The company should resist making it all or none across a package of modifiers. If a CUBE is falling short within one category, the plan should not make him or her give up hope of meeting the mark in another.

In Summary…

Paying sales teams on net profit is vastly superior to paying them with revenue quota systems. Compensation plan implementation is sometimes tricky, but is well worth the effort. Salespeople are converted to Customer Unit Business Executives, making plans and decisions in alignment with shareholder desires. An entrepreneurial spirit and professional attitude permeate the organization. Most importantly, the company suddenly finds that the most successful producers are also the happiest members of the sales team, which bodes well for low turnover rates and overall team attitude.

This chapter completes the next implementation facet in the Semper Fortis model:

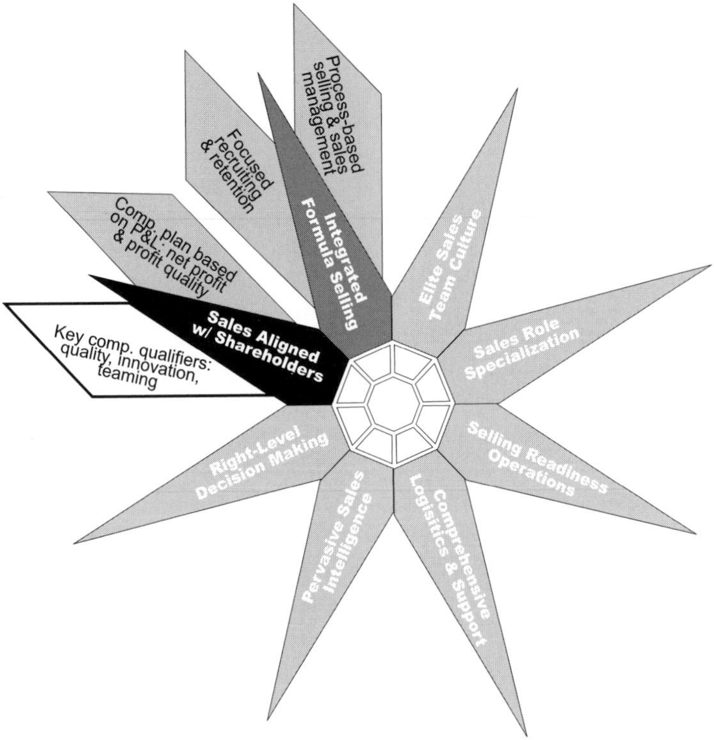

Section Three

~ ~ ~ ~ ~ ~ ~ ~ ~ ~ ~

Right-Level Decision Making

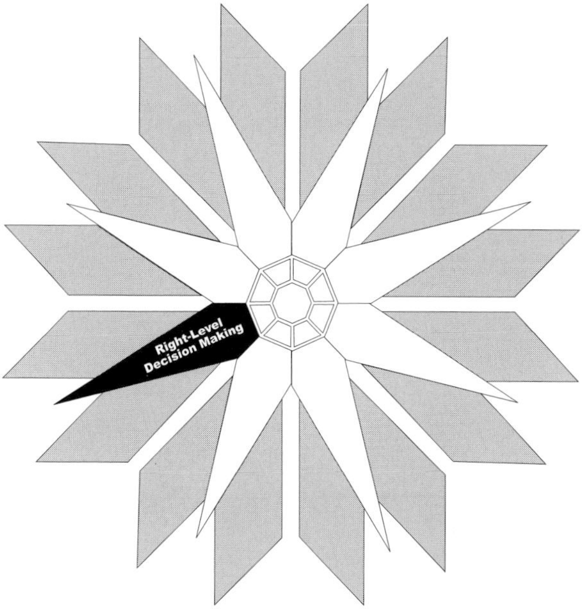

Empowering individuals to make a difference has a profound effect on the success of the enterprise.

Semper Fortis converts salespeople first into sales professionals, and then into all-around business professionals.

"Surround yourself with the best people you can find, delegate authority, and don't interfere."

- Ronald Reagan

Chapter 10: Forging Franchise Thinking

After a company commits to measurement, compensation, and motivation by individual profit and loss (P&L), the second half of the natural order is to empower worthy individuals with the ability to make the important decisions that affect the future of their P&L statement.

In order to succeed in its fullest, Semper Fortis focuses on building a culture of daily, superior effort, winning, and self-determination of one's destiny, all within a framework and culture of teaming. Empowering field personnel to make good decisions, asking them to review the logic behind their decisions with mentors and managers, and holding people accountable for the results is *liberating*. Most field personnel, once they realize that their destiny is truly their own, rise to the occasion, becoming entrepreneurs within the context of a larger business network.

When professionals are empowered to make decisions that matter, success accelerates dramatically.

Semper Fortis advocates "right-level" decision making. Many companies still follow the central command structures imposed by the earliest days of industrialization. While this hierarchical structure works well in certain types of enterprises such as transportation, generally, the more knowledge workers an enterprise has, the less effective centralized control becomes.

Sales professionals working in the Complex Corporate Solutions Environment (CCSE) are first and foremost knowledge-based workers. They have in-depth knowledge regarding buyer attitudes, personal and departmental needs, the requirements of the overall customer enterprise, and the competitors' positioning with regard to their particular prospect account. The sales professional's "value-add" is coordination, orchestration, politics, initiative, knowledge management, and serving as the catalyst of change. Because of this, certain decisions are best made in the field, just as long as compensation (see previous

Section Two) and measurement clearly align the "field decision maker" with the goals of the shareholders and executives.

Please note that within Semper Fortis, right-level decision making in the field and instilling a sense of franchise and entrepreneurship does not come at the price of organization and formula. Quite the contrary, the Semper Fortis team is keenly focused on establishing and using state-of-the-art processes and frameworks within each "franchise" territory to achieve superior success.

Semper Fortis achieves the best of both worlds: it combines the scrappiness and innovation of entrepreneurial franchisees with a winning formula and state-of-the-art process.

The same right-level decision making can be seen in a special forces mission against terrorists in the Philippines. While the President might green light an operation, the Joint Chiefs will determine the theater level strategy, the Commander-in-Chief of the Pacific will task ships and support units for the engagement, the captains of the ships will determine the best way to accomplish their role in the mission, while the leader of the Navy SEALs team determines the best tactics and runs the tactics of the operation once in country. The top brass must focus on the "what" rather than the specific "how."

Ultimately, while the operation is in full swing, the SEAL team on the front line takes temporary control of the entire supporting organization, requesting support and assistance depending on the dynamics of the situation. The military establishment, from the Joint Chiefs on down, stands ready to support the soldiers on the front line as the engagement is fought. This uncompromising support of the front lines during battle is another key Semper Fortis tenet, which will be discussed fully in the upcoming Section Five.

Decisions that are "in scope" of distributed sales decision making include:

- Most customer-level decisions, such as pricing, contract parameters, and service response,
- Travel and entertainment expense decisions, and
- Territory- and account-specific strategy and tactics.

There are other decisions in which the field CUBE may have great say but which should involve the concurrence of other interested parties in the company. There are many such areas, including at the very least:

- Custom product or software development required for a specific project,
- Partnership with third parties on a specific customer engagement that may or may not lead to partnerships on an enterprise-wide scale,
- Third-party integration efforts,
- Third-party content in a larger solution for a customer, and
- Legal contracts that are customized outside pre-approved norms.

The Semper Fortis formula does *not* advocate turning over all decision-making overnight as the new system is implemented. The next chapters will discuss implementing the change and controlling the probation period from one sales professional to the next, as well as the model for continuous monitoring and control of the decision-making on a permanent basis going forward.

Magic lies in convincing sales professionals, recast as field-level businesspeople, that they are entrepreneurial franchisees.

Empowerment is everything. When people feel that their destinies are in their own hands, magical things happen. Semper Fortis advocates empowering sales professionals to become Customer Unit Business Executives, fully ready to make key business decisions and take important risks while aligned with the organizational goals of profit and profit quality.

In the end, management's goal is to forge franchise thinking. There are remarkable differences in many of the daily activities a field professional must perform, depending on whether he or she views him or herself as a regular employee or as a special player, the owner of an entrepreneurial franchise. Consider the following snapshots that illustrate the profound difference this organizational structure can make.

Snapshot #1: Decisions on Offense (Pricing and Contract Terms)

In field sales, some of the most important decisions revolve around pricing and contract terms offered a customer when trying to win the project.

Today's Dominant Revenue Quota Model:

In many of today's professional sales forces, sales representatives are aligned primarily based on revenue and revenue-based quota. When a proposal comes up, the salesperson does whatever necessary to win the deal. While many in management believe that the salesperson will earnestly try to preserve profit, my research and experience show that this is rarely the case.

Sales reps face much greater risk in not winning a large quota-making deal than in taking a deal that comes in a bit shorter than anticipated with regard to revenue and profit. Ninety percent of something is a better "career survival equation" than a big goose egg in the quota attainment column.

In general, the fewer prospect accounts a salesperson has to call upon, as typically found in major account environments, the greater the tendency to forgo profitability in exchange for improved chances of landing the revenue. Yet, many firms count on large-scale accounts for most of their business volume. The salesperson's tendency is to bid as low a price as possible in these environments, even though the basement figure potentially hurts quota attainment. Ultimately, this dynamic results in a considerable "profit left on the table" figure, when measured across all accounts.

It is not surprising—or maybe it is to some executives—that in this revenue quota model system, the salesperson, in order to make his or her quota, becomes essentially a negotiating advocate for the customer. The salesperson will "magically" produce competitive pricing, add key details to the argument, and augment the statements made by customer management to ensure that he or she has presented an overwhelmingly solid case for maximizing the discount on the project.

Rarely—very rarely—do companies win deals at the most profitable price within today's quota-based sales operations.

Decisions on Offense and the Semper Fortis Model:

The tables turn dramatically when the CUBE is paid based on net profit and not on an annual quota. The CUBE is most interested in winning the business at the price point the prospect account will bear. All the intelligence regarding the prospect stays sided with the selling company and special pricing requests are much more often truly indicative of what is needed to win the business.

Snapshot #2: Longevity of Contracts

Generally speaking, it is much more efficient to run a business in which revenues, profits, resource requirements, and capital requirements are predictable fairly far into the future. Therefore, the longer term the contracts are with customers, the easier it becomes for management to anticipate needs and plan ahead.

Today's Dominant Revenue Quota Sales Model:

Within today's systems, salespeople are generally drawn to signing shorter, fast-hitting deals rather than longer-term, multi-year contracts. The reason is straightforward: the goal is to beat one's annual quota, not to deliver more total profit over multiple years.

Quota setting is a relentless beast when it comes to business under a long-term contract. If a salesperson lands a three year, $10 million per year ($30 million in total) contract on this year's $5 million quota, he or she will become a 200% of quota superstar and receive accolades at the big annual sales meeting, but will face a new objective of $13 to $15 million the following year, often regardless of whether he or she has truly exhausted the primary opportunity in the territory by landing the big contract. Even if the professional beats the odds and outperforms expectations the following year, coming in with $17 million, surpassing that $15 million goal by $2 million only gives him or her a 113% final scorecard, while another salesperson with $5 million in quota but delivering $2 million more or $7 million in total comes in at 140% and wins the awards.

What's even more discouraging is that in many pay plans, the second salesperson at 140% attainment would earn more commissions than the first, even though the first delivered 250% more revenue and often more profit.

It is not surprising that the same sales professional finds him or herself discouraged and in career trouble in year three. The quota would probably come in 20 to 30% higher than the $17 million he or she landed. It becomes high time to transfer cities, go for a promotion, or leave the company. The quota system inevitably drives the best salespeople out of servicing a good base of customers where they have established relationships.

The result is that salespeople would prefer to land big-hitting projects with quick completion and no long-term contracts, a model completely out of alignment with the interests of executive management and shareholders. Given that the salespeople are usually the architects of deal structure, they often have the ability to draw these kinds of walls around business deals.

In the example above, the salesperson would have the ability to argue with his or her manager that the quick-hitting $10 million / six month project was an anomaly and that his or her original $5 million quota was truly a fair representation of the potential in the territory. If successful in the lobbying, he or she might come away with a 200% year this year, perhaps a mild 20% quota boost for the following year to $6 million, and still have an open door to land another quick-hitting, short-duration "anomaly" next year for another $10 million (and 166% attainment), paving the way for greater commissions, more awards, recognition, and open career-path doors.

It is clear that quota models are in conflict with the overall business goals of a predictable business model in which decisions regarding resources can be made with confidence well in advance of needs.

The Semper Fortis Model:

Within Semper Fortis, the CUBE is well aligned with the business. Instead of playing games for quota reasons, the business professional's only mission is to grow the franchise and maximize total business flow. The more long-term contracts become, the better prepared the franchisee and the overall enterprise are with resources, enabling excellent execution. When commission pay is based on net profit, not annual revenue or profit *percent* of quota target, long-term contract profit is better than short-term, given the added benefits of only needing a customer approval once and being able to plan the delivery aspects. The CUBE gets paid the same amount on $1 million in net profit, whether it is spread over six months or sixteen. Natural business gravity drives the CUBE to speed up delivery as much as possible, as all know that the longer a deal drags out, the more risk there is in completing a contract.

As an added benefit under the Semper Fortis model, there are no pressures to conduct "fire-sales" to move up a customer order a few weeks to make a quota cut-off deadline. In the quota system, customers come to expect "special" prices every year at the end of certain quarters. Just ask any large Cisco customer. I worked with customers that even went as far as directly asking about a Cisco salesperson's quota objectives to better gauge their negotiating power!

Snapshot #3: Decisions of Defense (Travel and Entertainment)

Salespeople are the primary decision-makers on travel and entertainment expenses in both models. The corporation typically sets guidelines across the board, occasionally modifying acceptable dollar amounts for lodging and meals by city.

Employees Under a Revenue Quota Model:

Employees under the revenue quota model spend as much as guidelines allow. First-line managers spend considerable time monitoring and controlling expenses, trying to ensure that travel and entertainment expense is well-used. Unfortunately, this is a difficult task, given that the manager is one step removed from the decision making. In general, spot audits do help send the message that the company will not tolerate blatant abuse, but few managers believe that expenses are 100% free of some minor abuse.

Franchisees:

When employees see themselves as franchisees, it only takes a few weeks before they realize that every dollar saved on expenses directly affects their paychecks. Guidelines are no longer viewed as a target but rather a maximum. Many suddenly take an extra one-way flight to Oklahoma City before catching a west-bound roundtrip to the Bay Area that saves the company (and their P&L) $1,124. Suddenly, customer golf rounds decrease dramatically, as they realize that taking the assistant junior application programmer on the project once every month is not a good payoff item.

Most importantly, first-line managers no longer find themselves in the weekly expense control circle—they merely employ the occasional audit to assure the CUBEs that the company is not asleep at the wheel.

Snapshot #4: Decisions on Adding Resources

One of the fundamental decisions companies must make is whether to add resources and capability. The trade-off is always the same, no matter if the discussion concerns plant, people, or equipment:

- What is the minimum required return on investment?
- What are the odds of achieving the required return on investment?
- What are the risks?
- Does the (best case / probable case / worst case) return justify the risk?
- What are the alternatives?
- Can we afford it right now?

The equation is often rife with unknowns and approximations. The art of being a good decision-maker is being able to make prudent decisions based on imperfect information.

For the context of the sales discussion, let us take a look at adding human resources in the field.

Employees Under a Revenue Quota Model:

Under the revenue quota model, sales employees in the field lobby for adding resources such as pre- and post-sales systems engineers, project managers, and customer service reps. Generally speaking, the more resources there are to be leveraged, the better the salesperson's life becomes, even if the new resource is not well-utilized—there is no personal financial downside risk under the revenue quota model.

Managers must make the risk assessment decisions independently, relying somewhat on the information provided by the salespeople. Yet depending on how the manager's compensation works, he or she too may have little to lose by adding more investment (or cost) to the area.

In this model, two unwanted outcomes tend to occur. Either too many resources are added, resulting in poor payback, if any, for the headcount, or too few are added, because upper management becomes overly cautious. In other cases, centralized executives make headcount adjustments far from the action, demanding that first-line managers find ways to comply, resulting in little correlation between the size of field groups and the opportunities and scope of work in the area.

Franchisees in Semper Fortis:

Adding human resources can be one of the more frightening decisions that the P&L-owning franchisee can make. He or she must weigh his or her investment carefully to ensure the payback will be there. When faced with imperfect data, he or she may seek council from mentors and managers and then ultimately make the call.

This is exactly as it should be. The decision-maker is the CUBE closest to the action, the one with the most insight. Checks and balances are in place to make sure his or her argument is well-founded in logic but the ultimate decision for more field resources is made in the field.

A group of CUBEs can influence the sales director to add shared pre-sales or post-sales personnel. In the pooled process, they commit to put any additions to profitable use, ensuring that the investment is justified. These pooled resources are often allocated across sales professionals, as they and their related expense are 100% dedicated to sales activity in the field.

In my years of experience of working within the franchisee model, I witnessed an extremely high success rate with human resource investments in the field. I believe the rate is much higher in a franchisee model than can be found where the sales personnel and first-line managers have little to lose by adding more overhead cost.

As with everything, there are two sides to this coin. Some CUBEs will be extremely hesitant to take risks. Sales directors and area VPs must recognize this tendency and be tasked with putting more "investment dollars" to work. In these cases, they must proactively sell (not override) the CUBE on the idea of expanding his or her group and capabilities over time.

Snapshot #5: Working Smart versus Filling Time

A key aspect of productivity is how intelligently employees work, in other words, how well they allocate their time. Typical management tactics are to pile additional work on each person, until he or she becomes so busy that a natural, at least in theory, parsing of the list occurs, and the person ends up doing the most important things.

Employees Under a Revenue Quota Model:

Under a revenue quota model, the quota dominates the scene. Even before work begins in earnest, reps waste weeks waiting for the final numbers to be assigned, since most companies wait for the final year-end results as an input to the quota-setting process, and then waste more weeks finding loopholes in the freshly modified pay plan formulas that have come out of headquarters' MBA financial analysts.

A rep with an unrealistic, unachievable target will typically work to fill time, waiting until the latter half of the year to spool up efforts, with a goal of putting some orders "in the drawer" ready for the start of the next year and a new, lower quota objective. At the other extreme, salespeople who beat their quota early may slow efforts as well, especially if faced with an artificial "limiter" on their total compensation. Unless each quota is set perfectly with the true opportunity in the territories and the salespeople see the opportunity and the achievability clearly—and this never happens—there is little reason to believe that all salespeople will hustle and work smart year-round, maximizing their potential.

No matter the reason for work slowdowns in revenue quota models, managers cannot effectively manage each salesperson on a daily basis. If a person wants to look busy, it is simple enough to do and determining if that "busyness" is smart or not cannot be solved by anyone other than the salesperson, at least not on an ongoing, sustainable basis.

Franchisees in Semper Fortis:

In Semper Fortis, the core item that matters is net profit. It doesn't take long for CUBEs to understand that all work that can result in more profit is good and to be tackled first, as opposed to all other work that does not add value nor lead to landing more profit. The plan doesn't change year to year so there is no sit-around-and-wait time. Orders “in the drawer” won't earn the CUBE more money next year than this year—in fact, there is risk in waiting to deliver. The CUBE acts as and effectively is an owner of the business.

Snapshot #6: Career Path Options

Many employees have career ambitions to move into management, yet management hierarchies are becoming ever flatter and leaner in this hyper-competitive business environment. Simple math reveals that most will be disappointed.

Employees Under a Revenue Quota Model:

In the quota system, all the years of hard work and success don't necessarily give the veteran salesperson any numerical advantage as he or she faces his or her twenty-second year of selling with a new, unattainable, poorly-set quota. He or she tried but missed making it into management ranks. It is not surprising that a salesperson sooner or later looks to change companies in the hopes of greener pastures such as more reasonable quotas, or perhaps finding a district manager position or getting a “piece of the action” with some smaller outfit.

Under quota systems, interesting, unwanted phenomenon can appear. For example, at NCR in the 1980s, a tradition took hold where those with a tarnished quota achievement record fell off the list for promotion into management. In other words, a high-volume, major-account salesperson who made their large quotas twelve out of fifteen years, delivering revenue and profit in the top ten percentile of all salespeople, but missed the quota mark by only a few percentage points in the three "unsuccessful" years, was effectively off the list as a management candidate, while another, with a perfect albeit far shorter six for six record, in a small territory producing meager profits remained a top candidate for moving up.

The end result is that anyone with the talent and drive to make it into management quickly learns that someone who *manages* sales results to deliver a slow-but-steady year-over-year increase has a better chance of promotion than someone whose goal is annual achievement maximization, which naturally results in much greater fluctuation of quotas and higher risk of failure. Unfortunately, the company would be far better off if all the most talented salespeople tried to maximize results.

Franchisees in Semper Fortis:

A long-term Semper Fortis franchisee has built a lasting business over the years. Existing streams of revenue continue on the basis of maintenance contracts, existing customers continue to purchase upgrades and so forth. The business has grown large enough to support more human resources and the veteran enters every year with a good idea of his or her income level and potential upside.

Even though he or she may have missed making it into regular management, the salesperson is generally unconcerned, given that his or her franchisee outperforms and as a result, the salesperson outearns a great number of traditional managers within the corporation. The sales professional gets the respect from the executives that the size of his or her unit deserves.

In Summary…

There are many examples of the differences between salespeople who see themselves as employees trying to beat an annual quota, subject to the whims and biases of managers and the newest corporate initiatives, and full-fledged sales businesspeople running their own franchises.

The CUBEs are given a process discipline to follow, a formula that helps make each franchise successful and efficient. Those who innovate within the framework are rewarded and their input is often used to fine-tune the formula for all. However, those who do not follow a best-practice discipline in their sales efforts quickly find that management steps in to firmly correct the situation, and if need be, remove the decision-making license.

A company makes an important leap when it turns everyone's perception into one in which the salesperson, armed with P&L statement in hand, believes he or she is essentially building a franchise and is thus essential to the success of the company.

The concept of superior performance rooted in "feeling essential" is not new. To quote Knute Rockne, the legendary football coach who built Notre Dame into a national power back in the 1920's:

> ***"An automobile goes nowhere efficiently unless it has a quick, hot spark to ignite things, to set the cogs of the machine in motion. So I try to make every player on my team feel he's the spark keeping our machine in motion. On him depends our success."***

Semper Fortis tries to achieve this with every member of the sales team and all the supporting cast.

One of the biggest keys to this thought is bonus pay, based on pure meritocracy and profit. The franchisees must believe that if they double the net profits, they will receive roughly twice the compensation. More realistically, the franchisees must see that through building a larger organization that can achieve good year to year net profit growth, they have the potential to be set for life, running a substantial business within the virtual walls, the value-add, financial, administrative, cultural, and brand support of the larger enterprise.

To forge franchise thinking, executives must sell the sales force on five key facets:

1. CUBEs will manage their own P&L and be compensated based on their business results.

2. CUBEs will have the power to make nearly all of the decisions (some may require second-level concurrence) that can effect their P&L.

3. The company will not change the basis of the P&L or derivative compensation unless there is an overwhelming, mutually beneficial, or truly necessary reason to do so. If such a course is needed, the company's executives will take the action with extraordinary sensitivity to gain CUBE acceptance without losing the franchise culture.

4. The company will provide well-developed sales and field processes to help each CUBE succeed.

5. The executives remain the right level for all decisions involving strategy and theaters of targeted operation, while first-line managers remain the right level for specific tactics and resource allocation.

Once empowered, the sales professionals become hard to stop.

Creating franchises is the next key step or facet of the Semper Fortis model:

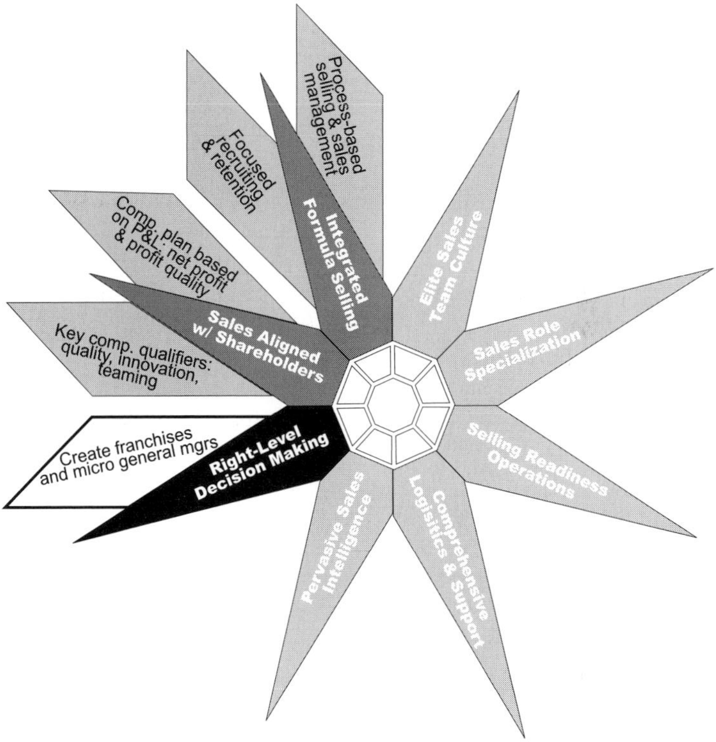

Chapter 11: Implementing Right-Level Decision-making

There are six keys to implementing right-level decision-making (RLDM) in the field while maintaining corporate focus:

- Transfer responsibility and accountability to the field Customer Unit Business Executive (CUBE).
- Define the decision-making processes and use flow charts to help guide the team.
- Institute probation periods and management reviews, by which CUBEs earn their decision-making freedom over time.
- Assign mentors and consultants to the CUBEs while encouraging peer sharing of information and advice.
- Create an intranet system to enable enterprise-wide visibility and lasting record of decisions made.
- First-line sales directors must be transformed from primarily a control function to a coaching and motivation force.

RLDM Implementation Key #1:
Transferring responsibility and accountability to the CUBE.

As discussed in the previous chapter, there are numerous benefits to transferring greater responsibility to field decision makers. In Semper Fortis parlance, the process converts field representatives from salespeople to Customer Unit Business Executives or CUBEs. Many executives are surprised at how easily salespeople take to greater decision-making authority. Most salespeople have been frustrated over the years, knowing in their hearts what decisions they want made, but having to sell the chain of command to gain the green light. In many daily activities, the CUBEs take to decision-making like fish to water.

Semper Fortis immediately turns over most daily field decision-making to the CUBE after he or she is accustomed to having his or her own P&L and understands the compensation ramifications of different actions. A flow chart is provided by type of decision, clearly showing the CUBE which decisions he or she can make on his or her own, which clip levels require additional review by the first-line manager, and which decisions must be reviewed by others, such as contacts in the Sales Intelligence Group (SIG).

It is of utmost importance is that the CUBE believes he or she has given a franchise to build. Armed with the P&L, able to make decisions that impact the P&L, having the support of the overall enterprise, and having clear documented processes that exist not for bureaucracy, but to maximize the chances of success while minimizing the chances of failure, the CUBE becomes an entrepreneur—with guidelines and means—on a mission.

RLDM Implementation Key #2:
Define the decision-making processes and flow charts to help act as guides for salespeople.

By providing process flowcharts by decision type, the company can institute clear guidelines, easing the new decision-makers into their expanded role one level of responsibility at a time. CUBEs learn to walk before running. Any number of levels or flowcharts can exist, each changing the financial clip levels of decision-making authority.

Below is an example of a flowchart for "pricing help desk services." The clip levels in the diamond decision blocks ("Is contract less than $250K" and "Is contract less than $1M?") change as a CUBE earns higher levels of decision making authority:

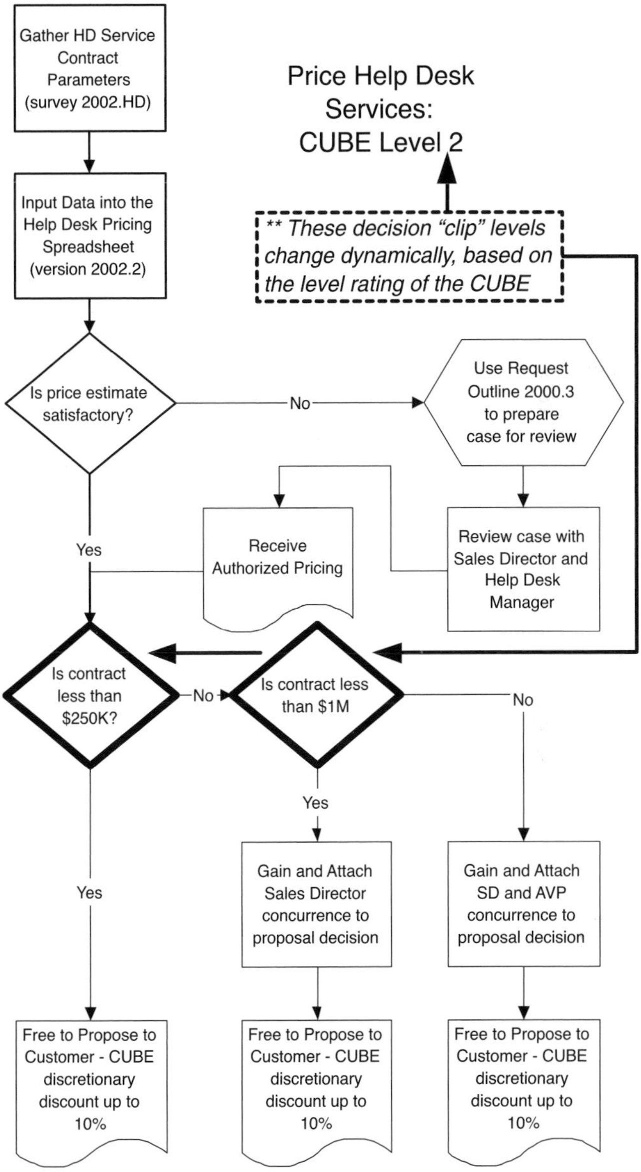
Gather HD Service Contract Parameters (survey 2002.HD)
Price Help Desk Services: CUBE Level 2
Input Data into the Help Desk Pricing Spreadsheet (version 2002.2)
** These decision "clip" levels change dynamically, based on the level rating of the CUBE
Is price estimate satisfactory?
No
Use Request Outline 2000.3 to prepare case for review
Receive Authorized Pricing
Review case with Sales Director and Help Desk Manager
Yes
Is contract less than $250K?
No
Is contract less than $1M
No
Yes
Yes
Gain and Attach Sales Director concurrence to proposal decision
Gain and Attach SD and AVP concurrence to proposal decision
Free to Propose to Customer - CUBE discretionary discount up to 10%
Free to Propose to Customer - CUBE discretionary discount up to 10%
Free to Propose to Customer - CUBE discretionary discount up to 10%

RLDM Implementation Key #3:
Implementing Process via a Computerized Sales Force System

Semper Fortis advises the construction of a computerized sales force system for sales automation, opportunity management, process guidelines including decision-making flow charts, and information exchange. There are a number of packages in the customer relationship management space: the current leader is Seibel Systems, with others like SAP, Oracle, and internet portal Salesforce.com vying for greater share. No matter whether a company uses an application from a vendor or develops its own, using a computerized system offers many advantages regarding the ability to control and secure this all-important knowledge asset, consolidate the opportunity radar upwards, upgrade functions, and communicate within the sales force. While instituting graphical process charts typically is not standard within the canned packages, such functionality can be added relatively easily using existing web-based technology.

As CUBEs demonstrate growing acumen, the company can loosen the reins, giving them more room to decide without checking with their sales director. Typically, a CUBE's title doesn't change as he or she demonstrates good judgment, but internally, the company assigns decision-making "sergeant stripes." Based on a salesperson's decision-making rating, the flow charts and clip levels change dynamically (the levels in the diamond shaped blocks on the previous page) for each CUBE, clearly communicating the company's expectations.

RLDM Implementation Key #4:
Provide assigned mentors and consultants to the CUBEs while encouraging peer sharing of information and advice.

While sales directors serve as the first point of contact for consultation, management also assigns other decision-making mentors to each CUBE. For example, tricky financial ramifications or the development of intricate return on investment models may spur the CUBE into seeking the advice of his or her assigned finance department mentor.

CUBEs are encouraged to solicit advice and bounce ideas off their mentors and managers when faced with tough decisions.

Mentors are provided basic training in professional selling, so that they better understand the process and keys to selling success. This is an important step in warming the entire organization up to the idea of a superior pro-sales ideology. CUBEs are encouraged to officially recognize the efforts mentors have had on their successes, making heroes throughout the enterprise. In the end, many departments within the company begin to take part and benefit from their teamwork with the direct sales force.

RLDM Implementation Key #5:
Management Control and Enterprise Visibility

Once any customer-level decision is made, the Semper Fortis program suggests having the CUBE enter the decision in an internal intranet portal, using a simple headline and one-paragraph explanation format. Required data elements include company name and specific customer contact name(s), providing a permanent record of all decisions broken down by customer or by CUBE. The data then is logged on dynamic screens for first-line management, rolling upwardly to the commander-in-chief of sales and other executives.

See a sample decision log simulation at www.SeizingShare.com/log

Generally speaking, most companies will choose a traditional hierarchy for decision review, where the first-line sales director sees all the decisions in his or her area, then the area VP sees all in his or her domain and so forth. Filters are provided allowing management to look at subsets of the data by account, salesperson, or geography. Decisions requiring a second approval from first-line management automatically notify the sales directors of the need to add their concurrence.

The Semper Fortis model advises proactive yet controlled information sharing through the development of a world-class Sales Intelligence

Group, or SIG (discussed in the next section). The decision-making logs are fully visible not only to the commander-in-chief of sales but to the SIG leaders, who are responsible for ensuring that CUBEs in current sales battles learn from other CUBEs' successes and setbacks in similar situations.

In the end, company executives can watch the field decision-making activity in near real time on the secure intranet portal, with views for today, this week, this month, and so forth.

RLDM Implementation Key #6: Ramifications for Management

The conversion of field sales personnel to CUBEs has a great number of implications for the way managers—especially first-line sales directors—approach their duty. The next chapter addresses this developmental issue.

In Summary…

Implementing right-level decision-making is not difficult once the sales professionals understand their P&L and the ramifications of decisions. Semper Fortis focuses on process and visibility of decisions on a near real-time basis to the entire sales management team. The benefits of entrepreneurial thinking and energy drive extraordinary results.

We have now completed the second facet of the Right-Level Decision-Making pillar in the Semper Fortis Model:

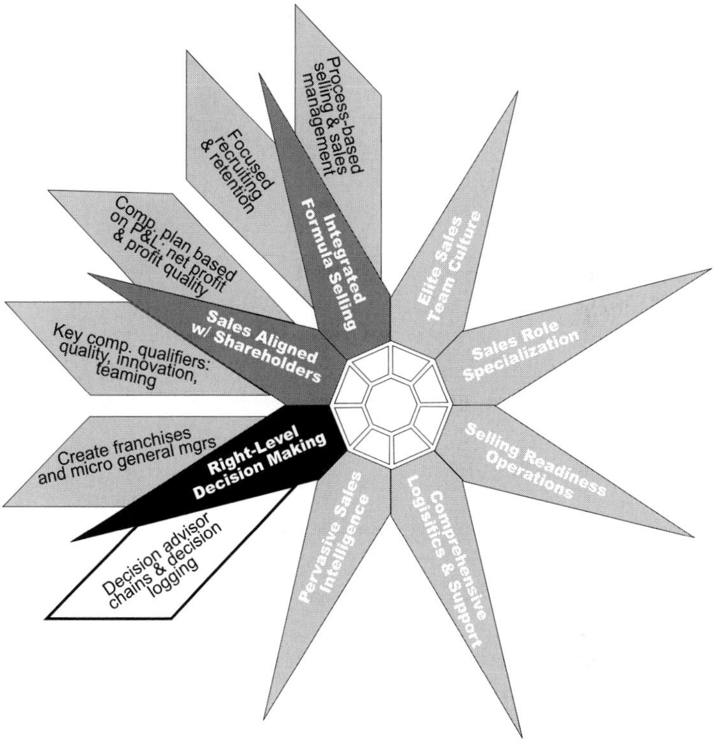

Chapter 12: Optimizing First-Line Management

The transformation of salespeople to Customer Unit Business Executives (CUBEs) is a substantial one, driving significant change upstream. The greatest change, after the entrepreneurial fire ignites within the professional sales ranks, is at the first-line manager level.

Just as the individual sport coaches are the heart of the U.S. Olympic Team's effort, the first-line managers, or sales directors in Semper Fortis nomenclature, keep the sales force on the right track. As CUBEs become adept at decision-making, the role of the manager changes to one of coach and leader.

Coaching and teaching are the foundations of great leadership.

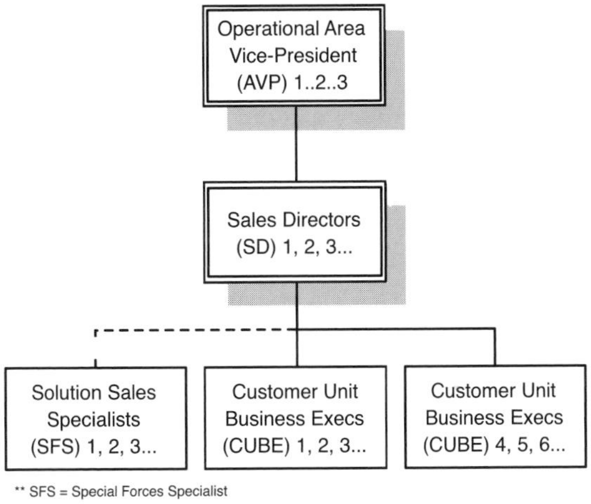

(see complete organization chart model in Appendix A)

The following are important aspects of coaching that redefine the manager's role on the sales team.

1) Recruiting and retaining the best sales talent is a must.

As we discussed in Chapter 7, paying strict attention to recruiting and landing the best players is an important pursuit. Nowhere is this more evident than in America's dominance of international basketball. The Dream Teams did not win through superior coaching and practice but rather through overwhelming the opposition with talent. Coaching can sometimes overcome the talent advantage but talent, if the shortcoming is substantial, will win the majority of the sales battles.

2) Managers should focus the team on daily, consistent, superior sales effort, not signed contracts.

When managers and salespeople focus on the end result, many obstacles, a good number outside a person's control, can stand in the way of landing contracts. On the other hand, the quality of the effort is 100% within the control of each player. First-line sales directors must instill this concept in all the CUBEs and field support personnel, allowing everyone to concentrate on what they can affect instead of wasting precious time and energy on outcomes they cannot.

3) Keep the company processes lean and sales message as straightforward as possible.

Complexity rarely helps success. Yet too often, companies forget to focus on simplicity and clear differentiation.

Nebraska has put together an extraordinary multi-decade record of college football success. They have accomplished this feat not by focusing on trick plays and great variety. Quite the contrary, Big Red focuses on a simple but well-executed attack that pounds competitors backward play after play.

A company that sells on twenty or thirty equal points will find that most of its salespeople are unable to clearly communicate and verify that each point is well-framed in the prospect's mind. The customer, with many vendors calling on him or her, rarely will retain even half the twenty points and in truth, may retain none, as nothing outstanding will be foremost in mind. On the other hand, by finding and emphasizing the right three key issues, a customer will easily be able to tell others why they buy from the vendor. The sales directors must stay vigilant and ensure that each salesperson is articulating the same concise and focused message.

4) Practice with precision.

The upcoming Section Six is dedicated to the concepts of practice. The process is a continuous circle of learning, practice, execution in real life situations, debriefing, and starting all over again. Sports teams practice each play dozens of times for each time it is run in a game situation.

Corporate sales forces rarely practice at all. Most learning happens in live customer situations. Semper Fortis changes this sad state of affairs. The sales directors are the key drivers, ensuring that practice is taken seriously.

5) Avoid the emotional roller coaster—Stay focused and professional.

An organization that stays focused on maintaining a high level of effort, quality, and professionalism wins more games than one that lives for the rush of adrenaline. It delineates the professionals from the amateurs. Semper Fortis forces move quickly, with precision, not missing key steps, and giving their "A" effort every day, every week. First-line management's role is to ensure that the effort stays consistent, that morale stays high, and professionalism never suffers. If an organization gets in the habit of expecting and delivering nearly the same level of superior effort every day, that company is well on its way to success.

6) Great leaders teach.

Managers must see themselves as leaders and coaches. What that really boils down to is becoming teachers. Teaching allows the insight of one person to enable hundreds, even thousands of others to succeed beyond what they could have done without that instruction and understanding.

Teaching requires that the coach be highly competent in his or her craft, earning the respect of the team members. After that, it simply comes down to:

1. Clearly communicating the what, why and how of the lesson,
2. Showing people how to do it—often in live customer situations,
3. Having the student imitate and practice first, then
4. Support them in live customer arenas, and finally
5. Correct and drill them until the skills become second nature.

Corporate managers seem to avoid this all-important duty much of the time, instead delegating instruction to paid third-parties, who always have “outsider” challenges that they can never truly overcome—for one thing, outsiders never go on live customer sales calls.

7) Let salespeople sell, especially when the stakes are high.

All too often, a company's players don't get the opportunity to play in the big game. When a critical deal comes along, upper management steps in, believing that they and they alone can ensure the deal is won.

If coaching has been done as it should have been, the coaches can and should step back and let the players win mostly on their own. It builds self-confidence and keeps the troops motivated. Without a doubt, there are times where managers and executives must play specialized roles in big sales and meetings, but care must be taken to ensure that the CUBEs and other specialists play their role to the fullest extent possible. Certain times will require the senior executive to seal the deal, but in those cases, the CUBE must make the call, request the executive assistance, and direct the action.

8) Adapt and Overcome. Fail with Forward Momentum.

The first-line sales director is the absolute key to fostering a learning environment. Companies have a nasty habit of celebrating success for only a short moment, and sweeping every mistake under the rug in Watergate fashion. Debriefs of successes in the corporate world are rare and are almost unheard-of on failures unless an event was so spectacular that executives demand forensics, often resulting in head-hunting, instead of learning. It's not surprising that organizational learning is poor in corporations.

Making mistakes is good. It shows that the team is striving, doing new things. A company that makes no mistakes is typically dormant in its approach and missing opportunities. But it is of the utmost importance that the same mistakes never happen twice. The company must take prudent risks and make mistakes to learn. This is difficult because a sales force is typically scattered all over the country or countries, and communications between pockets is not always free-flowing.

First-line sales directors are chartered to conduct extensive debriefs of what worked when things go well, and what could have been done differently when things go awry. Then, this key data must be passed to the SIG and upper management for documentation, dispersion, and additional follow-up. SIG's charter is to stay situationally aware of the detailed activity everywhere and proactively route information where it can make a positive impact on other sales efforts.

The Semper Fortis model thrives on pushing the envelope and learning from mistakes. Few companies institutionalize failing forward.

9) Teamwork is mission-critical.

The upcoming Section Eight is dedicated to teamwork. Teams invariably tend to beat individuals. Yet today's sales forces rarely exhibit flawless teamwork or, for that matter, any teamwork. This failure is normally driven by corporate cultures that sometimes talk "teams" but do not insist on teamwork in daily operations.

The teamwork culture of Semper Fortis is built and anchored by the first-line sales directors.

10) Processes must be followed. Processes that do not help achieve excellence should be changed, not circumvented.

Process often has a poor reputation in the chaotic environment of sales. The reason is that getting process right—in other words, having process help, not hinder work flow—is a difficult task. But processes can be good or bad, depending on whether a company is firm in its resolve to adhere to them and fix parts that don't make business sense. Process must be focused on making sales happen, not just as a control mechanism for upper management.

If a company wants repeatable success across a large number of employees, process is a must. The first-line sales directors must ensure that this part of the culture is deeply ingrained, and must provide continuous feedback regarding changes that should be implemented to accommodate the workflow even better.

11) Adjust to the salespeople, not vice versa.

Many coaches generally understand that every player doesn't achieve maximized performance from the same instruction, yet business management often tends to try to apply one-size-fits-all measures, envisioning Patton-like dictatorship. This is especially prevalent in a manager's first promotion into the management ranks.

For a coach to achieve the best results, Semper Fortis encourages understanding what approach works with each sales professional and adjusting to maximize the result. In fact, Semper Fortis uses specialist coaches for certain types of issues in which a salesperson's direct manager may not have the best skills. For example, if a salesperson is struggling with stand-up presentations, the company may decide to use another person as the coach or even send the person to outside classes to drive improvement.

12) Preparation paves the road to consistent achievement.

Indiana University's basketball coach Bobby Knight, once said:

"The will to win is not nearly as important as the will to prepare to win."

He was right. Corporate America mistakenly believes it is too busy to prepare and as such, opens the door of opportunity for those few who have greater will and fortitude.

13) Management must be decisive.

How often have you watched a coach on the sidelines hesitate, unable to make the call on a critical 3rd down play in the Superbowl? The answer is never, because football teams cannot win without crisp decision-making in a highly dynamic environment.

Yet corporations often breed indecision and delay. Managers wait for more data, unable to make the call. Within the Semper Fortis model, coaches and leaders are trained to make the call and move on, as it is usually much better to err on the side of action than inaction.

14) Being a leader is not a popularity contest.

Leadership is not a popularity contest. Tough calls must be made. Leaders must often make those calls. The goal must be to strive for mutual respect and trust with the salespeople so that decisions are made with an eye toward "making business sense" and fairness, not favoritism and political ends.

So that there is no mistake, let me state clearly that fairness is not the same as equality. Fairness is giving salespeople the consideration they have earned, based on their track records. A sales force is not the place for absolute equality. It is the home of absolute meritocracy. CUBEs with extraordinary records of achievement, dedication, integrity, and teamwork have earned more leeway than those who have not contributed nearly as much to the cause. The trick is for the entire company to understand this definition of fairness clearly, so visible inequalities are understood by all.

15) Clear communication is mission-critical.

There is no such thing as over-communication in a knowledge-based environment. Invariably, some people tend to hoard information under the mistaken notion that "knowledge is power." The commander-in-chief of sales must ensure that his organization genuinely talks and collaborates.

Information must flow freely both up and down and peer-to-peer. Semper Fortis focuses on clear communication in four ways:

1. **Top-down flow**—Important notices from upper management must flow steadily to all the players,

2. **Bottom-up flow**—First-line management and the SIG collaborate to ensure that all important data is captured, recorded, analyzed, and used to help progress,

3. **Peer-to-peer flow**—Weekly or bi-weekly idea sessions are scheduled via conference call to inspire peer-to-peer discussion. CUBEs and specialists report on their activity while others with similar situations later contact their peers for additional information if needed,

4. The **Sales Intelligence Group** oversees the capture and analysis of information, drawing attention to any issues encountered with free-flow of knowledge.

16) Most of a sales director's time is spent concentrating on his or her own people, message, and value-add, not on the competition.

It is easy to lose focus and start worrying about the competition and its message. No doubt that this is an important aspect of selling, but many of the issues cannot be addressed by the sales force. The game is won more often by making your criteria, areas where your offering is strong, top criteria for the decision by a prospect.

Sales management should be focused on continuously improving the sales force and the message. SIG and commander-in-chief of sales must be the ones who analyze and adjust strategy in relation to competition.

In Summary...

Distributed decision-making in the field offers the organization tremendous benefits. First-line sales directors are crucial to achieving world-class teamwork, results, process, and communications. With right-level decision-making comes entrepreneurship and simultaneously the opportunity for each CUBE to play the game far differently from what is called for in the organization plans. First-line management must keep everyone focused while communicating the best innovations to executives for introduction into the company's formula for success.

The result is that first-line managers are converted from a control focus to sales directors, focused on coaching and leadership alignment. Only by developing superior field officers can a company achieve optimum results.

Section Four

~ ~ ~ ~ ~ ~ ~ ~ ~ ~

Pervasive Sales Intelligence

Success in professional selling requires superior knowledge of of the customer, the competition, the industry, and one's capabilities.

Semper Fortis focuses on developing and leveraging intelligence, ensuring that sales professionals are well-armed as they battle competitors.

"If you know the enemy and know yourself,
you need not fear the result of a hundred battles."
- Sun Tzu

Chapter 13: Establishing the Sales Intelligence Group

Intelligence operations often have bad connotations in the business world. Too many James Bond films have filled people's minds with images of illegal activities and high-risk missions. In today's world, the electronic-sourced intelligence problem is sorting through a tidal wave of easily and legally-obtainable information *in time* to make smarter decisions. However the other side, human-sourced intelligence from employees, is often even more important. As more and more of a company's value-add becomes knowledge and relationship-based, recording and *using* that intelligence becomes paramount to success.

Every company possesses a great amount of knowledge and understanding regarding customers, competitors, strategies and tactics that work or fail in various situations. Unfortunately, this information is too often completely decentralized and "off-line," locked inside the heads of the salespeople, managers, and field support personnel. It is not well-developed, written down, organized, indexed, or managed as an asset.

There are many reasons for this:

1. As discussed in Section Two, most companies operate under a quota plan that prevents forthright sharing of key nuggets of information.

2. Sales management tends to not demand a regimen of formal sales planning and process. When sales plans are big, annual, static documents created only for the largest accounts, few clarification questions are asked or if they are asked, it happens only once each year and the answers are typically not written down.

3. These data elements inside people's heads are not only guarded as secrets, but they are not developed nearly to the extent that they could be. No techniques are taught, no checklists are followed, few questions are asked, and as a result, salespeople do not learn nor develop more information steadily over time.

In the 1980s and 1990s, knowledge was recognized as an asset and today, hundreds of books and software packages are vying for thought-leadership on the topic. Companies are busy appointing Chief Knowledge Officers, but, in sales, many of these efforts come up short. Unless a company changes compensation and recognition to align the goals of the sales force with the goals of the company, unless human intelligence specialists are put in place to help these customer relationship management software packages succeed, unless management makes sales force learning and candid communications a daily priority, the knowledge officers will not achieve their full objective.

Once the first three foundation pillars of Semper Fortis are in place, the road is paved for information sharing. The sales professionals must be convinced that management is committed to "entrepreneurial franchises" and the net profit meritocracy model for the long term. If concerns still exist that the quota system may be reinstated in the next couple of years, the company will not be able to get much data from the force.

Semper Fortis advocates the creation of a centralized intelligence collection and analysis group that serves as the right-hand of the commander-in-chief of sales. Looking at the generally poor record of customer relationship management software implementations, there is little evidence that rolling out sales force automation software will result in much benefit unless dedicated resources stay on top of the project. Most companies have serious intelligence short-falls, whether they come from human or electronic sources.

If a company's sales group is small, and the technology and competitive landscape is slow-moving, it may be possible for the commander-in-chief of sales to operate in this role based on personal interactions. However, more often than not, operational demands, organization size, employee turnover, fast-changing product and competitive landscapes, and dynamic customer environments outgrow the ability of the leader to maintain excellent situational awareness.

The core differentiators that separate excellent intelligence groups from poor ones are the quality of its analysts, the quality of its information gathering, and the quality of its knowledge base system. Staffing the Sales Intelligence Group (SIG) with second-string players is a mistake, but this happens often enough, as leaders prefer to keep the best salespeople selling and avoid promoting them to staff roles, even if the staff roles are important enterprise-wide.

Under Semper Fortis, the intelligence group size varies by the size of the organization supported. At its smallest, the SIG group can be one seasoned sales professional who leads the effort and focuses on human-sourced intelligence, a technical analyst who applies his energies to electronically sourced intelligence, and a prolific administrative assistant who documents continuously. A group of this size would typically support a sales group of thirty or fewer salespeople. This ratio is a good rule of thumb in determining the SIG staffing for sales professionals and administrative assistants, even though considerable variance exists depending on the dynamics of an industry sector. The technical analyst position does not grow beyond a few people for some time, as external information is gathered primarily from electronic sources.

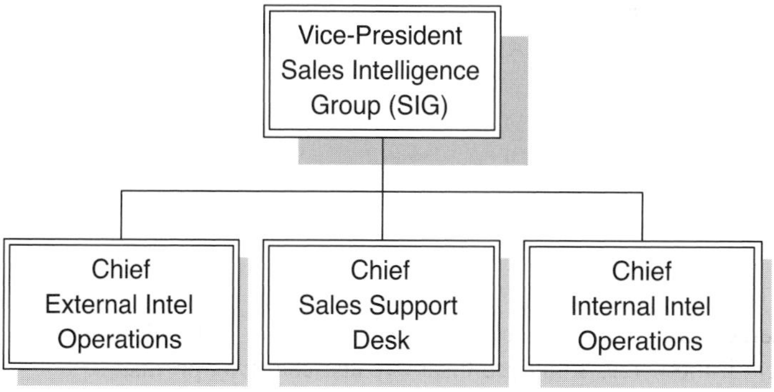

The SIG's former sales professionals must be intimate with the industry environment and must have individual records and reputations that permit CUBEs to see them, at a minimum, as worthy peers. Without this experience and reputation, the gathering of information is compromised as CUBEs either pull the wool over the SIG operatives' eyes or refuse to cooperate during the short, weekly calls that are part of standard operating procedures.

By splitting the intelligence function off from operational management, the commander-in-chief of sales gains a valuable second set of eyes and ears trained on the field, as well as a second opinion to that of first-line managers who are sometimes biased, as they are often deep in the heat of the battle. A key aspect of winning leadership is maintaining a positive bias. Nearly all successful sales leaders will be quite optimistic. The job of the SIG is to stay neutral, pragmatic, or even have a slight negative, questioning lean, helping the leaders see other plausible sides of any issue.

If the sales force professionals do not receive value-add from the SIG, the intelligence operation will not achieve its goals.

For the SIG to succeed, it must balance and accomplish the following objectives:

1. The SIG must develop trust individually with every salesperson and first-line sales director.

2. The information flow must be bi-directional—the salespeople offer their information freely and the SIG contacts reciprocate with information the salespeople need to help them with various opportunities.

3. The SIG must implement a system to store the information so that it is well-organized and accessible, while critical data elements, such as individual customer's pricing terms, are secure and available only when truly needed.

4. The SIG must understand the salesperson's mission as well as management's, helping both with timely information.

5. The SIG must serve as the center of knowledge exchange, proactively forwarding information to the people who can use it, based on possessing a superior situational awareness of the operations within the enterprise.

6. The SIG must develop methods to capture information directly from operations in the field without causing more administrative overhead on the CUBEs.

7. The SIG must train and maintain excellent relations with first-line managers, since they are tasked with helping the SIG succeed and serve as the first-line for initial debriefs and intelligence leads.

Intelligence operations invariably become too broad, losing effectiveness. The SIG must stay focused and not expand without a clear plan of why the additional information will offer payback benefits.

Clearly, the mission of the SIG can become too broad. Without a doubt, the operation cannot possibly cast a wide net and have any hope of success. The key is to focus on the 10 to 20% of intelligence work that offers the most benefit. Semper Fortis advises that the SIG's charter is written to focus 80% of the effort on human-sourced intelligence and 20% on electronically-sourced intelligence.

The benefits of internal knowledge flow typically outweigh the importance of information that can be leveraged from outside sources. For example, electronic-sourced intelligence might yield a user manual to a competitor's product, but human-sourced intelligence, specifically through Fred, the CUBE in Detroit, might yield the ten biggest selling points of that competitor's story. The company would find out that the competitor is de-emphasizing features, spending all their effort selling service aspects, warranty, ease-of-installation, and return on investment. Clearly, the latter intelligence is more useful to Sally, who is entering into a similar contest in San Diego this week.

Unlike other initiatives, the SIG is a bit more difficult to clearly justify based on hard dollar payback. The cost of the minimum-sized, three-person SIG operation is around half a million dollars. The fact that justification is difficult is precisely why most competitors do not invest and why the Semper Fortis company seizes the opportunity. Many miss the clear fact that superior knowledge and understanding are the primary tools of a sales force. Without intelligence, a company is sending its salespeople into a championship basketball game without knowing the opponent's strengths and weaknesses. With intelligence, the players are better prepared, know who the outside shooters are, know that #21 always drives to his left, know which match-ups should be targeted, and know who to foul based on free-throw percentages when only seconds remain in the game.

Despite the difficulty, the SIG can be justified. There are numerous benefits that offer hard dollar savings, but measurements are typically not sophisticated enough to determine exactly the impact of the SIG programs versus general management and other initiatives. If the sales leader is not seduced by the corporate folly of over-analysis, clear intuitive benefits include the following items:

Justification #1: Improved "Cost of Turnover"

> Whenever a salesperson, especially a senior one, leaves the company or a territory in pursuit of greener pastures, a difficult transition takes place. The incoming salesperson must turn into a forensic specialist, following vague clues as to how to re-engage and develop existing relationships at the various customers, wasting considerable time trying to understand the projects, competitor's positioning, and his own company's tactics-to-date at each prospect.
>
> With the SIG and the continuous sales planning process in place (discussed in detail in the upcoming Chapter 23), the

transition is greatly simplified. Most relationships and projects are well documented, as are the strategies the outgoing sales person was pursuing, as well as any understanding of the competitors' plans. The incoming CUBE gets fully briefed immediately, without losing months of productivity.

Justification #2: Organizational Learning from Wins and Mistakes

Having the SIG formalizes the debrief and documentation of successes and setbacks. The Semper Fortis organization avoids the typical "cover-up all mistakes only to repeat them again and again" corporate game plan.

Given the scarcity of resources, avoiding time-wasting futile sales efforts or wasting capital on projects with low probabilities for success can easily pay for the entire cost of the intelligence group.

Justification #3: Learning Competitor's Strengths and Weaknesses

The SIG is in a great position to consolidate an understanding of competitors' strengths and weaknesses. In selling, the ability to pre-position a prospect's key purchase criteria away from a competitor's sales story and strengths is a giant step on the road to a win. Given the importance of major accounts, one additionally won project each year can pay for the cost of the entire intelligence arm of the sales force.

Justification #4: Opportunity Cost of Missing Moments of Advantage

There are many moments of opportunity for every company in every solution arena. Without the consolidated view that the SIG enables, many are missed because only tidbit hints of the opportunity pop up in individual territories. The SIG helps the commander-in-chief of sales recognize and seize the opportunities that always appear.

Justification #5: Seeing New Competitors and Threats Early

Few successful companies are nimble in reacting to changes in their marketplace. Many books, from Andrew Grove's *Only the Paranoid Survive* to Clayton Christensen's *The Innovator's Dilemma* all point out how difficult the agility challenge can be.

The SIG helps, serving as an early warning system for new threats. Leadership must still react but the SIG can save the company from becoming irrelevant in today's fast-paced environment. If the SIG is instrumental in the company's reaction to competitive threats, it not only justifies its own existence but perhaps saves the entire enterprise in a crisis moment.

Implementing Semper Fortis on a Tight Budget

Within the Semper Fortis model, no function is more important than the SIG.

Even when implementing on a tight budget, the SIG is the one area where a full-time effort by a highly energetic professional is a must. However if budget and resource constraints make this impossible, I have seen success by starting the SIG as a centralized sales support desk, manned by entrepreneurial executive assistants.

By focusing the effort on pervasive knowledge and never reinventing-the-wheel, the back and forth information flow starts. If the chief of sales encourages support from sales directors, much ground can be gained.

Justification #6: Benefits for Internal Training

The smaller a sales force, the less likely formal training materials have been developed. An important side-benefit of the SIG's documentation efforts is that organizational how-to is captured and available in briefs and white papers for the sales force. When this information is combined with the "process" flow-charts that are part of Semper Fortis' franchisee operating formula, new recruits become productive quickly. Once again, one additional major account win justifies the annual cost of the SIG.

Justification #7: Soft Benefits of Focusing on Intelligence

A final important benefit is the effect a dedicated SIG operation has on the overall field force. Personnel become more attentive to listening and developing information. Over time, the continuous repetition of debrief and documentation becomes second nature. Sales calls are planned better, missing nuggets of data are systematically uncovered, and customers are impressed by how well the Semper Fortis enabled company listens and understands their problems.

In Summary…

Semper Fortis recognizes that having a smarter sales force is of paramount importance. Instead of adding yet another secondary responsibility onto mainstream management, the formula creates an overlay intelligence operation that focuses on the development of human and electronic sourced intelligence.

The initiative can be justified intuitively based on a number of factors, but the difficulty of exacting measures stop many firms from taking advantage of a focused, dedicated group. However, any firm that implements a Semper Fortis SIG will see tremendous benefits within two years and often less, arming their Sales Olympian force and upper management for combat, exploiting advantages offered by competitors, and learning and profiting from success and failures in the field.

Chapter 14: Gathering Intelligence

A common denominator found in most top-tier sales professionals is that they know more about their customers and prospects than competing salespeople from other companies. The depth of information on both the business and the personal level is often several times greater than the information an average performer develops. From interviewing hundreds of sales professionals and sales managers, I found that the top-tier professionals tend to have an organized information gathering and documenting process. They typically use personal checklists, ask great open-ended questions, develop call plans before entering meetings, and listen attentively.

Even though this facet of successful selling is well-known, and it is by no means rocket science to consolidate the activity into daily operations, few *organizations* institutionalize the collection, organization, and development of this information. Semper Fortis follows a simple formula to initiate the intelligence process and build its momentum over the years.

When the Sales Intelligence Group (SIG) is first established, immediate steps are taken to begin the flow of information after understanding what, if any, information is already documented. One interesting phenomenon is true of all salespeople: no matter how useful documentation and planning exercise may be, initial homework requests are met with great resistance, even if the field representatives understand the eventual benefit.

Step #1: Establishing a Foothold for Gathering Information

The SIG and sales management must approach their sales force in small steps, in order to not overwhelm salespeople with a large mountain of work. If taken in steps throughout the first year, the documentation effort will not seem nearly as difficult. The first step in the Semper Fortis formula is to ask salespeople to fill out the following simple matrix for each of their customer or prospect accounts.

Top Ten Key Customer Contacts, for Account (XYZ Co.)

Contact (Name, Title)	**Contact's Manager (Name, Title)**	**Rate in Order Of Importance To Us (1-10)** (10=critical)	**Rate your Relationship (1-10** (1=poor, 10=great))
1. Joe Smith, CFO	Bob Slate, Pres	2	6
2. Jim Doore,VP,IT	Joe Smith, CFO	1	8
3. etc... thru #10...			

Step #1 is also completed by the field-based personnel that surround and support the salespeople, including project managers, systems engineers, service managers, and others. The SIG soon has a pretty good view of who knows which contacts in each customer account.

Step #2: First Pass at Adding Color to the Key Contacts Picture

As a follow-up to Step #1, SIG specialists then place a telephone call to each salesperson, asking some clarifying questions regarding the data turned in during Step #1. Semper Fortis advocates always asking for more information every step of the way: people tend to have much more information than they realize or are willing to enter into a computer screen. By proactively asking for more, the spigots are turned on and data flows quickly. This information is documented and added to the original data, which is then copied back to the salespeople for their own use and correction if necessary.

As a final round to this Step #2, salespeople are e-mailed and asked to fill out one form per contact named in Step #1, with as much basic information as they know off the top of their heads, due in one week. Data in this round includes basics such as e-mail address, telephone numbers, and key elements such as those found in Harvey MacKay's 66 questions, available in his entertaining bestseller, *Swim With the Sharks Without Being Eaten Alive.*

For a look at Mr. MacKay's complete 66 questions, see link at www.SeizingShare.com/mac

Step #3: Establish a Foothold for Understanding the Prospects' Environment and Current Projects

Step #3 calls for documenting an initial "light" survey of the environment and discuss projects underway at each of the customers and prospects. In my experience, the best method is to conduct a "territory review" meeting with each of the salespeople, providing them an example template to follow for their formal presentation. Once again, asking too much in one round, especially in the formal written preparation phase, can prevent open data flow. The key is to ask just enough about the customer's environment to understand what products are in place from incumbent vendors, as well as identify what project "titles" may exist at each. A good rule of thumb is that the salespeople should spend less than four hours preparing for the first review meeting.

During the meeting, I recommend audio recording the comments and having the contents transcribed by one of the SIG's administrative assistants. The SIG administrative assistant should be present in the meetings to monitor the recording and take notes, enabling the best possible transcript reproduction. It is stunning how much detail is lost when no one is chartered with comprehensive note-taking, the current status quo in most business reviews. It is helpful if SIG administrative assistants have court reporter training, allowing them to keep pace with meetings in real time.

As part of the review, management and SIG "peel the onion," asking probing questions regarding relationships, customer politics, competitive position, and the salesperson's assessment of his or her company's strengths and weaknesses in relation to the prospect. By the end of the meeting, a clearer picture has formed and through the efforts of the SIG, has been documented in a lasting file on each account.

Step #4: Developing the Picture as the Game is Played

Step #4 is for the SIG, the first-line sales director, and the CUBE to collaborate and identify what information is needed but unknown at each account or prospect. This forms the beginning of an ongoing weekly effort to focus field personnel on asking specific questions and reporting back the answers, fleshing out the picture. The CUBE is ultimately responsible for determining how to best land the data.

As part of this effort, SIG introduces a sales call plan and structured debrief processes to help organize the initiative. Salespeople are encouraged by their managers to take fifteen minutes to produce a written sales call plan for every substantial sales meeting, no matter whether it is in person or on the telephone. As part of that plan, salespeople develop open-ended questions to ask during each meeting, filling in the gaps in the knowledge base (the upcoming Chapter 23 discusses the sales call plan in detail).

The Semper Fortis formula requires that each call plan be forwarded to the sales director and a salesperson's SIG contact, normally one full business day before the meeting. A solution sales specialist also sends the plan to the CUBE who maintains the leadership role at any given customer account. The sales director or SIG has an opportunity to suggest questions to consider for the call plan, forwarding their comments back to the CUBE or solution specialist. The field professional then executes the plan during the meeting. The Semper Fortis formula asks the sales force to take as many notes as feasible during meetings, which aids the official debrief later.

After the meeting is over, the salesperson follows a SIG pocket debrief card and the call plan, recording as much of the meeting detail to a digital voice recorder as he or she can remember. Several models are available from Olympus and other brands. These advanced units allow the voice files to upload via USB connections to salespeople's laptops, and provide desktop software that permits the digital, compressed files to be retrieved via the network in the background, and delivered to the SIG administrative assistant for transcription. Typically, the written debrief is available back to the salesperson within 24 hours, allowing them to add more comments and corrections while the memory of the meeting is still fresh.

As always, the SIG will typically follow up on all important sales calls with a quick clarification phone call on the quest for additional insight. Clearly, Step #4 is an ongoing process.

A great side benefit for sales management is offered by the call planning and debrief process. Many companies struggle with determining the best way to check sales activity levels. Decreased activity often points to a variety of problems, including the need for training, loss of motivation, possibility of departure from the firm, and so on. By requiring salespeople to produce and share sales call plans and the debrief results, it is easy to spot performance issues early: no one goes through the trouble of faking sales call plans and sales calls to show activity.

Step #5: Building the Company's Sales Radar Screen

The SIG's goal for the first six months is to document an excellent situational awareness of the customers, prospects, and projects. This focus helps salespeople ask better questions, listen better, and unearth more potential in their territories while identifying relationships that need attention.

Step #5 calls for building individual sales radar screens for each CUBE and solution specialist, reflecting the project potential of each territory. The territory sales radars consolidate upstream to sales directors, regional area VPs, and the commander-in-chief of sales, giving the entire organization a view of the potential and the hot spots of activity. From the enterprise war room view, the commander-in-chief of sales, SIG leader, VP of Special Forces, Human Resources chief, retention specialist, CFO, or president can drill down to the detail of an opportunity with a click of the PC mouse. This enterprise sales radar becomes a key planning input for resourcing, allocation of special forces, executives, and financial forecasting.

Some customer relationship management software packages offer a sales radar or sales pipeline function. An example of an individual's sales radar is offered below:

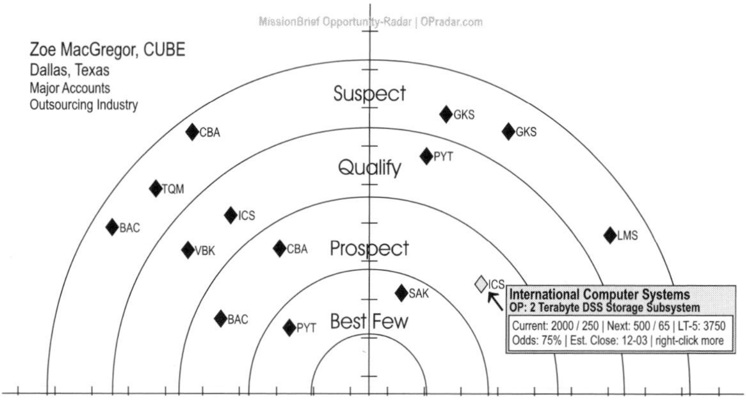

Step #6: Scheduled Mini-Reviews

Semper Fortis recommends quarterly mini-reviews of sales territories with sales management. New technologies permit the use of video and teleconferencing, simplifying the process of bringing together all the required players, no matter where they are in the world at the time of the meeting. The Internet permits many people to share the same PowerPoint presentation while using simple telephone conferencing for clear, real-time audio. The SIG participates, keeping track of missing data, finding out nuggets regarding competition, and documenting all the detail of each call with its prolific administrative assistants.

Step #7: Peer-to-Peer Share Sessions

CUBEs and solution specialists are charged with the task of sharing strategy and tactics learned from wins and losses in a monthly peer-to-peer teleconference. SIG and first-line management help pick the best examples from debrief work performed during the month. As with most SIG activity, the information is recorded and cataloged in the centralized knowledge base. Over the year, the SIG produces a number of "The Best of Peer-to-Peer" video / audio tapes to provide learning for all, especially as the Peer-to-Peer sessions are rarely heard by the entire force at the same time.

Step #8: Achieving the Semper Fortis Six-by-Six, by Key Customer Contacts, in Year One

In addition to gaining excellent situational awareness of the relationships, the customer environments, and ongoing projects, the Semper Fortis formula strives to accurately discern the answers to six key questions that help frame what is perceived as value-add in the mind of each key contact. These six questions become the primary focus for the latter half of year one.

The Semper Fortis six key questions are:

Contact Name:________________ Company:______________
Contact Title:________________ Reports to:_____________
Last Updated:________________

(1) What are the six most important issues that you and your department are facing and must solve over the next 12 to 18 months?
1.1) ____
1.2) ____
1.3 through 1.6...)______________________________

(2) What do you believe are the six most important issues that your company and your top executives are facing and must focus on over the next 1 to 4 years?
2.1) ____
2.2) ____
2.3 through 2.6...)______________________________

(3) What are the six most important personal career goals that you hope to achieve over the next 5 years? How about six goals outside the workplace?

Career Goals:
3.1) ______________________________
3.2) ______________________________
3.3 through 3.6...) ______________________________

Personal Goals:
3.a) ______________________________
3.b) ______________________________
3.c through 3.f...) ______________________________

(4) How do you perceive our company in the industry? What six words or sentences sum up where we stand in your mind, in the industry, and as a vendor or a potential vendor to you?

4.1) ______________________________
4.2) ______________________________
4.3 through 4.6...) ______________________________

(5) If you were to give us advice, what six things should we do or change to earn more of your business?

5.1) ______________________________
5.2) ______________________________
5.3 through 5.6...) ______________________________

(6) Who are the six most influential decision makers and decision influencers on projects where we compete, and how are they aligned with or against each other?

6.1) ______________________________
6.2) ______________________________
6.3 through 6.6...) ______________________________

Undoubtedly, getting good answers requires a concerted and cross-referenced effort by salespeople, sales managers, and executive contacts. Gathering this information requires many meetings and informal events. The SIG focuses the effort, inspiring the CUBEs to orchestrate the collection effort.

An ongoing verification process follows, ensuring that this critical data stays fresh. Once in place, the roadmap to becoming a value-producing, consultative vendor that solves key customer problems comes into better focus.

Helpful Hints in the Early Stages of Information Collection:

Salespeople are the world's worst at starting or finishing homework. Helpful hints for pulling off any knowledge management or strategic planning project with a sales force include:

- **No leaks:**
  All sales people get the same step-to-be-completed at the same time.
- **Approach projects in discrete baby steps:**
  Small steps make easy first downs.
- **Take salespeople offsite to succeed in finishing painstaking parts of a project:**
  Don't leave them in their own cell phone / e-mail environment.
- **Provide an incentive:**
  For example, conduct a two-day meeting offsite, but offer a surprise round of golf if the step is completed before 10 a.m. on day two.
- **Lead by example:**
  Don't leave it all up to the sales representative. Sales management needs to help do some of the painful homework.

Intelligence Parallel Efforts in Year One:

Competitive Information from Internal Sources:
As the SIG collects intelligence and documents the situation faced by the sales force, a parallel effort to document the sales stories, pricing strategies, strengths, and weaknesses of the competitors is underway.

Sales Fitness Evaluation:
The SIG also develops personnel evaluations that are shared with Human Resources and retention personnel. This information helps the Semper Fortis-enabled company identify which field personnel may need specialized coaching and development.

Proactive Assistance:
Building reciprocal, mutually beneficial relationships between the SIG and the field CUBEs, solution specialists, and first-line sales directors is of utmost importance to internal-sourced intelligence success. The SIG makes a special effort to assist in whatever way possible to help CUBEs and solution specialists win, including visits to the field for important sales calls or proposal moments.

Steps in Year Two:

Once the recommended year one SIG agenda is completed, the momentum of information takes on a life of its own. As sales management asks more questions, the SIG determines the best areas upon which to focus human-sourced data collection.

In Summary...

Human-sourced intelligence is priceless. The SIG serves a key role in developing an organized initiative, keeping the momentum going, building an intelligence-gathering habit enterprise-wide, and documenting details in a centralized system. If a company accepts the Semper Fortis methods for building sales intelligence, it will be well on its way to arming its sales force with critical data that will show bottom-line results in more wins.

Knowledge is one of a company's most important assets. The time has come for companies to invest in a Sales Intelligence Group, not just customer relationship management software, to make sure that knowledge is documented and, more importantly, used for competitive advantage.

We now add the next facet to the Semper Fortis model:

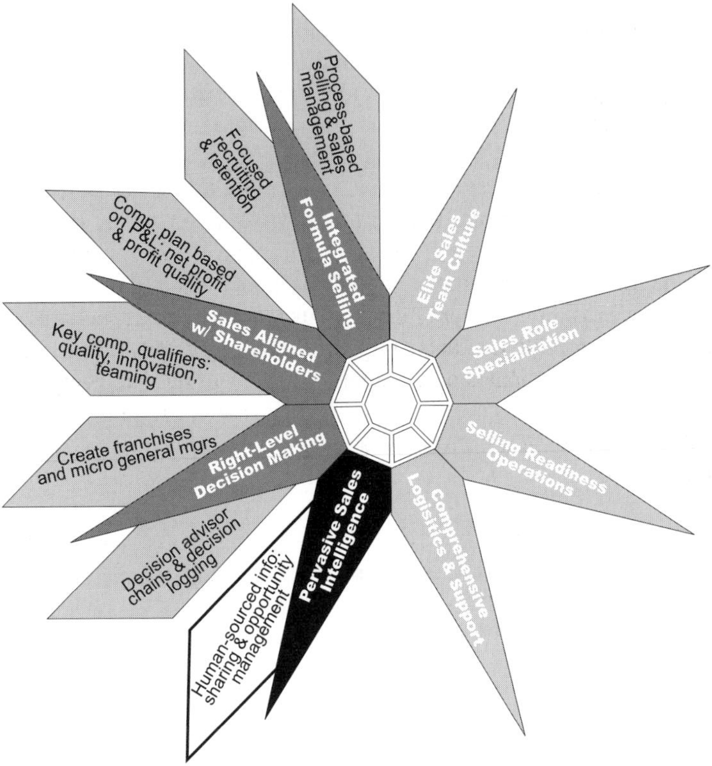

Chapter 15: Using Electronic-Sourced Intelligence

The world is swamped with data. Pervasive networking has made data instantly available. The challenge for winning the external-sourced intelligence game is to listen, filter, and deliver information *in time* to make a difference.

In the Semper Fortis formula, the SIG (Sales Intelligence Group) has one or more electronic intelligence analysts who serve two duties. First, the analysts are chartered with designing procedures and systems to store all information, no matter what the source, in the enterprise's sales knowledge base. Second, the analysts monitor external sources of data, culling valuable tidbits, storing them, and proactively sending the data to field professionals or managers who need it. As with everyone in the SIG, the analysts must stay situationally aware of the information needs and activity of the entire sales organization if they are to be effective in delivering valuable information in a timely fashion.

Given the vast resources available, SIG analysts work in a way some may see as backwards, first determining what intelligence data is needed by their CUBE (Customer Unit Business Executives) and sales management "customers." The analysts then tap a variety of sources to get the data flowing in a timely fashion.

While the exact needs may vary from one company and industry to another, the Semper Fortis formula for electronic-sourced intelligence concentrates on seven initiatives in year one.

Step #1: Identifying Sales Opportunities Intelligence Stream

One of the first initiatives the SIG takes on is to listen for opportunity. The nature of the connected, internet world is that companies leave substantial trails or press releases, news, and financial filings with government bodies. By checking free sources of news such as Yahoo and CBS MarketWatch, and by subscribing to premium services such as LEXIS / NEXIS and Edgar, it becomes easy to monitor industry activity. For example, if Switzerland's economic minister announces revamping the country's power grid to include more diversified power generation sources, it sends a clear signal that they will have to purchase engineering services, and construction goods and services, to meet their stated goal, opening the door for competitors from nuclear to hydro to fuel-cell technologies.

Step #2: Understanding Customer and Prospect Data Streams

There is no reason that sales professionals can't read every printed word about each one of their customers and prospects. Yet many do not, since they do not have the initiative to watch even a simple service such as Yahoo.

The SIG ensures that they see everything by automatically routing weekly briefs by account via email. As part of the process, each article asks the reader to rate its applicability to his or her job, and the feedback routes back to the SIG analyst. Over time, the analyst understands what articles will be of great interest versus those that will not be useful.

Step #3: Gaining Insights About Competitors

Competitors offer a wealth of information on their websites and in their tradeshows, brochures, and user manuals. Often, only a little bit of effort can yield important intelligence, especially when combined with information harvested from human sourced intelligence efforts.

The SIG analysts attend industry conferences, trade shows, and meetings to document the sales story of competitors. They subscribe to sources such as the Gartner Group for third-party evaluations of competitive products. This information is brought into focus with effort on the human sourced intelligence side: SIG analysts conduct company-wide conference calls, often concentrating on one competitor a month, to harvest and organize additional data, including any known competitive pricing and proposal specifics.

Step #4: Delivering Information of Interest to Customers and Prospects

One of the ways a salesperson improves his or her "value-add" rating with a customer contact is to serve as an interesting information source. A common trait of many successful sales executives is that they carefully clip and forward magazine and news articles to their contacts that they believe will be of interest to them.

The SIG steps in, polling the sales force for each contact and what articles are of interest to them for "forward to customers" purposes. For example, George Walken, a VP at Gulfstream may want to see articles about new advances in avionics, even though the Semper Fortis vendor may be in the telecommunications business and have little to do with airplane manufacturing. By setting up automated data collection and filtering programs, avionics articles are accumulated directly on the salesperson's PC in a folder dedicated to George. The salesperson previews the content as a final check of applicability and interest, then forwards good ones on to George via e-mail with a short cover note, or orders a reprint if legalities require it.

Step #5: Trends and Advances in the Industry Intelligence Stream

Another value-add that builds the credibility of salespeople is awareness and competence on industry topics. The SIG collects all sources of industry articles, the analyst reviews them to ensure applicability and quality of content, then forwards good ones to the appropriate salespeople for review and feedback rating. Sales management often charges the SIG with watching for specific areas of interest that ultimately may become new offerings for the company. The salespeople stay current and educated on the industry. They also have the ability to forward interesting articles to key contacts, further building their standing with clients.

Step #6: Education on the Latest Guru-Speak Intelligence Stream

Building the salesperson into a consultative force is not complete without building a keen understanding of the Ivy League topics of the day. These ideas tend to be some of the best ways to build rapport with the executive layers of companies.

The analysts in the SIG use readily available services to offer summaries of key business books to the sales force. A program is instituted for suggested reading, audio books are made available via the corporate thought-leadership library to be used on airplanes or commutes and so forth. Certain articles are offered as reprints out of magazines such as the *Harvard Business Review, McKinsey Quarterly*, and others. Many are forwarded to the sales force training specialists, to become information used for "thought-leadership" training sessions and video tapes.

Building the SIG Knowledge Base

Building the Internal Knowledge Base:

By staying in lock step with the human-source intelligence side of the SIG, the analysts build an extensive electronic knowledge base of information on each customer's and prospect's account. It is important to complete this activity without adding any substantial work on the part of the field personnel.

At a minimum, the following documents are added into the database, refreshed on an ongoing basis:

1. Key Contact Data, including the Key Six-by-Six Matrix
   (see Chapter 14)
2. Sales Call Plans
   (see Part Two, Section Six)
3. Structured Sales Call Debriefs
   (see Part Two, Section Six)
4. Environment Surveys
5. Territory Review Data
6. Sales Radar Funnel Data
7. Strategic Account Plans
   (see Part Two, Section Six)
8. Opportunity Plans
   (see Part Two, Section Six)
9. Sales Presentations Archive
10. Customer Requests for Information and Requests for Proposal
11. Project Survey Data
12. Proposals
13. Important letters and e-mails regarding any customer account or prospect
14. Franchise Decision Logs
    (see Part Two, Section Three)
15. Competitive Sales Story Data
16. Competitive Pricing

The analysts secure data that is sensitive, while summarizing data in generic terms for distribution to the rest of the sales force. However, when an opportunity demands in-depth knowledge, analysts work with the CUBEs and solution specialists to ensure that everything that needs to surface does, in order to help win the opportunity. The only issue is to ensure that bulk data is not downloadable without managed oversight, as the danger always exists that a salesperson may be leaving the company and is trying to gather data on the way out the door.

Building the Internal and External Knowledge Web Portal:

The SIG analysts produce an information portal on a secure, logon-controlled intranet / internet site to aid in the distribution of intelligence as well as organizing requests. The portal becomes the first stop for reading industry news, understanding what the organization learned this week, and more.

The same portal technology is then extended (optionally) out to the customers, in an edited format, allowing them to gain value from the Semper Fortis company's intelligence operations. The name of the game remains adding value and electronic intelligence delivers.

In Summary…

When a company implements electronic intelligence gathering, care must be taken to focus on information needs first, and not the supply. The supply side in our globally connected world is immense. The VP of the SIG must constantly question whether certain intelligence streams are useful and serving the intended purpose. However, if implemented well, true value is delivered to the sales force and to the customer.

We now add the final facet to the Pervasive Sales Intelligence pillar of the Semper Fortis model:

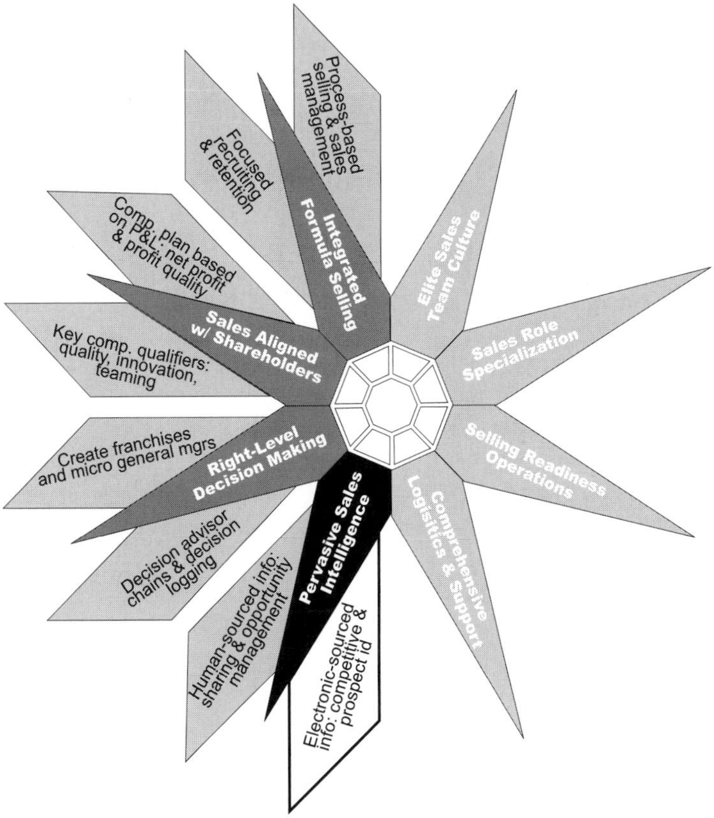

Section Five

~ ~ ~ ~ ~ ~ ~ ~ ~ ~

Comprehensive Logistics and Support

Many corporations do an inadequate job supporting the sales force.
Salespeople are often forced into quality assurance roles,
taking time away from the pursuit of additional opportunities.

Semper Fortis focuses on leveraging all available resources to
keep the sales professional at the peak of productivity.

"When executives send brave salespeople into battles,
the enterprise has a clear duty to support them fully in the endeavor."
- Bruce W. Travis

Chapter 16: Providing Comprehensive Sales Support

In military combat, excellent, timely support is a life-and-death issue. Every exercise focuses on delivering support where and when it is needed. Tanks become sitting ducks if they run short of fuel. Troops become casualties if they run out of ammunition. America's dominant military would not be dominant if the support logistics could not keep up with the rapid deployment of soldiers.

When troops are in battle, the military hierarchy exists to help the soldiers on the front lines succeed and survive. Everything else takes a back seat—even the walls of bureaucracy between service branches become irrelevant.

Corporate America has much to learn about supporting the battle front. Field personnel are fighting various sales battles continuously around the globe. Yet, many executives lose focus regarding where the battle is won or lost, on the customer front lines, against competitive vendors. Headquarters priorities tend to become a bigger and bigger portion of everyone's daily work load.

Too often, the next prospect opportunity is seen as more unwanted work by supporting departments.

In the Semper Fortis model, this focus is regained and institutionalized, but not at the expense of higher-level strategy.

Right-Level Decision Making

As part of Right-Level Decision Making, the top executives keep focused on strategic questions at the organizational level, such as:

- "What products should we invest in?"
- "What types of markets and customers should we target?"

- "What is our true value-add to various types of customers?"
- "What types of environments should we avoid?"
- "How can we as a company better support the front-lines?"
- "What process changes will make the sales force more efficient and effective?"
- "What changes can be made to improve the growth potential of individual sales franchises?"

Area VPs allocate precious resources for maximum effectiveness, work on plans for addressing their territory, and fine-tune the sales process to maximize effectiveness while avoiding bureaucracy.

First-line sales directors coach, teach, and motivate the sales professionals, play a key role in intelligence gathering, and help their CUBEs overcome issues that prevent them from focusing on their primary objectives.

Finally, the CUBEs manage and grow their individual franchises and P&L statements, while operating as part of a closely knit team.

This hierarchy exists for normal business progress. However, Semper Fortis draws and publishes two organizational charts internally, a traditional one called the Strategic Organizational Chart as described above and another called the Tactical Organizational Chart, where the CUBE is placed at the top, and everyone else in the organization aligns below them.

This inversion clearly shows everyone that many people from the CUBE down to the president and CEO, are all responsible for success in tactical battles once the firm is engaged and determined to win. The tactical chart also shows that certain traditional lines of reporting should be skipped; for example, a CUBE should contact the departmental sales liaison in Development or his or her Finance Department analyst directly, avoiding the overhead of contacting his or her sales director, who in turn would escalate to the area VP and so on.

Publishing two organizational charts sends a clear, concise message regarding the value a company associates with customers and sales progress.

As highlighted in previous chapters, the sales effort is typically run without defined process in many companies. In this environment, the sales professional spends and inordinate amount of time and effort on quality assurance and herding cats. Without process, each engagement is handled differently and few in the company feel or claim responsibility for any particular step. A salesperson spends time developing opportunities, then when one is landed, spends most of his or her time troubleshooting the project. The proverbial wheel is reinvented month after month and year after year.

Today's companies continue to win deals, but often through the Herculean efforts of sales heroes. It should not be surprising that less than 20% of salespeople have the right stuff to be heroes and then it should not be surprising that 20% of a sales force often delivers 80% of the revenue and profit. Executives have heard of the 80/20 rule so often that they believe that the situation is optimal, but it is not.

Process is the key to ensuring that the rest of the organization feels great personal responsibility for the success of every project. Great care is taken to make sure that various groups buy into the sales effort, hand-offs of work are clear and communicated to the entire community, and quality is built into the discipline, not an overlay function that gobbles up selling time.

People react to how they are measured and compensated. Even though Semper Fortis is focused on improving the sales force, a world-class sales effort cannot exist without the gung-ho cooperation of everyone in the company; therefore, “sales impact” measurements must be put in place for all key players in departments that support selling.

Supporting department personnel must be measured on how they rate with CUBEs and sales directors.

In most companies, few departments outside the sales force feel the heat if customer satisfaction wanes. When salespeople are trapped performing quality assurance for the ordering and billing process, many CFO's continue to rejoice at their "below the industry average" General and Administrative Expense overhead, not realizing that by farming quality assurance out to sales, valuable sales hours are lost every week that, if leveraged as designed, would mean more revenue and profit overall. The *cost of quality* is large but few companies measure the real opportunity cost and report it to the executives and the board of directors.

If a company is to maximize its potential, five important goals must be achieved in the organization:

1. Salespeople must spend 90%+ of their time on activities that can directly result in more business for the company.

   First-line sales directors must be the watchdogs, seeking out all "overhead" work that is getting in the salespeople's way and finding ways the company can eliminate those distractions.

2. Pre-sales support personnel must be in place to ensure that the pre-sales efforts are invented only once.

   Newly developed marketing materials must be available to the entire sales force and the invention of new materials must be continuously underway under the direction of CUBEs. Leveraging what has already been done before is a task few companies perform efficiently in the sales department.

3. Pre-sales processes must be followed. This is the only way to ensure the organization is well-aligned and bought-in on each sales effort. If the process is no longer meeting its objective or is wasting people's time, the process should be fine-tuned to fit the environment like a glove.

4. Post-sales support and resources must be in place to ensure laser-like precision and execution of projects.

   There will always be some quality assurance, but that should be handled mostly by individual value-adding departments and as last resort, the delivery project manager. The totality of the effort by the project manager on quality assurance should be 20% or less of the job, not the majority of the job as often found at many companies today.

5. Post-sales processes must be defined and followed stringently.

   Often, the difference between a profit and a break-even or worse yet, a financial loser of a project, is flawless execution. Nowhere is discipline more important. Flawless post-sales execution should be the lifeblood of companies. Unfortunately, chaotic execution is the ridiculous state-of-affairs that dominates the status quo at many companies.

In Summary…

In many companies today, sales professionals spend 50% or more of their time making up for deficiencies in quality and lack of process. Many executives are oblivious to this.

The current situation is similar to a football team where the starting quarterback spends half of his time planting and mowing the grass on the field, painting yardage lines and end zone logos, and cleaning the stands. While everyone immediately recognizes that the quarterback's time would be better spent studying films of the opponent, practicing plays, keeping up his physical fitness, and going to physical therapy for the tendonitis in his elbow, senior managers don't always recognize the parallel situation that exists in sales.

The CUBEs are the quarterbacks of the company's sales efforts. Each opportunity is another football game to be won. The amount of practice, preparation, conditioning, and game time a CUBE gets directly influence the number of touchdowns and wins on the scoreboard. Companies that allow their salespeople to get dragged into various quality assurance activities are giving up valuable preparation and game time. No other employees outside the sales force are chartered to be rainmakers, so if others have “extra” bandwidth, the time is not spent on searching for more business opportunities.

Semper Fortis uses a comprehensive model for support, both before the sale and after. When a sales contest is underway, the organization stands ready and willing to help, no matter what unforeseen assistance may be needed, ensuring that the Sales Olympian team takes its best shot at winning each engagement.

Chapter 17: Delivering Support Excellence

After surveying many sales execs from a variety of companies while documenting the corporate status quo found in Chapter 2, it has become clear that even firms considered to be the top echelon of sales professionalism still have plenty of room for improvement on the support issue. More often than not, salespeople are left to their own initiative to solve a great multitude of issues and challenges on the road to a successful sale, especially on the pre-sales side of the equation.

Many parts of most organizations believe that they have little responsibility *before* a contract is signed. In fact, given that landing new sales is one of the company's primary missions, ensuring that projects are won, fit the company's competencies, and will be delivered profitably, is many peoples' responsibility. The sales professional without a doubt serves as the catalyst, leader, and foremost spokesperson for each engagement, but support and team effort are the differences between winning most, or only a few, of the opportunities.

Some pre-sales support is conducted by groups developed for that specific purpose, like the Sales Intelligence Group (SIG), but many of the tasks are assigned throughout the company. Semper Fortis advises clearly assigning champions for the following pre-sales support areas to each CUBE, so that he or she knows not only whom to call, but that the person called understands that helping win the sale is a key aspect of his or her responsibilities.

Below, please find a Semper Fortis pre-sales support chart for a software solution vendor. Ensuring that the CUBE maximizes his or her "selling" time and achieves his or her maximum business potential requires a lot of help from the extended company team.

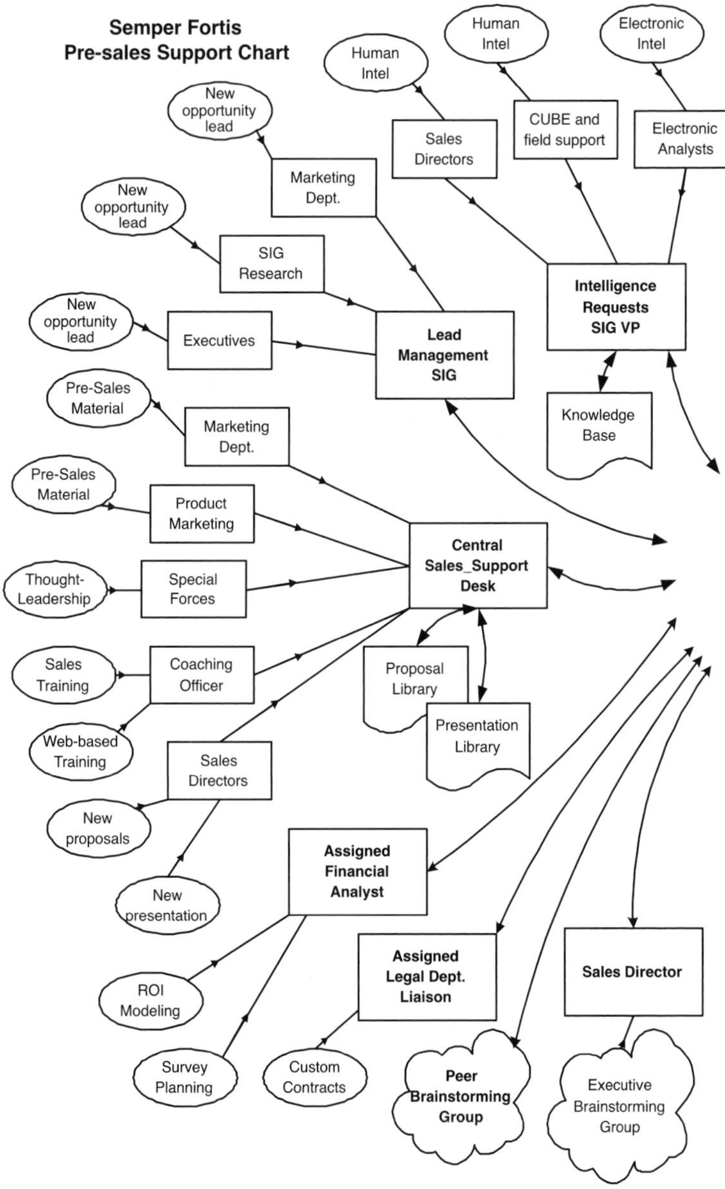
Semper Fortis
Pre-sales Support Chart
Human Intel
Human Intel
Electronic Intel
New opportunity lead
Sales Directors
CUBE and field support
Electronic Analysts
Marketing Dept.
New opportunity lead
SIG Research
Intelligence Requests SIG VP
New opportunity lead
Executives
Lead Management SIG
Pre-Sales Material
Knowledge Base
Marketing Dept.
Pre-Sales Material
Product Marketing
Central Sales_Support Desk
Thought-Leadership
Special Forces
Sales Training
Coaching Officer
Proposal Library
Web-based Training
Presentation Library
Sales Directors
New proposals
Assigned Financial Analyst
New presentation
Assigned Legal Dept. Liaison
Sales Director
ROI Modeling
Survey Planning
Custom Contracts
Peer Brainstorming Group
Executive Brainstorming Group

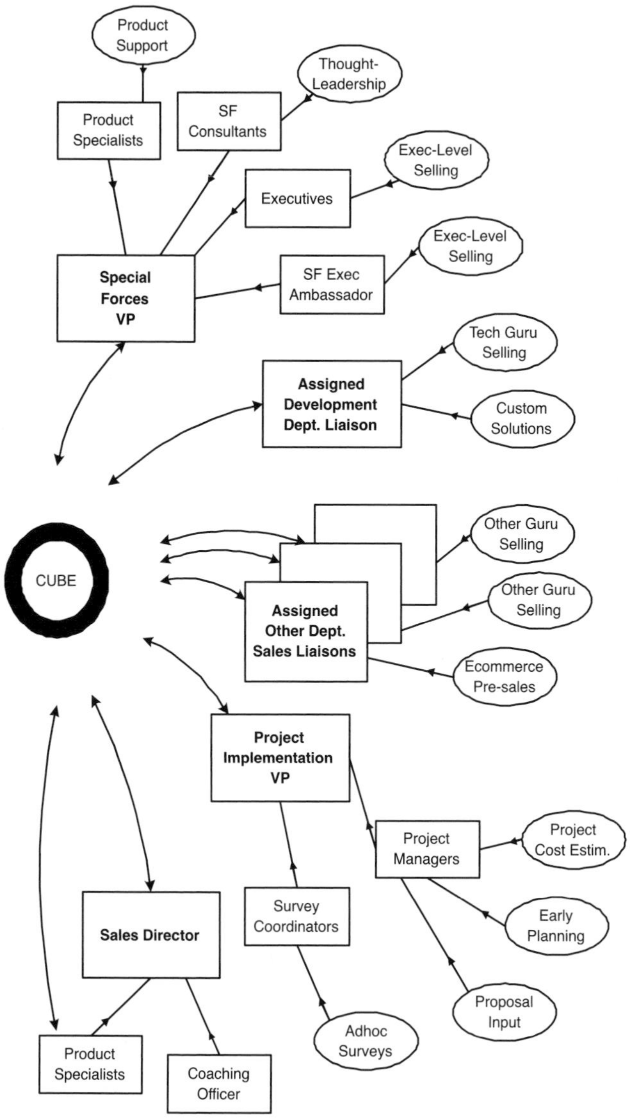
Product Support
Product Specialists
SF Consultants
Thought-Leadership
Executives
Exec-Level Selling
Exec-Level Selling
Special Forces VP
SF Exec Ambassador
Tech Guru Selling
Assigned Development Dept. Liaison
Custom Solutions
CUBE
Other Guru Selling
Other Guru Selling
Assigned Other Dept. Sales Liaisons
Ecommerce Pre-sales
Project Implementation VP
Project Managers
Project Cost Estim.
Early Planning
Survey Coordinators
Sales Director
Proposal Input
Adhoc Surveys
Product Specialists
Coaching Officer

A number of the supporting roles will be discussed in upcoming chapters. For readers that would like a greater level of detail on the various functions outlined within the pre-sales chart, please refer to the SeizingShare.com website and download my *Presales Excellence* brief.

For greater detail on
pre-sales support,
see link at
www.SeizingShare.com/pre

Support After The Sale

The greatest inhibitor for a successful salesperson staying productive and winning additional sales is the distraction of supporting existing contracts. The salesperson typically does not get paid commissions until the customer is invoiced, and if bills are not paid, charge-backs typically reverse transactions and commission bonuses. Many companies do not have a formal plan and oversight function for completing projects; therefore, salespeople gravitate to filling the gaps, serving as quality assurance players in the delivery of projects.

Unfortunately, this "safety valve" activity pulls the salesperson away from the full-time pursuit of new business leads. Given that the average sales cycle in complex corporate solution environments is more than a year, an individual's sales opportunity radar must be worked to receive a constant flow of new projects, or the results will be periods of feast and famine. The company's goal must be to keep the salesperson focused on selling.

Semper Fortis advocates turning over all substantial projects to a dedicated project manager,
and smaller deliveries to a customer service coordinator,
freeing up the salesperson to continue selling.

The skill set of a project manager is typically different than that of a salesperson. While both areas require initiative, communication, and problem solving skills, the project manager must gravitate toward detailed planning and follow-up, using logic and discipline to overcome all challenges. The salesperson, on the other hand, often deals in the grey zone of people's perceptions and desires. Not surprisingly, few people possess all these traits.

A company with good project managers will typically succeed in two ways over a longer timeframe:

1. It will score higher in customer satisfaction and loyalty, enjoying greater repeat business.

2. It will find and develop more sales wins and additional clients, growing the business at a superior rate.

At a high-level, project management best practices incorporate the following nine steps:

1. Objectives of the project must be clearly defined and agreed to, in writing, by both vendor (and all of a vendor's internal departments) and customer.

2. A central point of contact and responsibility must be assigned and empowered to function, most often called the project manager.

3. The assumptions and environment for the project must be documented, including risks, timeframes, resources needed, contingencies, and more.

4. A comprehensive statement-of-work must be created and agreed to by the parties.

5. Measures and responsibility definitions should be developed to ensure the project stays on track without breakdowns in process or quality.

6. A detailed project plan must be developed, which includes costs for costs, resources, and timeframes.

7. The plan must be executed while monitoring progress and learning and adjusting the process over time.

8. Formal customer acceptance should be obtained in baby steps throughout the project at predetermined milestones, avoiding a momentous final acceptance potential roadblock.

9. The team should conduct a structured debrief and analysis of the project once disengaged, placing everything learned in the company's knowledgebase for future use.

Care must be taken when turning projects over to project managers—the salesperson must maintain a close connection and relations with key influencers and decision makers during the delivery. The project manager will develop similar relationships that the sales professional already may have and both must compare notes, understand the play-by-play of the delivery project and ongoing sales efforts, and help each other's cause when possible. Involving the project manager early, often before the project is sold, and setting proper expectations, helps achieve this goal and can offer the additional benefit of gathering information from a different perspective.

In the Semper Fortis model, a separate group, headed by the VP of Implementation, specializes in the delivery of projects, and ultimately reports to the commander-in-chief of sales. The purpose

Implementing Semper Fortis on a Tight Budget

Often, companies I talk with have concerns about the cost of the supporting cast around the sales professional. In the pre- and post-sales arenas, there are generally few new costs—the resources typically exist but are not used as fully for sales support. When resource must be added, every hour a project manager is used for the coordination of fulfillment directly results in an hour the salesperson is freed up to pursue new business. More profit, more revenue, and faster growth result—the cost of the project manager is invariably much less than the opportunity cost of not pursuing more business.

for reporting through the sales function is to ensure that project managers are acutely aware of their role in the company achieving subsequent sales at the customers.

The VP ensures project managers are trained well, pool knowledge and techniques, and are balanced across projects, while a "dotted-line" reporting structure is put in place to the CUBE during any particular implementation. Reporting to two people does not cause issues because the organization ensures that the goals of both are exactly the same: flawless, efficient customer implementation while setting up the company for subsequent business opportunities.

Successful implementation of projects involves many steps. Additional information is available in my *Post-Sales Support Excellence* Brief, available on www.SeizingShare.com.

For greater detail on post-sales support, see link at www.SeizingShare.com/post

In Summary…

Corporations often do not realize that excellent pre- and post-sales support makes a tremendous difference in sales professional productivity and ultimately company success. A great number of areas can and must be plugged into the equation. Most are not net-new functions and costs; rather, most of the support comes from the existing organization refocused on winning business as a prime directive.

Important side-benefits of organized, world-class pre-sales support is greater cohesiveness and a feeling of responsibility throughout the company, better pricing and delivery assumptions on proposals, and better ultimate execution of the post-sales implementation phase.

By turning over the delivery of projects to dedicated project managers or customer service reps, the salesperson is able to keep a consistent stream of new sales projects in the works, ultimately delivering more revenue and profit to the company.

We now add two more facets to the Semper Fortis world-class sales model, completing the fifth pillar, Comprehensive Logistics and Support:

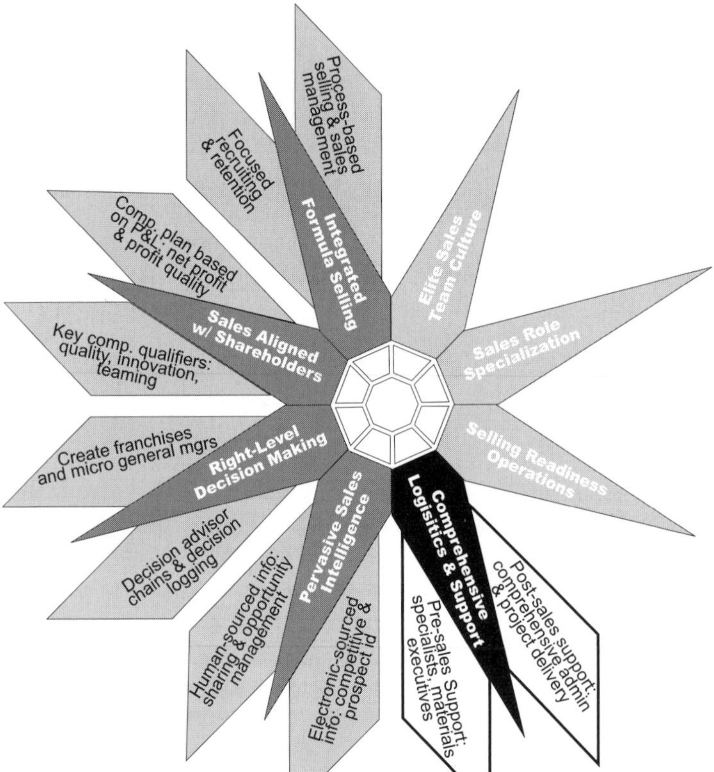

Section Six

~ ~ ~ ~ ~ ~ ~ ~ ~ ~

Selling Readiness Operations

The selling readiness of most sales forces is unknown to management. Salespeople generally are tempered by live duty in front of customers. Planning, preparation, and practice are almost unheard of, and management often only has a vague understanding of whether a particular salesperson knows his or her stuff on a specific subject.

World-class selling requires more—much more.

"Before everything else, getting ready is the secret of success."
- Henry Ford

Chapter 18: Achieving Championship Readiness

The one area that championship sports teams and professional selling differ the most is preparation and practice. No matter if one looks at team sports like football or individual sports like tennis and golf, the will to *prepare to win* is the hallmark of achievement.

In the corporate world, preparation of salespeople is almost non-existent. Everything is learned during the contest, vying with competitors in front of live customers. The fact that many sales managers see their role as controllers and activity pacesetters, rather than as teachers and coaches, is a complication. No substantial sales education is offered at colleges and universities, and many companies' training programs are woefully lacking.

Practice

In recent times, practice seems to have been trivialized. Even if the salesperson is facing one of the pivotal presentation meetings of his or her year, all effort is focused on putting the PowerPoint slideware or hand-outs together, and not on the delivery and objection handling.

The Semper Fortis discipline advocates one full day of dry-run practice, if possible, two or three days before the customer meeting. In the practice session, the sales director, several peers, and support team members act as the customer executives, asking tough questions while trying to find weaknesses in the pitch. The sales director enforces rules to make sure that the practice is taken seriously, that no one breaks his or her role, and that there are no "timeouts" to readjust in the middle of the practice effort. For the practice to really be a learning experience, it cannot be any easier than the meeting will truly be. The practice meeting should be video recorded, allowing the CUBE to study and adjust his or her approach after reviewing areas where he or she stumbled. In the end, by practicing well, the teams perform much better at these critical juncture events.

The salesperson also enters into the continuous Field Coaching Cycle that will persist for the rest of his or her days in the direct sales force at a Semper Fortis company. The cycle includes the following steps, through which the sales professional and associated field support personnel such as pre-sales system engineers participate under the guidance of the sales director:

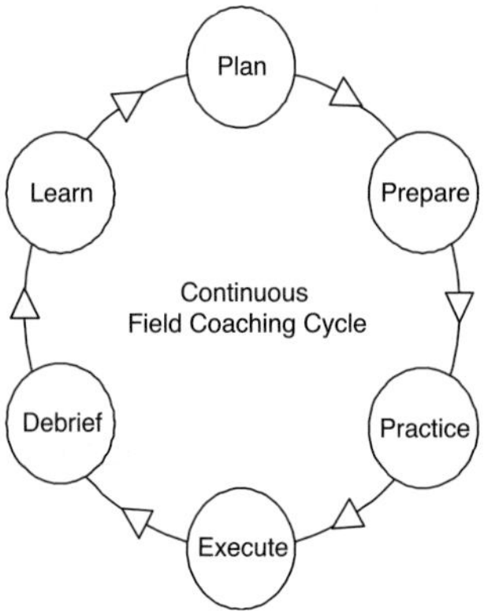

Becoming Better Coaches

Sales directors, too, face their own educational challenges. The company focuses on developing each manager's skill as a coach and leader, sometimes using third-party programs to mix in fresh ideas. Peer sharing is institutionalized and area VPs serve a key role in determining how each sales director can become more effective with his or her CUBEs and other field personnel. Additionally, intranet systems help gather feedback from subordinates, giving the sales director and his or her manager feedback from the troops.

Great selling and great coaching are much like great golf. There are a never-ending number of nuances that make a big difference in the score, and there is always more to be learned and practiced.

Testing and Certification

Important checkpoints in achieving superior sales force readiness are certification and re-certification. Many companies do not test their salespeople and other personnel for fear of running a few of them off. This is a risky decision—an uninformed salesperson can damage customer relationships or, in some cases, even spawn legal battles for misrepresented expectations on contracts. It should not be surprising that the level of knowledge varies dramatically in these companies from one salesperson to the next. Other companies offer some level of competence tests, but they are usually self-study courses on products, and I often have seen the most "challenged" salespeople have one or more friends huddled around the PC screen to help them pass.

Playing with kid gloves does not help forge a world-class level of competence within the force. The expectation must be that every team member, including sales support personnel, will know the following items perfectly:

1. The professional sales process as it relates to their company.
2. General business principles and how they relate to the franchise P&L.
3. Corporate financial statements and investment analysis methods for justifications.
4. Specific details regarding the company's products, services, and solutions.
5. The company's best-case sales stories.
6. The best-known competitor's sales stories and the vendor's designed answers to these items.
7. The top 25 most-repeated objections and the vendor's designed strategic answers for handling the objections well.

Executives often wonder why I advocate investing sales training effort and expense on system engineers and customer service reps. Prospects look to many sources and details to double-check that a vendor is truly credible. By having everyone on the team clear on the objectives and the appropriate sales story, every touch-point with the customer is harmonious and complimentary. As an important side-benefit, the entire team becomes conscious of information sought in the quest to gain sales advantage. Many wind up gathering valuable clues that ultimately pay off in upcoming contests.

Semper Fortis approaches certification by breaking the concept down into smaller parts. Each primary piece of "base-required" knowledge has a certification test. For example, a CUBE at a small software firm may need certifications on each of the five software modules offered, another on the services offering, two more on internal sales processes and franchisee operations, and three on various sales stories, just to remain in his or her position. By including base knowledge requirements into certifications, the Semper Fortis company clearly communicates to the employees that information competence is a must for them to succeed in their mission.

Re-Certification and Readiness Checks

The competitive landscape and product environment is ever-changing. To ensure that sales and support personnel stay current, video refresher courses and re-certification tests are required to keep a certified status. To encourage timely re-certifications, employees who miss the window may be required to retake the longer course. There is value to be learned from our driver's licensing bureaucracy after all!

Additionally, area VPs focus on keeping troops ready for selling combat through occasional surprise drills. It is not unusual for an area VP to ask a salesperson to give him or her a five-minute introduction about the company or Product X without any advance notice. If there are concerns regarding readiness, the sales director may get a one-day warning to prepare his or her group to give a two-hour presentation with hypothetical assumptions to the area VP or commander-in-chief of sales, who role plays as the discerning customer.

Many sales forces first revolt when faced with testing, just as high-school teachers do when confronted with competence testing—they simply are unaccustomed to internal challenges. It is often best to introduce the concept slowly, at first requiring only one or two certifications, such as one for the primary sales story and another for the foremost product line, and then add more tracks later. The initial resistance will wane. In line with meritocracy of pay, the most competent salespeople become happier in an environment that demands better performance from all, while the weakest reconsider their employment. As said before, this is a good dynamic in the longer run.

To maintain the constant pace of learning, a dedicated training coordinator, called the coaching and readiness officer works with Human Resources and the centralized sales support team to ensure that all facets of sales are represented in the courses and certifications. While study materials are available on the SIG's intranet site, testing is offered only in a monitored environment, ensuring honesty in the evaluation. While the coaching and readiness officer and the liaison within Human Resources are responsible for logistics, delivery, and scheduling, the sales directors are responsible for adjustments to the courses, based on the ongoing coaching effort within the territories.

Visibility and Recognition

Peer pressure is under-utilized as a motivator in most companies. Something deep in the human genome produces a drive to keep pace with peers. Semper Fortis does not ignore this effective motivator.

As part of recognition, which is covered in greater detail in the upcoming Section Eight, each salesperson's certification status is posted on an internal intranet website for all to see, along with accolades, awards, and of course, the sales results scorecard. Each company can experiment with posting testing scores or just certifications, but if the testing is rigorous, successful certifications are usually sufficient.

Unlike the academic environment, questions answered incorrectly must be resolved, as an incorrect understanding may wind up causing missed expectations on a customer engagement. Sales directors use the completed certification tests to go back and talk through missed answers, even if the final score was a pass.

Qualitative Management Measures

In addition to certifications, sales directors complete confidential Sales Fitness questionnaires regarding the readiness of their salespeople, which are updated once per quarter. The questionnaires produce two documents, a Salesperson Feedback Report that informs the salesperson of the manager's opinion of his or her sales fitness, and a management-only fitness report, that may contain additional comments directed to the commander-in-chief of sales and area VPs.

These fitness reports, when combined with certifications and documented coaching plans and progress, enable the commander-in-chief of sales to judge the sales force's readiness across the entire geography. It may become evident, for example, that the force is not ready to take on another product because few salespeople have mastered the previous product introduction from five months earlier. Or, coaching and SIG attention might have to be focused on competitive sales story coaching, as many salespeople are failing in their attempt to recertify on the competition track. I have seen, first-hand, management add product after product to the sales force's solution portfolio, without ever asking about the readiness of the force to accept and learn more offerings. Such moves are a mistake, diluting the overall effectiveness of the salespeople.

In Summary...

Semper Fortis is a discipline that requires participants to perform with great competence. Sales professionals must unequivocally know their stuff and stretch in various ways to learn more each year. Sales directors must know and practice becoming excellent coaches and teachers, in addition to understanding every aspect of the sales professional's world. Working with the coaching and readiness officer, they are chartered with creating programs that teach and test each salesperson's competence in a variety of ways, from product knowledge to on-the-fly objection handling to prepared presentations.

These demands are much greater than those found at most companies, where the only "practice" is in fact on-the-job training in front of live customers. Following a formula of "failure to prepare is preparing to fail," Semper Fortis companies spend more time practicing for the big game than playing in it. This is made possible and *profitable* because the Semper Fortis firm relieves much of the support work with excellent pre- and post-sales support. The dynamics of preparation increases close rate percentages, ultimately delivering more revenue and profit per sales professional.

In Semper Fortis, the daily routine is part of a continuous cycle, in which the sales professionals learn from every event, personally coached by their sales director. On an annual basis, the routine also includes formal education, certification, and re-certification to ensure that a salesperson's base of knowledge is clear and correct.

We now add the first facet to the Selling Readiness Operations pillar of the Semper Fortis model:

Chapter 19: Forging the Career Sales Professional

After base knowledge and a good understanding of work flow are achieved, culture plays a pivotal role in building a higher-than-average performing organization. The Semper Fortis strategy puts sales force development and competence at the forefront of a company's quest for competitive advantage. Forging the needed gung-ho, professional attitude starts the minute a new candidate joins the company, and continues through a career which offers excellent options for success both in company management and within a new area of culture leadership.

The primary steps in a sales professional's career at a Semper Fortis company are:

- Candidate (Trainee)
- Cadet (Apprentice)
- Account Manager | Solution Sales Specialist
  (positions may have internal ranking (1, 2, 3...))
- Customer Unit Business Executive (CUBE)
  (positions may have internal ranking
  (CUBE 1, 2, 3...))
- Sales Director | Special Forces operative | SIG specialist
  (positions may have internal ranking)
- Area VP | Special Forces VP | SIG VP |
  VP Project Implementation
- Commander-in-chief of sales

Candidate (Trainee)

Before a candidate is hired, Semper Fortis recognizes that the recruiting and interviewing process is poor in many companies. Instead of reinventing the wheel, I recommend that the recruiting arm, in addition to the observations offered in Chapter 8, leverage the methodologies outlined in the excellent book *TopGrading* by Bradford Smart. Dr. Smart's methods involve much greater depth and detail when analyzing candidates than current norms. Approaching the interview professionally will dramatically increase the survival rate of candidates within the sales force, while sending a clear message regarding the professionalism of the firm to the potential new hire. I believe the company should sign agreements with new hires that outline that the first six months with the company are probationary, simplifying dismissal if it is required.

For more info on *TopGrading*, see link at www.SeizingShare.com/top

No matter whether a new hire is a graduating senior straight from college or an experienced salesperson recruited from a different company, every candidate must attend and graduate from Semper Fortis Initial Training. Many companies skip formal training for experienced recruits. Given that the Semper Fortis culture is so important to ultimate success, I believe that all should attend classes to learn the sales basics, sales process, product information, basic operating procedures within the company, and indirectly but importantly, the prevailing culture of team work, professionalism, and weekly habits for success.

While the agenda will be different for various companies, some of the typical components of a rigorous one-month initial training curriculum include:

- Culture I — Introduction to the company's culture.
- The strategic sales process.
- Conversational selling skills.
- Presentation selling skills.

- Basic finance in selling—return on investment, internal rate of return, leasing, et al.
- The franchisee model and making decisions.
- Product and services offerings (provide pre-training study guides).
- Industry break-out sessions (if applicable), touching on industry background, current industry issues, and company solutions within the industry.
- Public speaking crash course.
- Introduction to business golf.
- Teamwork at the firm.
- The company master index—where to find what kind of help and info within the company.
- Living a balanced life (Steven Covey's *Seven Habits* or equivalent).
- Culture II — Start and end with what is most important.

The company should consider providing recommended reading for the weeks before initial training starts, and require the candidates to write book reports summarizing each text. Throughout the training, culture is a dominant theme, as is inspiring and testing teamwork, evaluating "adapt and overcome" instincts, gung-ho professionalism, and the coachability and versatility of the candidates.

The last three days of initial training are certification tests. In addition, the director of initial training writes a detailed report regarding each candidate. Whether there is a full-time director of initial training depends on the volume of new hires; sometimes, the coaching and readiness officer can pull double-duty and serve in this role. If a candidate completes all the testing and the written report does not find serious flaws in the new hire, he or she graduates to the active workforce as a Cadet.

Cadet

During the Cadet phase, the Cadet is assigned to a full-fledged, model CUBE or solution sales specialist in an apprentice relationship. During the six to twelve months, the Cadet learns from his or her mentor in real-life field situations. Working with the sales director, the Cadet is challenged to plan strategy and tactics, conduct meetings, give parts of presentations, work on proposals, configure solutions, and more. At the same time, a rigorous schedule of self-study classes and reading is prescribed with testing and book reports, to help fill in the detail that the initial training overview started.

The goal is to harden the Cadet into reacting appropriately in various situations. Much like teaching someone a golf swing, nothing beats repetition once the right techniques are learned. The mentors are picked and coached for excellence in process, approach, and culture. To keep "seniors" motivated, the company offers substantial deferred bonus pay, which vests when the Cadet graduates and succeeds for several years on the force, giving the senior a long-term vested interest in a cadet's success.

Nearing the end of the Cadet term, a number of tests and simulations are completed in a "hell week" format. A specially convened board of testers of sales directors and CUBEs then approves the promotion. The company should make a big deal about successful graduation with recognition, rewards, and celebration, building confidence and a sense of achievement within the gung-ho Semper Fortis culture.

Account Manager or Solution Sales Specialist

Cadets are promoted to one of two possible positions. Account Managers serve as junior CUBEs, working for veteran CUBEs on existing major accounts. Solution Sales Specialists report to the VP of Special Forces and focus on supporting CUBE efforts to sell particularly complex offerings. Care is taken to give each some free-standing non-buying accounts to prospect, allowing them to develop their own territory and learn from their own experiences.

Throughout the term, the salespeople are given training on industry and general business principles. When the sales director feels he or she is ready, the Account Manager or Solution Sales Specialist can be nominated for promotion to a CUBE.

In order to achieve the rank, the promotion candidate completes another round of testing regarding the additional aspects of managing the financial welfare of a territory. A highly-targeted interview process, once again modeled after the work found in *TopGrading*, is completed, followed a day later by a promotions review board meeting. This process strives to rank the candidate's capabilities on fifty or so key criteria, and specifically focuses on how the candidates have matured since the same criteria were evaluated when they were new hires. If the candidate is approved, they move on to what a Semper Fortis company considers a position of great importance in its long-term success.

CUBE

As a CUBE, the employee is transformed into a business owner, keeping a portion of the profit from their territory. They are empowered to hire personnel, make important decisions, and even take the company in new directions. Semper Fortis advocates assigning levels to CUBEs, signifying the size of the franchise they are responsible for, in terms of revenue and profit.

Given the unlimited nature of "building one's own franchise," many sales professionals realize that there is little reason to claw their way into company management. A great career can be built staying in place, as more and more fruit is harvested from seeds planted years earlier.

A tricky management issue arises when a territory outgrows the servicing capability of a CUBE. In such a case, upper management must develop a plan to promote the CUBE to a sales director and split the territory into several smaller ones; promote the CUBE to another key area like Special Forces or SIG and split the territory; or convince the CUBE that the territory must be split for the welfare of the customers. There rarely is one right answer, but often CUBEs negotiate a deal to keep most of their existing accounts while giving up non-buying opportunities.

Sales Director

Many firms make a huge mistake with how the first-level manager is paid and treated in the organization. Often, a great sales professional must take a pay decrease to move into management, hoping to make up for it with future promotions.

Semper Fortis makes sales management an easier transition. The first three years in the job, the individual makes 10% more than their last three year's average. If the territory performs much better than previously, the manager has the ability to take pay based on a numerical formula, if that figure is greater than their sales average. In Semper Fortis, first-line sales management is the heart and soul of a world-class organization. In recognition, it is rarely the case that a CUBE doesn't want the challenge for fear of earning less than staying where they are.

Positions Parallel to Sales Director: Special Forces and SIG Specialist Directors

Most positions in the Special Forces and the Sales Intelligence Group are organizational equivalents to field-based sales directors.

The Special Forces are used primarily for industry thought-leadership, specialized executive selling, and managing complex solution selling resources across a broad group of CUBEs. Its operatives play key roles on CUBE-driven teams, helping set the stage for success by capturing customer mindshare. Even though the internal title is director level, the external titles used may vary, designed for opening the right doors at customer sites. The next Section addresses sales specialization and the Special Forces in greater detail.

We discussed the SIG in detail in Section Four. The SIG's primary operatives are previous CUBEs who have decided to take on a new challenge.

Area Vice-President, Special Forces VP, SIG VP, VP Project Implementation

The area vice-presidents report to the commander-in-chief of sales and are typically the top of the sales hierarchy for tactical decisions, while serving as key collaborators with the commander-in-chief of sales on strategic decisions and program design.

The VP of Special Forces and VP of SIG run their respective departments and are organizationally at the same level as area VPs. The VP of Project Implementation is responsible for all project management and fulfillment efforts.

Commander-in-Chief of Sales

The commander-in-chief of sales is the theater commander, primarily focusing on strategy and high-level improvements to the company.

Many times, executives take too active a role in daily activities. The commander-in-chief must design the firm's approach in attacking markets more than 50% of his or her time, not spend 100% of their time fighting fires.

An Overlay Sales Culture Organization

In George Lucas' *Star Wars*, the Jedi Knights were few but highly effective ambassador / peace makers throughout the galaxy. They trained and achieved true mastery of a number of skills and balance in life to serve as models, embracing the "good side" of the Force.

Semper Fortis creates an overlay organization in the same model with ambassadors called SemperForte (pronounced sem´-puhr fôr´tay´), composed of just a few exceptional sales professionals who are the best of the best, both in the business game and as all-around citizens. Typically, the SemperForte position is honorary, with the professional having a full or part-time position within the sales organization. From time to time as conditions allow, special projects may be taken on by the SemperForte, requiring the sales professional to serve full-time on the engagement.

The SemperForte members accept a five-pronged mission:

1. Advance the state-of-the-art of the professional selling within the company,

2. Serve as visible heroes, propagators, and protectors of the Semper Fortis culture of teamwork and professionalism,

3. Develop best-design approaches to selling various aspects of the company and its solutions,

4. Serve as super-level mentors for key engagements and events,

5. Remind all in sales that quality in life requires balance between work, home, spirit, and health.

Much of a SemperForte's time is spent traveling the country and influencing sales professionals. In keeping with Item #4 of the mission, the SemperForte serve as an elite team for the top-tier opportunities. Depending on circumstances, some of the SemperForte serve full-time while others have duties within the regular organization and participate on an as-needed basis.

Each SemperForte develops a mastery of certain aspects. For example, one may become the company's master presenter. Service requires that the SemperForte write and publish internally and externally, practice balance in their lives, teach culture above everything else, and inspire superior personal mission within individuals.

Any professional CUBE or higher can be eligible for acceptance to the ranks of the SemperForte. Successful appointment is the embodiment of true meritocracy. The commander-in-chief of sales or SemperForte captain must nominate a candidate. The candidate is evaluated based on experience, wisdom, results, integrity, cultural excellence, and a host of other facets. Current members of the SemperForte must approve the candidate for him or her to achieve the honor. While the company does not offer greater pay for SemperForte service, important perks such as quarterly retreats for culture strategy development and clear recognition within the sales force suffice. The trade-off is that a SemperForte is expected to continue to earn greater degrees of proficiency in strategic selling through diligent study, thought, publishing, and public speaking, until they reach the very pinnacle of the profession.

In Summary…

Many companies quickly lose their best and brightest sales stars to management ranks, where they often make less direct impact. The Semper Fortis model of franchises and pay based on profit makes developing a territory a great career option.

Additionally, sales directors occupy an immensely important and respected position, once again offering career-minded personnel a great place to stay. The trick to keeping superstars is rewarding them based on earned profit, not using the carrot-and-stick methods found with quotas. Sales directors are paid on net profit results and year-to-year growth and improvement, not quota-based systems.

By creating paths such as service on the SemperForte council, sales professionals are less likely to pursue career paths that take them to other companies without a pro-sales focus.

Chapter 20: Developing and Refining Sales Plans

Sales planning is currently practiced at most companies, but in an occasionally scheduled, generally static fashion. Account plans are typically updated once per year or once per review. Reviews rarely happen more than once per six months. These plans tend to be large documents, full of the basic "survey" information Semper Fortis keeps in the SIG knowledge base, and offer an incomplete picture when it comes to the project level and player relationship views. Salespeople update the plans usually only as much as is required to pass muster during reviews, and do not refer to the plans even monthly when working in the field.

In Semper Fortis selling, there are three levels of plans:

- Account-Level Strategic Plan
- Project-Level Opportunity Plans (several per account)
- Sales Call Plans (numerous)

These plans are supported by detailed information residing in the SIG knowledge base including:

- Account Environment Survey
- Key Contact Profiles (Semper Fortis 6x6 +)
- Competitor Survey by Account

The primary difference between a company following the Semper Fortis discipline and most others is that the three levels of plans are reflected in constantly updated, living documents, referred to by the sales professional, the support team, and the sales director on a daily basis. The plans serve as the backbone for all activity and management. From an implementation standpoint, the plans reside on a secure, centralized SIG informational portal server and are reviewed by everyone in sales leadership chain.

No other aspect leads to better quality activity than planning. When a salesperson is operating without thinking tactics out first, he or she tends to waste time and opportunities floundering through a project, reacting to other people's agendas. On the other hand, when a salesperson takes a few minutes each day to plan sales calls that support the envisioned sale and goal, when a salesperson spends a half hour updating account and opportunity level plans each week, field activity becomes laser-focused, producing progress every week. The planning yields dynamic, not static, documents for reviews.

A quote from Sun Tzu sums up the value of planning well:

Those who are victorious plan effectively and change decisively. They are like a great river that maintains its course but adjusts its flow... they have form but are formless.

They are skilled in both planning and adapting and need not fear the result of a thousand battles— for they win in advance, defeating those that have already lost.

<u>The Account Plan (A-Plan)</u>
Customer or Prospect Company Level

Not all prospect companies will justify an A-Plan immediately. Criteria that must be present to ensure that this time is well spent include:

- The size of the opportunity at that company,
- The number of projects that are winnable by the vendor,
- The number of years that account would be an important profit producer if won, and
- The synergies between the company's needs and the vendor's deliverables.

If a company only offers one opportunity to sell one distinct project, the A-Plan is typically deferred until the company becomes a customer. At that time, the CUBE and sales director re-evaluate the longer term opportunities and decide if creating an A-Plan above the project-level Opportunity Plan is worth the investment of time and effort.

On the other hand, some prospects are so large and clearly could use the vendor's offerings. In such cases, A-Plans may be developed years before a successful entree into a project-level opportunity is found.

The A-Plan bridges the gap between a number of project-level opportunity plans, defining the bigger picture of an account's potential value over the longer term. Typically, large account development takes four to five years to achieve excellent profitability. The first couple of years target establishing a foothold for sustained work, then expanding into other departments and processes of the enterprise. By years four or five, the successful vendor will have captured more than half of the available budget spending in the areas of their products and services.

Questions answered on the account-level plan include:

A-Plan / Section One / The Account's Strategy and Position

- What is the company's strategy within their marketplace?
- Whom do they consider to be their top competitors? How are they positioned in the same marketplace?
- How do we, as a vendor, fit with the strategy?
- Why is this prospect a great potential account for us?
- What are the top ten operational improvement priorities at an executive level at the account?
- What are the top ten priorities in each of the departments where our products and services apply?
- How is the company doing financially?
- What is the general state of mind at the company?
- How are we generally positioned in the minds of the key executives? What is our real value-add? What is our *perceived* value-add by the customer's executives?

A-Plan / Section Two / Projects—Overall Projected Account Value if Won

- What are the top opportunities / projects we foresee or suspect at this account?
- What are the values of those top projects?
- What's the combined value of the projects we are most likely to be able to win? What is the value of the projects including those that we have to stretch to win?
- How are the projects interrelated and dependent on each other? Which ones must be won in order to have a chance of winning others?

A-Plan / Section Three / The Players and Relationships

- What is the large-scale organizational chart of the enterprise?
- Who are our contacts, friends, foes, coaches within the enterprise?
- How are the contacts interrelated?
- Who are the players we must meet and recruit to permit our participation on projects?

The Opportunity Plan (O-Plan)
Project / Individual Opportunity Level

All engagements have an opportunity plan completed within the Semper Fortis discipline. The O-Plan drives all activity and strategy when striving to win projects and serves as a critical communications component between various facets of the vendor's organization.

Questions answered on the project-level opportunity plan include:

O-Plan / Section One / The Opportunity

- What is the opportunity?
- What is the hypothesis for our solution?
- How well does this solution fit our best-case sale profile?
- Why does the customer have to make a change?
- What are the odds the customer stays with what they have?

- What are the key justification points for our solution hypothesis?
- Who is the competitor(s) for this opportunity?
- What is the competitor(s) proposed solution for the opportunity?
- What are our strengths and weaknesses on this opportunity?
- What are our competitor's strengths and weaknesses?
- What is the basic schedule for a decision?
- What is the revenue / profit potential for this project this year / next year / five years?
- In what position is this project in the sales radar zone? (checklist should be completed to move the project closer and closer in the sales radar).

O-Plan / Section Two / The Players

- Who are the key buyers and influencers on a particular opportunity?
- What is the state of our relationship and knowledge depth of each buyer and influencer?
- What is each key contact's perspective regarding the problem / opportunity?
- What is each key contact's perspective / opinion regarding our company, our solution, and other competitors' solutions?
- What are the primary issues and advantages we have with each key contact?
- What are the primary issues and advantages we have with our proposed solution?
- What are the primary issues and advantages our competitor(s) has?

O-Plan / Section Three / The Tactics

- How do we best position this project to accomplish a high win-win rating for the customer and us?
- What are the top ten tasks that must be done next?
- What are the results of the previous tasks?

O-Plan / Section Four / History

Additional information includes a track of all changes and deletions within the plan to track how the vendor is "adapting to and overcoming" challenges. This historical perspective is important to really understand how the account team arrived at their current state and also plays a key role in the ultimate debrief and learning from the engagement.

The specific format can vary greatly for different implementations as well as the key data tracked. For example, if a company sells a static product that has tightly defined specifications, such as escalators, the O-Plan should include key statistics that describe the product delivery.

Semper Fortis selling puts this and all planning on a secure intranet site, ensuring visibility for the management team and lasting backup of activity in the field.

Sales Call Plan (C-Plan)
Individual Plan for All Substantial Contact Moments

Within the Semper Fortis discipline, every planned contact with a key contact is pre-planned, usually for 10 to 15 minutes. This discipline is critical and must be built into a habit. When sales calls are planned, missing information is discovered and documented, progress is made, and the customer's time is never wasted.

Questions answered on the one-page sales call plan include:

C-Plan / Section One / Meeting Details

- Who will attend?
- What is the planned duration of the call and its format?
- What are the logistics / date details for the meeting?

C-Plan / Section Two / General Direction for the Meeting

- What is the single overall objective for the account (from the account plan)?

- What is the single best-case interim objective for the account on the path to fulfilling the overall objective?
- What is the stated objective of this call?
- What are our meeting objectives (up to three) (may be stated or other)?
- What is the valid reason from the customer's perspective for this meeting (not wasting his or her time)?
- What are the best / ok / worst case first-downs to be achieved by the end of this meeting?

C-Plan / Section Three / Perceptions

- What is the customer's concept / perception regarding this project?
- What questions can be asked to validate our read of the situation?

C-Plan / Section Four / Searching for More Information

- What three open-ended questions should be asked for confirmation of assumptions and our understanding?
- What five open-ended questions should be asked for new information?
- What three open-ended questions should be asked for learning attitudes of the customer and others in the organization?
- What three open-ended questions should be asked for learning personal details about the contact?

C-Plan / Section Five / Micro-Agenda for Meeting

- What are the three to five agenda points for this meeting if it falls far off track and we have to rein it back in?

Creating the C-Plan should not be a great effort. Most experienced salespeople can knock out a good one in less than ten minutes. But having a plan makes a world of difference in the result of a meeting or teleconference.

After a call, the CUBE or solution sales specialist debriefs the results into a digital recorder, whose content is uploaded via the network to the SIG in compressed transcription files. The SIG personnel translate the recording into written text, returning it to the salesperson, the sales director, and inputting the data into the sales knowledge base.

The sales director then uses the plan and initial debrief data to have a short conversation about the call with the CUBE and often his or her assigned SIG specialist, to gain more insight and start the planning process for the next steps.

In Summary...

Planning is well worth the effort. Meetings with just fifteen minutes of pre-planning hit many more important points, have many more questions asked and answered, and offer greater value to the prospect contacts. Projects with living plans have greater chances of success, better coordination of the sales team, and deliver superior value to the customer in the form of a win-win contract. Accounts with strategic plans keep the vendor focused on the importance of customer satisfaction and partnership, eventually allowing a vendor to land a dominant share of the customer's budget in areas where a vendor competes.

The Semper Fortis discipline demands that all activity is planned, and that all CUBEs and solution sales specialists are managed to their own developed plans. The knowledge is recorded, allowing organizational learning and smarter approaches each and every year. Through planning and continues cycle of learning and practice, the firm achieves extraordinary readiness to tackle the next opportunities on the horizon.

We now complete the second facet of Selling Readiness Operations in the Semper Fortis model:

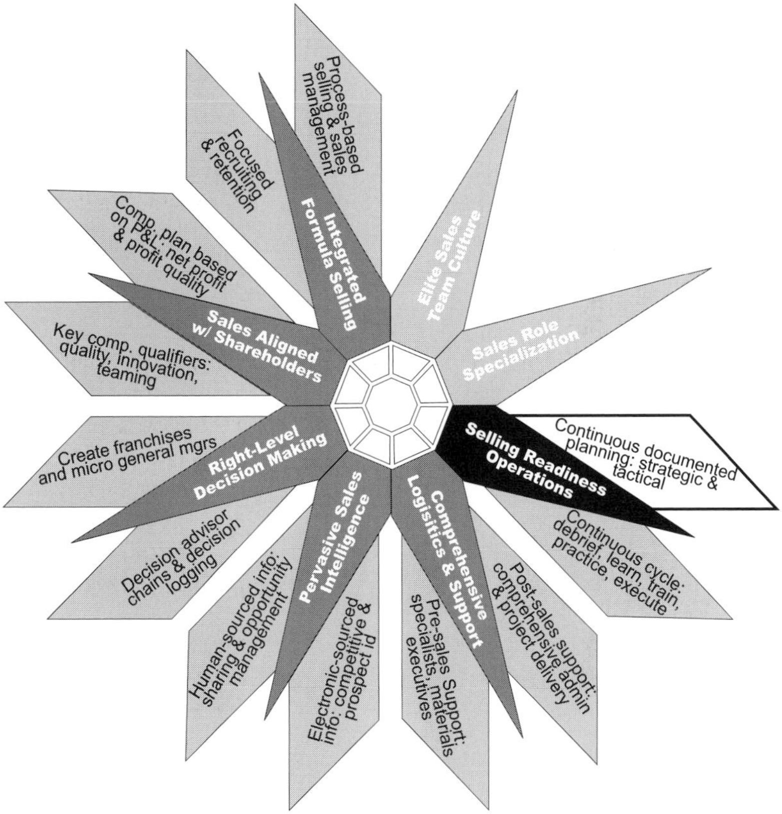

Section Seven

~ ~ ~ ~ ~ ~ ~ ~ ~ ~ ~

Sales Role Specialization

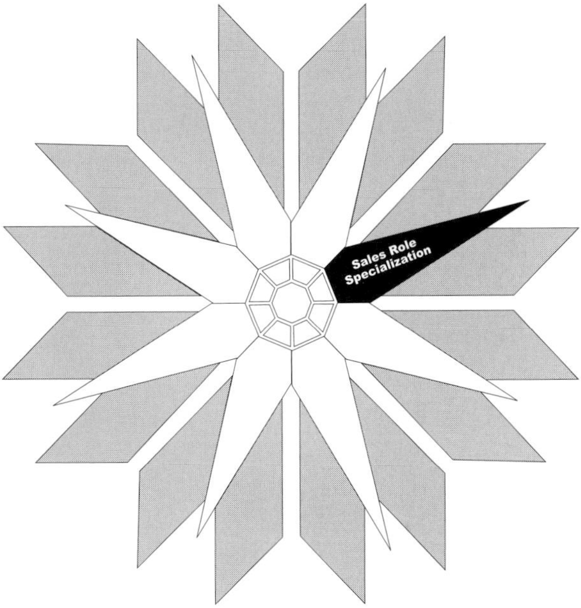

The professional sales effort requires applying various talents and capabilities across various opportunities.
Too many companies use one-size-fits-all-situations salespeople.

In fact, there is a broad range of specialization among salespeople. The company that develops and leverages a great mix outperforms its competitors.

"Each man is capable of doing one thing well.
If he attempts several, he will fail to achieve distinction in any."
- Plato

Chapter 21: Understanding Sales Force Specialization

Great teams are rarely composed of like, interchangeable players. Instead, players specialize and intertwine in complimentary roles. This truth is clearly evident in the Olympics and every team sport.

The game of sales is every bit as complex, specialized, and dynamic. Yet most companies play the game with individuals not teamwork, one-size "sales" players to fit all opportunities, not specialization and balance. This homogeneity does not lead to a world-class force.

An accepted notion within the sales profession is that there are two basic types of salespeople: "hunters" and "farmers." Hunters are adept at pursuing new opportunities in non-buying accounts, knocking down doors and blazing trails. Farmers tend to buying accounts, cultivating annual crops and maximizing the harvest. Hunters are typically rarer and more celebrated, while farmers contribute the vast majority of annual profit and revenue. In most cases, an account does not provide excellent profitability until year four of the business relationship.

Semper Fortis adds a third category of salespeople called "developers." The Semper Fortis discipline believes that finding top ten percentile sales professionals in each category is difficult, and that all three have key differentiating characteristics. Additionally, candidates in a world-class Semper Fortis organization must accept and thrive in an unrelenting environment of teamwork and continuous coaching. As discussed in Chapter 7, having the absolute best players on your team is one of the most important facets of winning any game.

When one looks at the three categories, there are a number of characteristics that all salespeople need. These include:

- Honesty,
- Integrity,
- Initiative,
- Excellent communication skills, and
- The ability to ask the right questions and listen well.

I advise creating a matrix of required skills and using a disciplined interview series to evaluate how each candidate stacks up versus the best-fit salesperson model for your company.

There are a number of skills that differentiate the various sales specialties and which then help steer the development of a sales professional into the best-fit job for him or her on the sales force.

For more info on
the skills matrix,
see link at
www.SeizingShare.com/skills

The Hunter

The differentiating skills and characteristics that an effective hunter practices and perfects include:

1. *Courage* to start high in organizations,
2. *Determination* when faced with false starts,
3. *Charisma* to maintain a foothold in an account when barely in the door,
4. A high personal *Teflon rating* that allows rejection to roll off his or her back,
5. Optimistic, unwavering *positive attitude,*
6. *Self-sufficiency*, as companies rarely provide comprehensive back-up until a project plan can be fleshed out,
7. *Quick thinking* on his or her feet, as many factors are unknown in new situations, even with great preparation,
8. *Quick read* of the politics and issues, allowing good decisions based on only a faint trail of clues,
9. *Creative* out-of-the-box idea person, demonstrating personal value to the prospect,
10. Excellent *industry knowledge*, further demonstrating value.

This list is not exhaustive but clearly, the hunter relies on having a great first-impression impact to stay engaged on the smallest of business reasons until an active project can be found.

The Semper Fortis company coaches hunters in key areas such as industry issues and knowledge to help hone their edge when penetrating accounts. The SIG strives to provide early, accurate intelligence regarding the inner workings of potential customers, giving the hunter better information going in, while allowing him or her to intelligently allocate his or her effort on the best potential entry points.

The Farmer

At the other end of the sales spectrum is the farmer. Often less celebrated, the farmer delivers most of the revenue and profit for the company, and is critical to continued customer loyalty and retention. The farmer's skill set is markedly different from the hunter, and includes:

1. Detailed *project planning* abilities,
2. *Ruthless* focus on *customer satisfaction*,
3. An eye for quality and logical *process*,
4. *Teambuilding*,
5. *Management and coordination* of a broad array of company, customer, and third-party resources,
6. Adept with *financial models* and justification,
7. Great *competence* regarding product and service offerings,
8. Expert at *efficiency*,
9. Has an *adapt-and-overcome* personal mantra,
10. Seen by the customer as, above all, *trustworthy and dependable.*

Many companies make the mistake of hiring and training hunters, then after they land a number of accounts, turning them into farmers, even though the hunter and farmer core skill sets are quite different.

The Semper Fortis organization supports farmers with many areas of the firm. One of the most helpful measures is customer loyalty surveys, where the farmer can track how well he or she and the company are perceived by various contacts within the customer organization. When trends turn negative, the entire company sees the erosion in customer confidence and plans are put in motion to reverse the sentiment before it reaches critical downward spiral trajectory.

The Developer

Semper Fortis recognizes a third skill set, that of the "developer." The developer is different from the hunter in that he or she often has less charisma and doesn't necessarily make an *extraordinary* first-impression impact. The developer usually has less bravado, preferring introductions rather than trying to break down doors single-handedly. The developer is a creative person who has the ability to remain focused, disciplined, and process-oriented, but not always at the level of detail found in farmers.

The developer's skills include:

1. Magnetic, prolific *networker*, leveraging relationships to make a great number of contacts,
2. *Leader with vision* that inspires team members to put forth their top effort,
3. *Persuasive* salesperson, able to position products and solutions for the best chance of success,
4. Adept *politician*, bridging gaps between the customer's various camps without ruffling feathers,
5. Great *situational awareness*, seeing the big picture, while gathering and analyzing key intelligence from many sources,
6. Highly *trustworthy*, gaining the confidence of internal coaches throughout the customer's organization,
7. *Patient*, waiting for the right opportunities and possessing a good sense of timing,
8. Highly-logical *problem solver* with a broad range of ideas,
9. Extraordinary *listener* that asks great questions,
10. Forges *relationships* that stand the test of time.

While there are dependencies based on the size of a sales organization, the Semper Fortis formula generally places developers as CUBEs that own the territories and customer accounts, hunters as solution sales specialists, and farmers as key Account Executives within large CUBE areas. Over the years, through promotion and attrition, a number of farmers make the jump to the CUBE level on producing territories while some hunters make CUBE, after demonstrating the balance of skills needed to lead a larger team.

Top Gun Hunter Teams

Sometimes a company will develop "Top Gun" hunters to break into new accounts. Once a successful beachhead is achieved, the accounts are transitioned to a developer CUBE, who has greater resources at his or her disposal to expand into other areas of the corporation. In such cases, the compensation plan is designed so that the hunters receive a substantial bonus for the landing, and a two to three year deferred stream based on the development team's success, while the hunters move on to other targeted missions. The developer CUBE carries the expense in his or her P&L until the stream is ended.

Project Directors with Political Savvy

Farmers often start out with the company as technical project directors who are then trained on advanced professional selling. Good candidates can be identified based on their communication abilities, political savvy, team leadership acumen, and initiative. Once nominated, the candidate is interviewed in depth using the *TopGrading* methods, and then management makes the call on whether he or she should enter the sales ranks by attending initial sales training and moving through the prescribed route as discussed in Chapter 19.

The Sales Director's Challenge

Once a company recognizes that one-size-fits-all sales hiring and training is not in its best interest, it becomes simpler to determine the best fit between a sales professional and an assigned account. Sales directors are chartered with using the right player in the right situation. While it is relatively simple to change coverage responsibility on non-buying accounts if the first hunter is unable to crack the code, few companies aggressively monitor progress and reassign freely. Semper Fortis advocates creating a clear, unambiguous message to hunters and developers: the company expects serious, focused effort or an account will be reassigned.

When an account is buying, it becomes mission-critical to ensure that the account is best covered for the company while not crushing morale in the field. The sales director must stay in touch with the situation, and, if reassignment is called for, the business reasons must be clearly communicated so that the CUBE losing the territory understands why it happened and what he or she must do in the future in order to not be exposed to such a possibility again.

If an account offers enough potential, a farmer should be placed on a developer's team as soon as it is financially feasible. The quality and focus is necessary to achieve high customer satisfaction, which leads to customer loyalty, retention, and expansion of business over time. Often, there is an opportunity to bundle customer billable project management, which helps justify the resource expense while furthering the vendor's account development goals.

Lastly, while the Semper Fortis discipline requires meritocracy pay, usually based on profit and profit quality, there is no reason that hunters, developers, and farmers must or should be paid on the same formula. Hunters will typically earn bonuses based on landings, the quality of landings, and the eventual development of an account. Developers earn commissions based on profit and profit quality of their P&L. Farmers usually derive more of their pay via base salary, with bonus for profit, profit growth, and efficiency of their accounts for the organization. None, however, should be compensated with a quota system, for all the reasons found in Section Two.

In Summary…

One-size-fits-all salesmanship results in pockets of strength and weakness for a sales force. Semper Fortis develops and trains three types of salespeople: hunters, developers, and farmers. By specializing, the company can accomplish different missions well across the entire geography. Numerically, developers and farmers outnumber hunters in most organizations. By focusing on placing developers in the key CUBE roles, a company sets itself up for continuing growth with good customer loyalty and retention.

We now add the next facet to the Semper Fortis model:

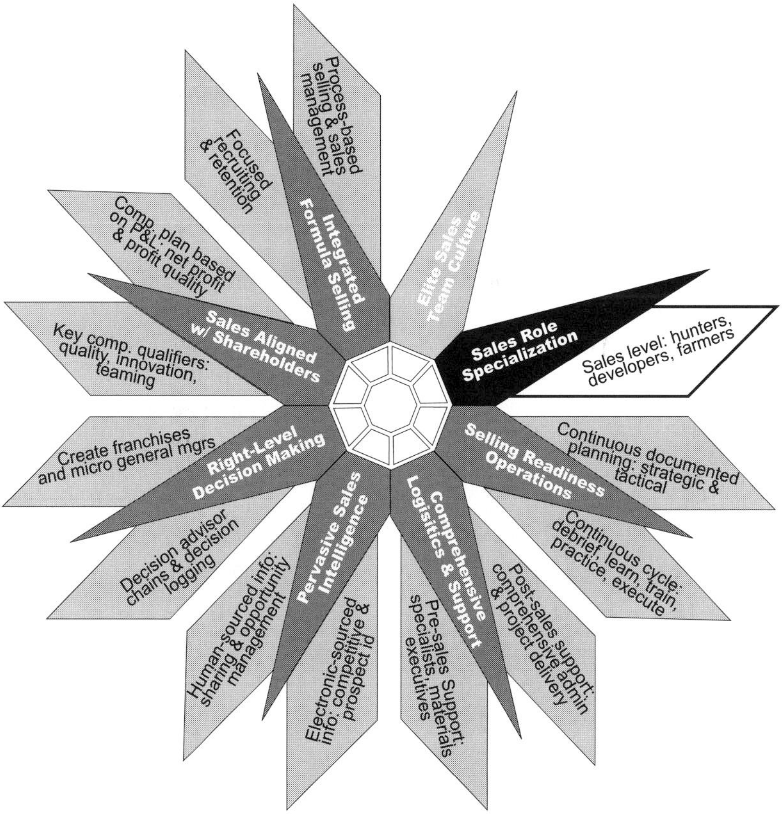

Chapter 22: Leveraging Special Forces

No matter how professional a salesperson is, few complex corporate solution selling environments are sold unassisted. Customers have come to realize that the salesperson is trained to make a positive impression, and typically reserve judgment until more clues are accumulated regarding the company and the product offering.

An obstacle to selling success is the growing difficulty to meet and establish relationships with top-tier executive decision makers. The corporate world has become hyper-competitive, resulting in a great increase of selling pressure from salespeople. Executives have become much more protective of their time.

In order to maximize sales professional effectiveness, the vendor must leverage assistance from a broad range of special forces. The single most effective of these is the adept-at-sales executive officer, because he is much more likely to be welcomed by customer executives, getting to the true decision makers. When executives take the time to make sales calls, customers perceive that the vendor is serious about earning their trust and business, which often serves as a key differentiator, especially when the difference between vendor offerings is painfully small.

The Semper Fortis discipline systematically develops a variety of special force operators and executives that are called upon to break sales logjams at critical times. The primary areas of the special forces group's focus include:

1. Executive officers.
2. Solution sales specialists.
3. Executive ambassadors.
4. Thought-leadership consultants.
5. Competitive experts from the Sales Intelligence Group.
6. Key departmental spokespeople.
7. Technical gurus with business sense and selling savvy.
8. Survey analyst field specialists.

9. Technical field-support system engineers.
10. Product marketing sales specialists.
11. Well-aligned third-party endorsers.
12. Board of directors members with broad networking reach.
13. Customer advocates.

In the organization scheme, the first-line sales director serves as the pipeline for the CUBE's requests to the VP of Special Forces, who coordinates the resources, *only a few of which report directly* to him or her. The VP ensures that all personnel available for "organizational selling" are up to date on basic product and sales training, in addition to their personal areas of specialty. The Semper Fortis system even puts together customized "selling skills" retreats, spearheaded by the coaching and readiness officer, for company executives who at times resist the idea that such training can help their approach.

1) Executive officers.

No one makes a bigger impact than a top-level executive making contacts and selling well at the executive level of customers. Unfortunately, a great number of executives are not trained as sales professionals and often do not feel comfortable in this role.

To assist executives in becoming proficient sales executives, the Semper Fortis organization provides special training classes and coaching. In keeping with the overall franchisee decision maker formula, a strict briefing formula is followed in which the CUBE outlines the mission and important details that compose the sales call plan for executive contacts. As always, the CUBE quarterbacks every contact with the customer, and the executives must stay within this system to keep the right-level responsibility and decision making in the field.

In addition to following sales call plans, the executive debriefs after the call with the CUBE, sales director, and SIG specialist, planning subsequent action. An executive tends to stay with a specific customer prospect as long as possible, keeping relationships alive and growing, while the SIG records activity in the knowledge base, enabling the company to not lose ground if another executive must later be deployed on the account.

The goal is not to outsource the mainstream of selling effort to a busy company executive but to ensure that the best possible message is being delivered directly to the primary decision-makers in the customer's organization. By using executives wisely, key logjams are often overcome in short order.

2) Solution sales specialists.

When a complex product or solutions offering is too complex to sell by CUBEs yet offers great potential for revenue and profit, the firm may decide to develop a few highly-trained solution selling specialists to assist CUBEs in the field with the effort.

The VP of Special Forces oversees the specialists, determining through conversations with sales directors where they can best be deployed, usually at an "internal" P&L billing rate to ensure that CUBEs only use specialists when the opportunity warrants the expense. Once involved in specific sales efforts, the specialists take their daily direction on any particular opportunity from the CUBE on that account.

While compensation can vary greatly, specialists tend to have a pay package that has a solid base salary and some bonus potential, but rarely offers the large upside of the CUBE plan. This reflects the fact that as a specialist, a salesperson's attentions tend to change over time and final responsibility for a project's success or failure always remains with the CUBE and assigned project delivery team members. Commissions are charged as an expense to CUBE P&L statements, while any remaining salary expense after internal fee recovery, rolls up to the commander-in-chief of sales.

3) Executive ambassadors.

Often, executives do not have enough time to cover all the sales opportunities that could use their attention and ability to vault higher in the prospect's organizational structure. Special Forces solves this issue by hiring a number of executive ambassadors into the group.

An executive ambassador is typically a semi-retired senior executive who has decided to serve part-time, focusing on sales assists rather than operations management. The Semper Fortis company gives him or her an impressive title, such as "Senior Vice-President, Northeast," without giving him or her direct responsibility for a large staff. The ambassador's entire mission is to serve as an executive sales professional, standing in for the company's operational officers and breaking into customers' executive offices. Because the ambassador is free from daily duties, he or she is able to cover more accounts, participate in sales strategy planning, ultimately building key relationships and lubricating the sales process.

For the program to work, the company must back up the ambassador executives with the same vigor as its normal mainstream operational officers. The ambassadors must appear to be key members of management in every way. Lastly, they must be used sparingly, across many accounts, to move relationships and sales efforts along, not to carry the bulk of the effort.

4) Thought-leadership consultants.

One of the best ways to differentiate a vendor when products are similar to competition is by presenting great visions for the future or prescient views of the industry trends.

The Semper Fortis discipline develops special in-house consultants who focus on these two aspects. By attending numerous trade conferences, keeping up to date on trends and challenges within the industry, training on the latest academic areas at executive sessions at institutions such as Harvard, Insead, Wharton, and Stanford, these special forces operatives develop presentations that draw excellent high-level executive interest and attendance.

In keeping with the sales goals, sales directors put together custom retreat or half-day programs using these internal top guns as keynote speakers. Follow-up often includes private sessions with customer prospect executives, once again moving sales forward by closely coordinating and planning sales calls under the direction of the CUBEs.

There is often no better way of positively positioning one's company than winning the thought-leader position among the competitors in a specific application area. In addition to special forces sales assistance, the thought-leadership consultants are chartered with publishing white papers, speaking at industry events, serving on industry committees, and helping the company's marketing and public relations efforts whenever possible. Along with the executive ambassadors, the thought-leadership consultants report directly to the VP of Special Forces.

5) Competitive experts from the Sales Intelligence Group.

Selling often involves a tricky topic: the competition and their offerings and claims. A Semper Fortis company will typically have developed excellent information regarding the competition. The SIG's operatives are often able to discuss the differences in features and function across many different products; in fact, the SIG conducts regularly scheduled internal seminars on the competition.

This knowledge allows the vendor to discuss the proposed solutions with a customer in a frank manner. The problem is that the difference between good insight and competition-bashing is razor-thin and must be handled delicately.

Special Forces overcomes this by training SIG analysts on how to best present the data, often using third-party information from sources such as the Gartner Group, in an effort to eliminate the implied company bias. Often, the best method is knowing what questions to ask, inspiring the customer to unearth the shakiest parts of a competitor's story, rather than simply pointing out the weaknesses directly.

The sales director and CUBE work closely with Special Forces and the SIG when this sensitive card is played. From numerous personal experiences, I know that this card can be played effectively, but must be positioned well, months in advance. If a prospect believes that the salesperson has genuine information that can help his or her decision but is hesitant to say anything, knowing that competition-bashing is often seen as “in bad taste,” the customer will do everything he or she can to pull the information out over time. By being able to conduct a conference call or meeting with an internal competition analyst who appears to not be a part of the regular sales process, the card can be played tactfully.

6) Key departmental spokespeople.

Customers look to every “touch-point” to evaluate the quality and professionalism of a new vendor. They often look past and around the first line of sales professional, sales director, and field pre-sales support engineers to try to gain visibility regarding the rest of the organization.

Semper Fortis ensures that this natural process works in the enlightened vendor's favor. Each department that will have contact with customer decision-makers, recommenders, and influencers appoints a sales liaison and spokesperson to serve as the focal point for customer interaction.

The sales organization sends this departmental representative through sales training, and follows up with sales coaching and the field coaching cycle process introduced in Chapter 18. The departmental spokespeople take their direction from CUBEs, developing sales call plans and participating in account planning sessions as needed. The department allocates approximately half of the liaison's time to direct sales efforts and the other half to serving as the sales champion within the department.

Through the trained liaison spokesperson program, customers are treated to subtle, top-notch sales professionalism by every department they touch, greatly lending credibility to the sales effort.

7) Technical gurus with business sense and selling savvy.

One of the goals of selling is demonstrating competence. A turning point of many sales is when the vendor can conclusively show better technical expertise than the closest competitor.

This can be accomplished by leveraging true gurus in customer-facing roles. Often, these resources are few, so rather than making the role a permanent position, the firm expends training effort to ensure that the gurus understand their role and how to help the sale from their angle.

Once again, the CUBE plays quarterback, conducting a pre-planning session that develops a clear sales call game plan for the guru to follow, while briefing her on the salient details of the account and opportunity.

As with all the Special Forces umbrella, helping account teams win comes with recognition and reward. Key contributors are recognized, and often small but nice awards, such as weekend getaway trips for the guru's family, are funded when key sales are won with their help.

8) Survey analyst field specialists.

A key step in the selling process outlined in Chapter 5 is the comprehensive survey. It often represents the first opportunity to show the customer the overall professionalism of the vendor's staff.

The personnel used for survey data collection and work are exquisitely coached on professional appearance, asking great questions, listening well, and soft-selling when appropriate. As with all the "touch-points," this early-stage impression is every bit as critical as the data collected.

The completeness of the survey drives two important objectives:

1. The customer must be surprised by the completeness, speed, and professionalism of the effort, including the final survey deliverables and presentation by survey field analysts, and

2. The company sales team and the SIG get one of the few "carte blanche" moments to ask probing questions and discover the breadth of problems that may eventually turn into sales opportunities in the future. The completeness of the effort, especially in documentation, often determines the "spring" in the opportunity "springboard," for years to come.

9) Technical field support system engineers.

After the salesperson, the pre-sales technical support engineers often have the most consistent contact with the customer.

Unlike many firms, the Semper Fortis organization invests in training and coaching the pre-sales engineers on selling skills. Often, the engineers are seen as more reliable by customer contacts, as the customer often questions the motive of the mainstream salespeople. By building relationships at a technical level, soft-selling the product and services offerings, and pre-selling the competence and reputation of other employees from the firm in order to pave the road for positive first impressions, the pre-sales systems engineer serves as a key assist player in the process.

While not officially part of Special Forces, reporting instead to sales hierarchy directly, the systems engineers are a vital stealth sales force for the Semper Fortis organization. The VP of Special Forces often "borrows" support engineers from one area and uses them in another to bring in fresh faces for the stealth technical sales effort on limited timeframe missions.

10) Product marketing sales specialists.

Customers generally love to have input and impact on product direction. One of the subtle weapons a sales team has is bringing out product marketing specialists to ask detailed questions under the banner of "future solution development" research.

Often, key details are revealed about competitor's products, the needs of the customer, and financial justification points. Product marketing accomplishes its stated objective, getting information it needs to develop future specifications that customers can financially justify. By conducting these product marketing surveys often and early, the sales teams learn much more about what it will take to win and develop an account to full bloom.

The VP of Special Forces ensures that the product marketing specialists are well-versed in selling while the CUBE coordinates the specific game plan onsite. The customer is given yet another professional "touch-point" regarding the vendor's operation.

11) Well-aligned third-party endorsers.

Endorsements by seemingly unrelated third parties are worth their weight in gold. In my own experience, tiny vendors with only a few employees have come from nowhere to win huge contracts because a sales representative from IBM mentioned them as a good source.

The Semper Fortis firm takes this concept a step farther, intentionally developing, maintaining, and tracking a network of third-party endorsers. Everyone from consultants to vendors are considered and recruited by the VP of Special Forces. This effort is facilitated by using a different "VP of Business Development" external title for the VP of Special Forces.

It is truly surprising how effective "pre-planned word-of-mouth" can be. Agreements are struck based on simple quid-pro-quo arrangements, whereby the vendor proactively refers its partners when possible. The VP primes the pump by actively starting the flow of "endorsement" favors, while ensuring that the "referred" know where the leads are coming from. Tracking the productivity and staying in contact with everyone in the network ensures success.

12) Board of directors members with broad networking reach.

In many industries, there is often a tightly knit "club" at the top executive level.

Smart companies can often add a few board members who can extend its networking reach immeasurably. Often, companies don't take the time to identify excellent candidates, even though industry trade magazines make it simple by always reporting the retirement of top executives. Depending on the industry, board members often cost less than $100,000 per year but yield great value in breaking down business barriers.

13) Customer advocates.

If a vendor can get its customers recommending the company to their peers, there is no greater endorsement. Semper Fortis institutionalizes this pursuit. Programs include:

- Top-quality user conferences, often with enough capacity to accommodate prospects who are not yet buying products,
- Customer newsletters that always include question and answer interviews with executives,
- Video-taped testimonial interviews, often included as a parameter in discounting terms offered in a sales contract,
- Visible placards on equipment that may be seen by other potential customers, also baked into sales contract terms,

Implementing Semper Fortis on a Tight Budget

Although not best, special forces can be developed by having managers accept a second role in addition to their primary role.

The chief of sales may assign a thought-leadership role (and title) to an existing sales director. The sales director would then be required to study and develop consultative material that he or she could be called to present when needed. There is little doubt that this part-time approach creates difficult challenges as key members of the team are asked to take on more and stretch their capabilities, but building these capabilities is key to forging a world-class sales organization.

- Customer visits between non-competitive entities,
- Credits for services if a site visit was especially helpful in landing a new customer, and
- Direct requests for an occasional favor.

While the VP of Special Forces coordinates and tracks this effort, all sales management participates in developing this key sales assistance aspect. Prolific customers are unexpectedly given additional terms or special treatment as a reward for their proactive help. Special care is taken to monitor the situation at every customer site, as often refusals to participate are early warning signals of a decrease in customer loyalty. By keeping a keen eye, the Semper Fortis vendor can often head off problems while they are still small.

In Summary…

Achieving world-class sales results and professionalism requires more than just the sales force. By providing well-briefed assistance from key areas, the productivity of the sales force often can be doubled.

Areas of Special Forces activity and coordination include:

- Executive officers,
- Executive ambassadors,
- Solution sales specialists,
- Thought-leadership consultant sellers,
- Competitive experts from the Sales Intelligence Group,
- Key departmental spokespeople,
- Technical gurus with business sense and selling savvy,
- Survey analyst sellers,
- Product marketing sales specialists,
- Well-aligned third-party endorsers,
- Board members with pristine networks, and
- Customer advocates.

We now add the second facet of Sales Specialization to the Semper Fortis model, completing pillar seven:

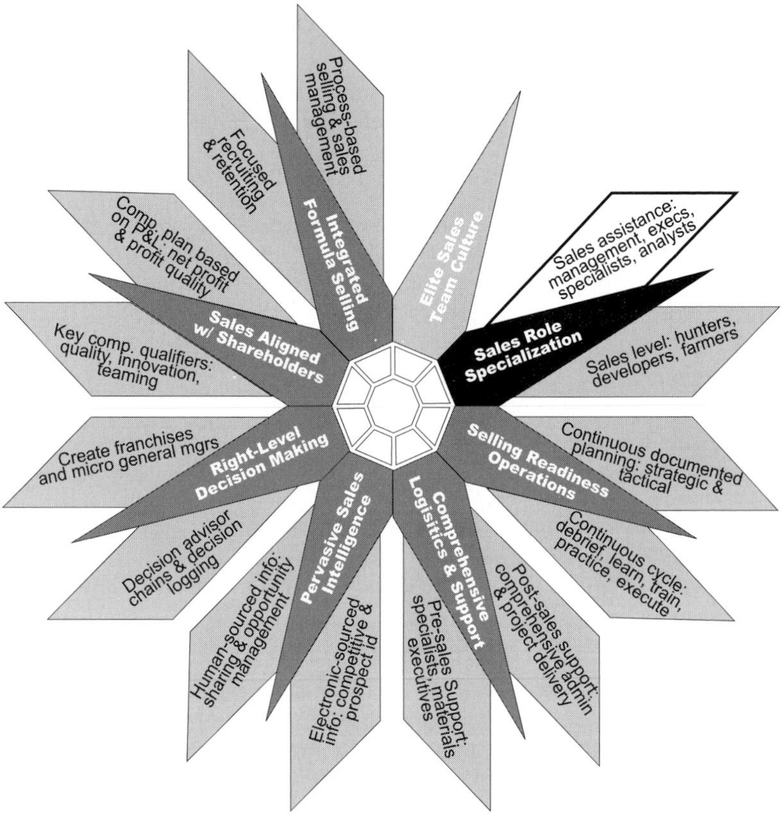

Section Eight

~ ~ ~ ~ ~ ~ ~ ~ ~ ~

Elite Sales Team Culture

Many corporations have tried to create flawless teamwork.
Rarely have the efforts succeeded.

Building a world-class selling company requires excellent teamwork within the sales force and between the sales force and all the other departments of the organization. Semper Fortis drives this effort through the forging of a superior teaming culture.

"Efforts and courage are not enough without purpose and direction."
- John F. Kennedy

Chapter 23: Inspiring Teamwork

America was forged by rugged individuals, coming to a new and wild land, to build, develop, grow, and prosper. Ever since the days of the rugged West, the individualistic maverick cowboy has been glorified by all. Unfortunately, too much of a good thing can become corrupted. Today's American society pushes people to be self-centered: *"What's in it for me?"* is an often heard phrase. This attitude causes many problems for companies. Few are able to break the code of individualism and really operate as a team.

Anyone who has played organized team sports understands that teams that work well together beat groups of hastily thrown together individuals nearly every time, even if the individuals are all-stars. Yet within sales forces, teamwork is rarely emphasized.

A Culture of Teamwork

The Semper Fortis discipline builds a culture of teamwork one step at a time, reaffirming the teachings every day a salesperson is with the company. One of the most important steps during recruiting is determining if a candidate has the ability to play well within a team framework and accept continuous coaching and teaching.

Once a candidate is onboard, teamwork is emphasized throughout initial training and beyond.

The first task is to build cohesiveness and a sense of being a part of the team. This is accomplished through a series of steps:

1. **Develop Pride in Sales Olympian Team Membership**

   During the recruiting phase, each candidate is exposed to a unified message from every person they encounter:

   "Our company's sales team is the best in the industry. It is a great place to learn the professional sales trade and a great

place to build a long sales career. We operate as a team. We accept only the best team players. If you prefer individualist heroism, you will save yourself a lot of anguish by going someplace else."

The recruiters set the tone. They also go above and beyond the norm, interviewing many people who the recruit names as references through detailed interviews, often looking for clues to how well they will operate in a team setting. The questions, of course, get back to the recruit. Long before the firm makes the employment offer, the "world-class teaming required" message has been sent loud, clear, and often.

2. Create the Organizational Identity

Once on board, the sales group must find themselves in an unrelenting team environment that is driven to be the best sales group in the world. There are no other goals—striving to be the best drives home the discipline to do the smallest of details, when needed, for a world-class achievement.

Training, coaching, and peer-reinforcement all combine to ensure that the weaker players all strive to rise to the level of the best. The best salespeople are heavily encouraged to help show all others the best ways to succeed.

3. Drive "Unit Level" Pride and Membership

Within the greater team, the Semper Fortis system creates individual unit-level team identities and pride. In a practical sense, it is difficult to achieve great unity when team size surpasses a certain size. A dozen or so members tend to be a good upside limit when creating units. Semper Fortis sets up each sales professional as a member of two teams: their immediate group, led by a sales director, and a peer "experience-sharing" group.

Once again, the drive to set new standards and to be the best, as a team, sets the tone. For example, one sales area may lay claim and defend the title of "best sales group for new customer penetration" while another claims "best new product development sales team" and so forth. Teams are encouraged to develop a commonly agreed working approach and purpose that will help each sales professional strive for improvement of his or her franchise P&L statement.

Inspiring friendly competition helps keep the teams motivated. At the same time, the firm uses cross-team special purpose groups to develop presentations and return on investment models, inspiring on-demand teamwork across units.

4. Focus on a Common Mission

Beyond individual goals, leadership establishes common purpose and mission for all the sales and sales support staff. One year it might be "design wins" for a new product line while another might be a 10% improvement in gross margins. Additional bonuses and recognition are developed around the team's special mission beyond the primary directive of consistent sales effort and net profit success. Through focus on the mission and clear communication, the team effort stays in the forefront, even as salespeople strive to improve their individual P&Ls and capabilities.

5. Recognize Great Teamwork

A good rule of thumb is that people react more to their pay plan than to recognition, but the recognition is a significant part of the game.

In the Semper Fortis formula, team reinforcement in the pay plan is often included as a modifier, to show that the company is serious about teaming. Additionally, the necessity of teaming is clearly articulated as a negative reinforcement item through well-advertised and feared territory reassignment measures, which can have substantial effects on a person's paycheck if enacted. Generally speaking however, recognition is the primary positive incentive for good team practices.

Recognition is handed out often, in numerous ways. The Semper Fortis company generally recognizes teamwork and effort several times more often than numerical results. Recognition is addressed in greater detail in the next chapter.

6. Build a Peer Learning Environment

Studies of military units have found that even scores that are inherently "individual," for things such as marksmanship, rise overall for highly cohesive units versus units suffering team work blues. The two primary reasons for this phenomenon are that:

- The better members of the team help the underachievers attain higher levels of proficiency, and
- The underachievers are more driven not to drag down their team when they feel strong camaraderie.

Semper Fortis encourages peer mentoring as much as possible, helping the entire team pull together and win borderline opportunities.

7. Prune the Bad Apples Decisively

Few things can ruin a team more quickly than a player with a poor attitude who drives infighting and division, or one who obviously will never make the grade and will drag down the performance of the overall unit.

Semper Fortis advocates hiring all candidates under a probation period agreement, facilitating separation of any bad apples. During training, the organization watches candidates carefully, looking for signs that a candidate does not have what it takes to work in the environment. If a candidate is having issues, he or she will be given stern coaching. If the candidate does not respond, he or she will be separated from the firm quickly and decisively. An important component of this effort is confidential surveys in which candidates grade their peers.

If a bad apple surfaces later, the organization must demonstrate the will to separate the sales professional, even if their production is numerically adequate. Such events must not be quiet or secret. The team must understand that teamwork is necessary if one is to stay and prosper with the firm. Once in a while, the company may be forced into litigation but the price of carrying the wrong employees on the team is often much worse. The wrong employees are like a cancer on the team, spreading and infecting many more if they are not surgically removed in a timely manner. Once again, confidential peer review is used to spot issues early.

8. Encourage Team Identity Building

At the unit level, teamwork is facilitated by creating team identities through symbols, mottos, slogans, t-shirts, and a variety of other identifiers.

All corporate events then feature some unit teamwork contests to set up bragging rights outside business issues. It is much wiser to have the competitive juices flow in a foosball tournament than in business, where teamwork must often transcend the unit level. Care is taken to ensure that the events feature all the members of the teams, and that teamwork is necessary to win any event.

9. Establish a Group Tradition of Being a Champion Through Teamwork

History is important. If a unit has a history and a documented tradition of winning, the inheriting members do not want to be the ones who break that tradition.

The tradition must be built for the company versus its competitors and for the units themselves. It is not unlike the feeling each Notre Dame or Miami football team has—with so many championships in the past, the current class's only choice is to keep the tradition of winning alive. The company must document and display the history to all, if it is to become a significant factor in motivating team spirit.

10. Encourage Outside-the-Workplace Bonding

Companies rarely institutionally encourage outside-the-workplace friendships, often on a misguided theory of keeping family and work as separate as possible. Yet, in most studies of workplace teamwork, the teams that saw each other and their respective families outside the workplace worked better together in the workplace.

The Semper Fortis formula encourages sales directors to put together frequent family events and team events outside the workplace, usually once a month or more. Softball leagues, picnics, camping, bowling nights, white-water rafting, skeet shooting, golf, even touring haunted houses in a rented limo, all qualify. Teams are encouraged to eat lunch together at least weekly and to work together to support community organizations. Few teamwork programs are as effective as blurring the lines between work and personal life just a bit.

Culture Starts with Leadership

Culture is infectious once built. Many companies will look at their current situation and not have any idea of how teamwork could be successfully woven into their situation. Rest assured, it can be done. It starts with leadership.

A common leadership theme for creating superlative effort is to convince each and every team member that they not only matter, that they are the spark plug that keeps the unstoppable machine moving forward. By themselves, they may not account for much of the company's sales, but without them, the effect on team results is outsized.

In Summary...

Teamwork is essential to a world-class sales program. Semper Fortis starts with ten distinct steps to build camaraderie:

1. Develop pride in membership,
2. Create the organizational identity,
3. Drive "unit level" pride and membership,
4. Establish leadership and focus on a common mission,
5. Recognize teamwork,
6. Encourage peer learning,
7. Prune the bad apples decisively,
8. Encourage team identity building,
9. Establish a group tradition of being champions through teamwork, and
10. Encourage outside-the-workplace bonding.

Once the sales force truly operates as a team, the results are extraordinary. Sales professionals learn from each other's wins and losses. Employee turnover plummets. The company, through great cooperation and coordination at the Sales Intelligence Group level, learns and documents the knowledge in its SIG knowledge base. The company's reputation starts to grow within the industry, helping with the efforts to recruit the best players to the sales ranks. Soon, the firm starts winning more close contests, and is well on its way to dominating the sales landscape in its industry niche. Positive results drive greater confidence in the disciplines and formula, which in turn drives more success and increases the lead between the firm and its competitors.

Chapter 24: Encouraging Esprit de Corps

Once camaraderie has taken hold, keeping a high level of esprit de corps is essential. Through expansion and recession, companies struggle to keep the best employees loyal and happy. The same economics apply to employees as to customers: it costs much more to replace a good one than to keep an existing one. Sales professionals are no different from any other type of employee in this aspect. While responsibility and pay are very important, morale plays an important part in motivation and loyalty.

Intrinsic to the Semper Fortis discipline and process are key aspects that help build morale. These include:

- Receiving clear, unambiguous communication from sales directors regarding the mission and suggestions for approach,
- Owning one's own P&L and franchise,
- Determining one's own financial destiny and greatness by being empowered to make the decisions that matter,
- Having the freedom to be creative in business,
- Inheriting a proven formula and process for success,
- Becoming part of a gung-ho team, dedicated to advancing a record of winning,
- Receiving truly world-class pre- and post- sales support to allow a continued focus on true selling activities, and
- Working within an organization in which executives under stand the competitive advantage great salesmanship offers.

Many organizations have discovered the extraordinary value of empowerment. Employees who make decisions tend to have much greater morale than those who receive orders from above.

Outside the ingrained DNA of the Semper Fortis system, a number of key elements are applied to maintain a high level of morale and esprit de corps. First is one that many business people seem to forget after only a few years in the corporate setting: be happy and have fun.

Having fun is not in conflict with running a professional team. Yet for misguided reasons, many companies avoid fun. Some managers believe fun will be expensive. It doesn't have to be. Others forget the value of team-building and morale until crisis levels are reached, and then no amount of effort can resuscitate the situation.

In truth, fun mostly requires a free spirit, some imagination, and some humanistic effort.

Combine Celebration with Recognition

Most executives understand the need for recognition but fail to take the next natural step: combining recognition with *genuine* celebration to achieve truly memorable events. Likewise, every celebration should contain a healthy helping of recognition.

The Semper Fortis sales organization recognizes people for milestones other than merely meeting or exceeding numbers. These aspects, such as superior effort, excellent teamwork, innovation, and improvement to process and discipline, are the foremost drivers of building a world-class team. Assuredly, numeric success is also highlighted, but in many ways, numeric successes are viewed as a healthy by-product of the former items.

True celebration is a great way to bring fun to the workplace. For those who may have forgotten, fun at work includes:

- Unexpected events,
- Contests, especially a good number of silly contests,
- Recognition of large and small achievements,
- Visible symbols of achievement, especially if the recipient gets two, one for the office and another to take home and show his or her kids,
- Pictures from celebrations posted in conspicuous spots, with copies for all associates caught in the pictures, as memories tend to fade quickly without them,
- Executives poking fun at each other,

- Unusual events, such as an occasional Friday afternoon matinee,
- Prizes that matter, like three-day weekend mini-vacations,
- Events that facilitate not only learning people's names but what they do outside of the workplace.

Fun starts by encouraging people to have fun. Southwest Airlines is the most vivid corporate example of combining celebration with workplace success. One of Southwest's mottos is *"Take yourself lightly and take your job and responsibilities seriously."* Adopting a playful attitude, being the first to laugh, laughing at yourself (especially if you are the CEO), and laughing with, not at, other folks, is highly contagious.

Here are some guidelines for celebrations that make a lot of sense, adapted from Kevin and Jackie Freiberg's book *Nuts*, about the Southwest Airlines formula for success:

1. Celebrations must be authentic. Often, I see celebrations that are not really fun, and come up short of showing genuine feeling and appreciation for the people recognized.
2. Celebrations must raise people's dignity and self-esteem.
3. The celebration must be done right. Southwest assigns roles—an imagineer, who visualizes the event, an artist that takes the concept to reality, and catalysts that draw people into the spirit of the celebration.
4. The celebration must appeal to all the senses. Music, food, decorations, costumes all matter.
5. The celebration must be seen as an investment, in morale, job satisfaction, productivity, spirit, and team building.
6. The celebration must be cost-effective. The question always asked is "what is the least expensive way to do it right?"
7. And lastly, leave a lasting impression with pictures, trophies, t-shirts, and more. It all matters.

Team-Building Events

Many companies offer an annual sales reward trip for high achievers. As the economics of hyper-competition have taken hold, the percentage of participants eligible for the trip has dwindled and the effectiveness of the trips for motivation and morale has waned. At IBM, for example, the sales force is no longer motivated by the trip, called the Golden Circle award, as only a few percent (less than 5%) of the salespeople qualify each year.

The Semper Fortis system calls for a different approach to such events: small, often, mostly-inclusive, and cost-effective. On a quarterly basis, teams do micro-retreats for one or two days, focusing on small but nice events like camping, white-water rafting, floating down a river, or snow skiing. The events often emphasize loosely-organized team-building exercises in addition to simply rejuvenating the troops.

A couple of times each year, special "weekend-winners" trips are put together, once again with an eye toward cost-effective-but-nice goals. Winners are those whose numerical results are tracking according to business plans for the year. Spouses are typically welcomed in the weekend-winners getaway format, and the goal is for every member of the sales force to attend at least one "weekend winners" event every year, keeping the goal attainable.

Unlike IBM's trips to faraway exotic destinations, the typical weekend-winners trip often features local resorts within an easy drive of many participants. By keeping it local, more people get to attend, and the trips are achievable, thus remaining effective motivators. In addition to CUBEs and solution sales specialists, key pre- and post- sales support personnel are also selected to attend the reward trips. Achievers are honored and recognized, with video and pictures later distributed throughout the company.

Leadership's Key Role

Esprit de corps is often a delicate item. The company's leaders must maintain a detailed situational awareness and take action to nip any morale issues early.

A number of serious leadership topics top the list of morale enhancers or detractors. Troops want leaders who *lead by example*. A president or CEO who sits comfortably in the ivory tower writing esoteric memos far removed from the daily battles will kill morale quickly. If the commander-in-chief of sales only takes easy, friendly meetings with customers, the force will notice almost immediately.

Leaders must lead with absolute integrity. If a top executive cuts corners with customers, the organization will worry that it is just a matter of time before they will be treated the same way. Trust matters most of all.

All managers must demonstrate genuine concern for the welfare of their subordinates. While the work is important, acknowledging the importance of the salesperson's mental, physical, and emotional fitness, as well as his or her family life, goes even farther. Unfortunately, many managers never take the time to understand all of the facets that one of their employees must balance to live a well-rounded life.

Lastly, esprit de corps is achieved by maintaining focus on the greater good of the whole enterprise, rather than on the results of any one individual. If a CUBE is putting up great numbers but, at the same time, is doing things that hurt the overall teamwork and morale of the company, he or she must be firmly corrected or separated for the good of the organization.

Team members who are clearly not carrying their weight must go as well. The NFL is a great example of meritocracy in action. With only a limited number of slots on each team, the coaches must pick the best players each year and cut the rest. In the long run, employees appreciate a clear line in the sand and consistent treatment of all.

In Summary...

High morale and esprit de corps is achieved through a combination of light-hearted attitude, recognition, celebration, and good leadership. Each facet must be genuine. Semper Fortis looks at recognition as the key driving force to encourage gung-ho teamwork.

We now add the first facet, "Continuous teaming reinforcement," to the eighth pillar of the Semper Fortis model:

Chapter 25: Creating a Pro-Sales Enterprise

The goal of the Semper Fortis formula is to develop a great Sales Olympian team. However, professional sales cannot succeed on its own in the complex corporate solution selling environment.

Almost by definition, complex solutions require customization, configuration, troubleshooting, coordinated delivery and implementation, ongoing support, and so forth. This list discounts the fact that a value-added product or service must first be developed to serve as the anchor for the overall solution. Clearly, a great number of non-sales departments are intimately involved in ensuring that the solution works well for the customer.

You Are What You Measure

I have seen a great number of companies where sales and the other departments are at odds. Each new prospect is seen as just more work for an overburdened quality assurance staff, development department, or staging group. The single most prevalent reason for this is that these departments are rarely incited by sales and growth goals, opting for other measures such as minimizing defects or maximizing lines of code per software developer.

For all the same arguments as presented in Chapter 8, the company must put measures and gauges in place that evaluate performance from the customer perspective for every department that contributes to customer efforts. Measurements must support the sales effort, which in turn is aligned with the goals of the owners of the company.

Some of the best measures are customer loyalty surveys by department / function. When designed well, the feedback is invaluable in determining if the company is delivering greater value and trending in the right directions from the all-important customers' perspective. The Semper Fortis system takes this a step farther, instituting internal versions of the surveys, whereby the sales professionals also evaluate the satisfaction ratings of the various departments providing service to the field. Departments quickly learn that working hard to please their "customers," the actual user of the solutions *and* the sales people servicing the customers on a daily basis in the field, is a good strategy for staying in good graces with executives.

The department-level measurements must filter down to the individuals in the department, and must serve as a component of pay raises, bonuses, and promotion. If not, consistent quality is difficult to achieve.

Sales Liaison / Department Spokesperson

When using the Semper Fortis discipline, each department appoints a relatively senior individual to act as the department's sales liaison. The liaison receives general sales and presentation skills training, attends Toastmasters for public speaking, attends industry classes and receives certifications, much as do the field-based system engineers.

The liaisons' primary roles are to:

- Serve as the official interface between the sales force and their own department,
- Project manage sales-driven requests to ensure timely and accurate follow-up,
- Act as the lead spokesperson for the department on customer conference calls and at customer meetings,
- Attend tradeshows, once again fulfilling spokesperson duties,
- Participate on special councils for feedback regarding new sales initiatives and presentations,
- Champion the sales cause within the department, and
- Conduct short briefings at departmental meetings, informing the department of sales progress and initiatives.

Depending on the volume of work, the liaison position may be full-time in some departments but part-time in others. Generally, candidates for the position are rotated out in one or two years, spreading the learning experience across a number of high-flyers. The high demand, high visibility position is used to determine the suitability for promotion of departmental stars to higher levels of responsibility. Given that success in the position nearly assures promotion, a clear message is sent across the company that good coordination and support of the sales effort leads to personal success.

Fostering Understanding

Professional selling is often a mysterious black art to those outside the field. Rarely do personnel within a headquarters department get a glimpse of all the process and steps required to pull off the highly complex, big-deal sale. The often two- or three-year effort leading up to a big win is invisible; instead, it looks like overnight success to many of the folks at the home office.

An important step to achieving cross-departmental teamwork is to foster understanding. Semper Fortis advocates creating bi-annual briefings, hosted by selected sales professionals for each department, training them on what goes on long before a big deal is announced and won. Care is taken to make sure people meet each other and put names with faces. If feasible, the company coordinates a celebration event, with fun items like a billiards or air hockey tournament and mixed cross-departmental teams, and of course, lots of pictures.

The power of understanding each other, and playing together, makes a lot of difference when a sales challenge demands extra effort later.

Departmental Recognition Programs

The centerpiece of building a pro-sales enterprise throughout all departments is the Semper Fortis Compski program. Many Delta Airlines frequent flyers have seen a variation of the program in action, when Delta distributes "Compliment" vouchers to its frequent flyers. The program makes it easy for frequent flyers to send in compliments whenever a Delta customer service associate does a great job.

In the Semper Fortis program, the sales professionals use a secure website to send in Compskis whenever any departmental associates do a great job helping the sales effort. The Compski routes not only to the employee's manager, but is posted on the Semper Fortis executive information portal, allowing executives to review compliments as well as the flow of decisions in the real-time decision log, discussed in Chapter 11. The information is also routed to human resources, and recorded for consideration during the next employee review.

When the sales professionals have such a direct and visible influence on the careers and prospects of employees in various departments, everybody realizes the importance of helping sales efforts succeed.

Extending the Rewards for Key Wins

From time to time, a non-sales employee plays a truly critical role in making or breaking a large sales deal. The area VPs have the ability and budget to financially reward such heroism in a very public way.

It doesn't take many $5,000 cash bonuses or seven-day trips to Europe (perhaps without having to use vacation time) to send a message that sales "assists" are noticed and rewarded. Giving a trip is preferable—cash often disappears into items like fresh paint on an employee's house, but memories of Venice and St. Tropez last a lifetime.

Celebrating and Honoring the Heroes

No matter whether the honor is small or large, trumpeting the heroes within all the supporting departments is important. Pictures and video footage should always be taken, and then spread throughout the organization. Including stories in company newsletters, posting write-ups on bulletin boards and news portals, and reminding people of accomplishments during introductions, all add to the honor of being a customer hero.

Going beyond the status quo "employee of the month" reserved parking slots, the Semper Fortis company has programs like "Key Sales Assist of the Month." Parking places are cheap—why not have many awards, not just the expected "employee of the month" one.

In Summary…

For sales to succeed, all the departments that support the cause must be pro-sales.

Semper Fortis accomplishes this in several ways:

- Departments and individuals are measured by selling progress and customer loyalty,
- Sales liaison champions are appointed and trained in every department,
- The sales team proactively educates and gets to know each department, fostering understanding,
- The sales professional–initiated Compski program provides direct, highly-visible feedback that can make or break careers,
- Sales VPs have the ability and charter to financially reward individuals outside of sales for key assists on critical battles,
- Heroes are recognized, celebrated and honored by all.

We now attach the final facet to the Semper Fortis teamwork pillar:

Part Three

Making It Happen

"It takes courage to decide to become the best, as such a public and
audacious goal sets one up for an important life's test:
the outcome can only be a glorious victory or a resounding defeat.

Many do not want to find out what they are really made of."
- Bob Sakalas

Chapter 26: Sparking Fusion

While all the pillars and facets of the Semper Fortis model work together, achieving program fusion is impossible without the spark of leadership. For a company to build a true, lasting competitive advantage in salesmanship, it must be committed to the vision, ready to adapt and overcome all challenges encountered on the way.

The discipline requires many changes, many of which affect other departments and operations. Support for the program must start with the top executives. The top executive in sales will not be successful if left to implement the program on his or her own.

One of the first transformations necessary to achieve fusion is the conversion of all in sales management to a new leadership and coaching focus. First-line managers are especially affected, as much of their previous control is transferred to self-managed CUBEs, who control their own P&Ls and serve as micro-general managers of their franchised businesses.

The Semper Fortis formula is generally a straightforward one, but building momentum until fusion is achieved takes tenacity. There is no magic time-frame for achieving success. One company may make remarkable progress in twelve months, while another may require thirty-six months. Each company's implementation will have interesting challenges and needs for customization. The program builds momentum in baby steps until it finally ignites upon reaching a tipping point. Executives will find that the initial steps are the most difficult, the initial year or two the most challenging, but in the end, self-directed sales professionals will produce extraordinary results, and the executives will find their jobs marked by guidance, fine-tuning, and the preservation of culture, as the engine takes on a life of its own.

Within the Semper Fortis system, the first-line sales managers, called sales directors, serve in a critical capacity. They are the "master sergeants," veterans that help keep everyone in a generally decentralized organization on course, driving all salespeople to significant personal improvement, and serving as management's eyes and ears in the field. Under this system, the sales directors must let go of their traditional management "control" thinking and adopt leadership, coaching, and coordination as their core tasks.

Well Before the Launch

Before launching the initiative, the commander-in-chief of sales must size up his or her managers regarding their capabilities to lead and coach. Those lacking these skills must receive training or be moved into special-purpose positions that can still help the sales team, in a different role. The formula generally requires fewer people in direct management in total than in the typical quota and control scheme. This dynamic allows executives to choose the best 70% to 80% of the candidates for operational leadership slots in the new scheme.

The first order of business is to conduct an evaluation that rates each manager on the following characteristics, called the Semper Fortis Leadership 30 (L-30). For each first-level manager, the L-30 evaluation is completed by:

1. Sales executives (area VPs and commander-in-chief of sales),
2. Peer sales managers, and
3. Direct sales and sales support subordinates who work for the manager.

Care is taken to assure that the information will remain confidential, in an effort to get the most candid evaluations possible. A special Human Resources department analyst reassembles the results, highlighting the scenarios in which answers varied dramatically from one evaluator to the next. The commander-in-chief of sales then is tasked with ranking his or her managers based upon leadership characteristics to determine the best candidates for the job slots.

The same L-30 evaluation is completed on area VPs by the commander-in-chief of sales, their peer area VPs, and the managers who report to them. Finally, the commander-in-chief of sales is evaluated by the area VPs and his or her peers within the executive ranks. These rounds help provide feedback to all the executives within sales and outline leadership development opportunities.

Some organizations will have a greater number of reporting levels. Under Semper Fortis, some flattening of the sales organization is desirable as compared to quota-based selling models, as a shorter and wider hierarchy fosters greater right-level decision-making clarity. With much of the day-to-day decision-making resting with the sales professional, each sales director can take on a greater number of salespeople. Excess managers can sometimes be retrained and re-tasked into highly-focused Special Forces' roles.

The L-30 Evaluation

The L-30 leadership evaluation includes rating each manager on the following characteristics of leadership. Not only is a candidate ranked according to his or her ability, specific notes are made outlining what a candidate must learn to do better, and what the odds are that the candidate has "the right stuff" to achieve required leadership capabilities.

The Semper Fortis L-30 characteristics include:

1. Honesty and Integrity

Honesty and integrity are mission-critical to success as a leader. The first time a leader is willing to bend the rules, the message reverberates throughout the enterprise, and many lose some, if not all, of their respect for their leader. In the longer run, many people in the organization tend to follow the lead: if shady deals are acceptable, all those who are willing to compromise their values will do so, and the ones who will not usually find other places to work.

2. Good Character

Character is the strength and the uncompromising backbone of a leader. The character of a leader is tested by the quality of his or her actions and intentions, especially during trying times. Good character does not change with the tides or prevailing winds. There will always be challenging moments and people will follow leaders whose good character is unflappable.

3. Discipline (for Professionalism and Excellence)

Leadership, per se, does not always require a discipline of professionalism. In fact, many leaders around the world are highly emotional icons. However, within the Semper Fortis model, where precision and discipline are hallmarks of consistent superior sales effort, discipline is most important. Semper Fortis demands adherence to a proven process, a consistent superior effort every day, and a focus on *how* results are achieved in addition to the results themselves. Therefore, leaders without discipline have a difficult time on a Semper Fortis team.

The leader must be disciplined in order to continuously question and improve his or her approach on the road to achieving and redefining excellence in the field. Semper Fortis is about dominating selling within a niche. The only way to dominate is to strive for consistent and ever-improving excellence.

4. Competence

All leaders must be highly competent, not just at leading, but in all topics that affect the operation of the company and the sales force, specifically regarding sales and sales process, company offerings, and industry issues. Incompetence immediately shakes people's confidence. Semper Fortis requires that leaders are certified on products and industry issues right alongside the sales force. In fact, the sales leaders must pass more stringent business "fitness" testing, as they are the first line of support and teaching for everyone else. The salespeople should know that they must strive for excellence and competence in part because their sales director is as qualified or more qualified than they are, setting a stringent standard. A Semper Fortis firm does not accept the all too frequent statement *"I've lost touch with the technical aspects since I was promoted into management."*

This one aspect can often test the mettle of a company's will to become a Semper Fortis champion. Many times, the resistance from first-line management to becoming highly competent will not be overcome by the executives, resulting in a quickly-aborted attempt to become world-class.

5. Communication Abilities

Oral communication remains the cornerstone of coaching. The candidates must have excellent skills and must be clearly understood by all. Within the scope of customer engagements, managers often attend difficult meetings, providing backup support for their sales associates. Excellent oral communication and nimble debate skills are critical to success.

As the "small planet" networking phenomenon continues to blossom, written communications, especially in e-mail form, continue to rise in stature. The leader of today, and even more so tomorrow, must have adroit abilities with the written word.

6. Direct and Open Style

An important quality within a leader is that he or she avoids ambiguity, approaching all situations and decisions in a clear, direct, and consistent manner. When their leader is direct, people know where things stand and can move forward without worry that decisions may change, or that there are innuendoes that must be read in the tea leaves.

Managers should be open with their teams. Secrecy should be avoided as much as possible. Too often, secrets are needlessly kept, fostering a cancer of distrust to grow within the ranks.

7. Ability as a Teacher

The Semper Fortis system changes first-line managers into coaches, mentors, and teachers. Managers who do not have the ability to teach simply do not fit the model. A key aspect of teaching well is adjusting one's style and approach to match the student's needs, as opposed to making each student bend to the teacher's methods.

8. Ability and Openness for Learning and Change

In order to implement a new system, many of the old ways must be questioned and undone, while new methods and inventions take hold. The leaders within a Semper Fortis force must learn many new things on the road to success. Semper Fortis leaders must have the ability, in fact the desire, to always question and improve the formula over time.

9. Vision

Leaders must have vision and must communicate it clearly. Semper Fortis narrows the focus to becoming the best sales force in one's market. To keep this singular focus, leaders within the organization must bring the common theme into every activity, ingraining the vision into the daily workflow.

No better example of vision exists than Ronald Reagan's vision of a great America. Inheriting the reins on the heels of the Iran hostage crisis, at a time when business leaders felt almost overrun by Japanese efficiency, America was questioning the truth of capitalism, wondering if state supported zaibatsu conglomerates were in fact impossible to beat in business, and gravely concerned about the USSR's growing strength and aggressiveness. Reagan's well articulated vision of the shimmering island of freedom and moral righteousness, turned around America's attitude. He went on the offense, building military might, convincing the Soviets that they could not win the Cold War or the arms race, culminating with the tearing down of the Berlin Wall. By the end of the 1980s, America, sparked by Reagan's vision, was the last standing military and economic super-power, and in every sense of the word, world-class among all nations.

The Semper Fortis vision is a parallel in the smaller scheme of companies and industries, in much the same way. The Semper Fortis sales force is both the company's military and the diplomatic corps. Up and down the chain of command, the leaders must forge the vision in the hearts of all company associates.

10. Team Player with Ideas, but Who Makes Orders Own

Certain people "push back" on most of the ideas and initiatives that come down from the executives. When these people finally move forward, they do so while subtly (or not so subtly) communicating to everyone that they are going along with the initiative but don't personally agree with it.

Underground push-back has no place in a Semper Fortis organization. Strong opinions should be welcomed at times of discussion and debate, but when a decision is made, the entire management team must execute it as if each manager put the orders out himself or herself. Sales directors and area VPs who cannot flourish in this type of environment will not be with the company long. In essence, the force does not need "yes men" or "no men." It needs strong, smart team-players and leaders.

11. Responsibility / Reliability / Openness

A good leader accepts complete responsibility for business failures and short-comings, while giving credit to his or her people for successes and wins. The more common corporate reality, unfortunately, is to take credit and pass the blame—the exact opposite style of what builds extraordinary teams.

Semper Fortis holds managers to a higher standard. An important aspect is learning from failures, documenting the lessons, and not repeating them as an organization. This can not be done where the leaders are not responsible and instead practice the well-known corporate formula of covering up all black marks immediately.

Responsibility and reliability go hand-in-hand. Subordinates know that their leaders will be reliable when they accept total responsibility. Through right-leveling decision-making, final say on most sales tactics rests with the sales professional. But the responsibility does not exonerate the sales director or those above him or her.

12. Relationship Sincerity / Listening / Empathy

Leadership does not mean that one must worry about being popular and liked by all. However, to become a great leader, everyone must believe that their relationship with the leader is sincere and that he or she truly cares about the subordinate's well-being. Listening and empathy skills, along with sincerity, serve a leader well, both with employees and customers.

13. Problem-Solving

In one way or another, leadership always requires problem-solving. Problems invariably bubble up the chain of command. A leader must not only make clear decisions, but decisions must be good ones more often than not. The L-30 evaluation pays special attention to the abilities each manager has in solving problems.

14. Good Judgment

Good judgment is making good decisions based upon imperfect data. Experience, good situational awareness, looking at the brutal facts, understanding one's own biases, and intuition all play a part. In business, there are few black-and-white decisions or answers. The best way to evaluate a manager's good judgment is by his or her track record over the years.

15. Passion / Energy / Enthusiasm / Positive Attitude

Passion and energy do not have to be loud and flamboyant. Passion speaks to belief in the company, its employees, its products, and its value-add to the clients. Energy and enthusiasm can be very personal or public for all to see, but they must be present to spark top performance. Leaders who really don't care deeply about the company's success have no place on a gung-ho Semper Fortis force.

Positive attitude is really the directional bias of passion, energy, and enthusiasm. One might be passionate and full of energy, but radiate negative reinforcement to the troops. Best performance requires an atmosphere charged with positive vibes, optimism, happiness, and even fun.

16. Courage

Courage is required to take prudent risks. Unless a company takes as many prudent risks as it can stretch and handle, it will not become great. But companies do not take risks—individuals and small teams really do, risking career and reputation in the process. Courage is required because it is always easier to settle into the known routine and not expose oneself to possible failure or difficulty. If the leaders of the sales force do not have and do not demonstrate courage, few of the salespeople will exhibit it on their own.

Courage does not mean trekking forth without fear or concern. As John Wayne put it,

"Courage is being scared to death, but saddling up anyway."

Few corporate situations are life or death, but concerns about "sticking one's neck out" and risking damage to either career or reputation prevent many individuals, and in aggregate companies, from achieving greatness.

17. Initiative

Sales and initiative go together like peanut butter and jelly. Most sales managers had initiative running through their veins early in their career, or they would not have been promoted. Given that customers' corporate habits are often set in stone, and that the essence of sales success is convincing people to change, initiative is a key component everyone could use more of on the force.

Sales professionals may tire or get distracted from time to time, pulling back on their effort for a few weeks here and there. The sales directors must serve as fountains of initiative, inspiring the salespeople to keep up the effort week in and week out. Additionally, the leaders must not only look for opportunities that the salespeople miss, but they must put on the full-court press when great ones are spotted.

18. Charisma / First-Impression Impact

Charisma is an interesting quality. Its core emanates from the ability a person has of making *the other person* feel important and good about himself or herself. Simultaneously, charisma consists of elements such as presence, an aura of success without pretense, charm, and even a touch of mystery. While difficult to define, a person's charisma, or lack of it, is easy to see and feel.

A leader in the sales group must be at a minimum likeable and must make favorable first impressions. By developing his or her listening and questioning skills, he or she can make the jump to becoming somewhat charismatic. Charisma ultimately is a foremost asset for the "hunter" specialists, as often this quality is paramount in enabling the salesperson to land a second and third meeting in the early stages of penetrating a non-buying account.

19. Commitment

Leadership requires commitment. Just as no athlete ever won an Olympic gold medal without whole-hearted commitment, no sales team will achieve world-class excellence without commitment as well.

People can sense commitment, or lack of it, from miles away. Leaders must be committed to the program, and to winning, or the organization flounders. Given that adopting the Semper Fortis model will represent a dramatic cultural revolution for many companies, the commitment of the leaders will be the glue that keeps it together, improving momentum each month.

20. Focus

Many pretty good salespeople fail when faced with too many opportunities and too many distractions. The sales directors must be adept at keeping people balanced in the work setting, focused on the important tasks that not only land business but keep the sales radar full of legitimate, good-fit opportunities. At the same time, the focus must not waver from building independent business men and women who follow a precise process for success and continued learning.

Managers who have scattered attentions have a difficult time in the disciplined Semper Fortis system.

21. Self-Discipline / Self-Sufficiency

Semper Fortis sets up an environment in which there is little daily management in the traditional control sense. If employees or managers require someone looking over their shoulders on nearly a daily basis, they probably do not belong on the team. While the team exists to further selling, it does not exist to keep people from having to paddle the boat themselves. Self-discipline, the kind that drives Tiger Woods to hit an extra 2,000 golf balls on the range when no one else is around, between tournaments, is required of all managers and sales professionals in the organization.

While the formula calls for team support, there are always resource shortages. The ingrained expectation must be that success will be achieved without excuse, and if resources are temporarily constrained, the individuals will find a way to adapt, overcome, and win, scrapping for every yard on the way to a touchdown, if need be. Sales people in companies with a blanket of support often find themselves incapable of moving forward when the support is unavailable.

22. Balance in Life

The Semper Fortis system calls for sustainable, superior effort. Sustainability is only possible if one practices superior balance across one's work, family, mental, physical, and spiritual life. The oft-used phrase *"work hard, work smart, not long"* applies. Workaholics tend to burn out, often becoming unproductive as their life at home craters from neglect.

Managers within the organization must live balanced lives and serve as both examples and counselors to the salespeople in their care. Only through harmony on all fronts can true happiness and sustainability be achieved.

One out-of-balance leader near the top can upset this dynamic. When the top manager starts demanding workaholism by setting that example himself, often because of a life-changing event at home such as divorce, the work-smart, gung-ho troops become work-long, gung-ho troops. In the short run, there is typically greater success, but in the long run, valleys of effort and employee turnover factors increase, esprit de corps is lost, and critical knowledge walks out the door, never to return.

23. Emotional Stability

Leaders must be stable and predictable. One who changes course daily, or bends too easily, winds up wasting valuable time as everyone continually tries to figure out how the game has changed from the previous week or month.

24. Situational Awareness

The need for situational awareness is paramount. Internally, morale and loyalty issues can be headed off by leaders who are in touch with the rhythms of the enterprise. Externally, good judgment and intuition start from being situationally aware of the dynamics between customers, competitors, complimentary vendors, and industry issues and initiatives.

25. Patience

Often, landing good deals at well-negotiated win / win prices and terms requires more patience than most people have. Selling is generally a vocation of initiative and impatience. Managers must help their salespeople practice patience and timing at appropriate moments. Often, the ability to walk away from the table for weeks or months is the difference between win / win and lose / win.

26. Fairness

Not only must a leader be fair to all salespeople, he or she must also be *perceived* as fair. This is a subtle but important observation. Managers often get pulled into referee roles during internal conflicts. The goal is to administer all situations consistently, avoiding any misconception of favoritism, not just by the participants, but all employees in the vicinity of the conflict.

27. Intelligence / Conceptual Ability

Selling is knowledge work. Nimble tactical selling requires one to be a quick study, able to pick up and leverage small clues to great advantage. While planning is important, the ability to think quickly on one's feet is critical as well. Intelligence is very important to winning the game.

28. Creativity

In the complex corporate solution selling environment, customers often turn to salespeople and sales managers who are creative and who are able to solve problems in innovative ways. Creativity is often necessary to financially justify solutions and to find new approaches when the tried-and-true ones are not getting the job done.

29. Political Savvy

Political savvy is another characteristic that is difficult to define, much like charisma, but shines when it is present.

Many are politically motivated, but few are adept at understanding and leveraging politics without appearing political at all. Building this wisdom takes years, often more years than many salespeople have been in the business. Consequently, the sales directors have to step in and provide mentoring and understanding of this important facet of selling.

30. Stress Diffusion

When striving to be world-class, there is always some stress, often self-induced by gung-ho professionals. Sales leaders must help diffuse the stress in positive ways, not add to it. Too many try heavy-handed techniques that wind up ultimately reducing long-term performance and decreasing career loyalty.

Development and Organization Plan

Once the L-30 is completed for managers, a rapid development plan is authored that gives the future sales directors and area VPs needed coaching on aspects where guidance is needed. As part of the plan, the sales management team is trained on the complete Semper Fortis program and its goals, customized to best fit the company's selling environment.

The sales managers also complete L-30 evaluations of all candidates for CUBE positions. Within this system, these sales professionals will serve as the leaders of the tactical sales effort, coordinating resources, making decisions, and becoming micro-general managers, empowered to succeed. By completing the L-30 for their direct reports, sales directors identify their perceptions of what is needed in each individualized coaching plan.

While this pre-launch phase is a lot of homework, putting the right people in the right places, creating development plans and awareness of expectations, and communicating the sheer depth of the change to culture is crucial. People soon recognize that no company would take such thorough, professional measures unless it was serious about attaining world-class status.

The Launch

Unlike many of the big-bang programs offered by management gurus, Semper Fortis involves a process of baby steps that builds momentum to a fusion tipping point, when it becomes almost self-sustaining. At the launch, a broad vision is presented to the force, with most of the message aimed at culture, not the specific steps that will be taken.

The launch message is simple:

1. We have a vision: We will become the dominant sales force in our industry.
2. We have distinct intermediate missions to reach the vision.
3. There are a large number of steps on the road, and we will not falter.
4. We will only become extraordinary as a team. If we continue only as individuals, we will not succeed.
5. There is no deadline or magic end date, but there is urgency.
6. We will prevail and become world-class.
7. We will seize share from competitors, building momentum.
8. We will not lose customers.
9. Our sales force will become stronger and stronger.
10. We will convert to a total meritocracy. Successful sales professionals will receive great rewards and management will no longer manipulate personal earnings potential.

First Steps

The first steps to the Semper Fortis program are found in the first three pillars of the model.

Pillar I: Integrated Formula Selling

A formal selling process is defined, developed, and produced as part of the franchisee operating procedures. All sales professionals attend formal classes to reacquaint themselves with the steps in selling strategically and within the framework of the company's planned selling process.

Sales directors coach and lead the salespeople, using only the information driven by the process, such as the account plans, opportunity plans, sales call plans, and sales radar as input. All other reporting is put aside until a clear need for the return of certain reporting elements is established and validated by the commander-in-chief of sales.

The area VPs, sales directors, and CUBEs collaborate to teach the professional selling process methodologies to supporting personnel, ensuring that the surrounding organization understands the remarkable change being implemented in the selling methodology. By requiring key sales professionals to teach, the company ensures that the concepts have been well understood and accepted.

Pillar II: Sales Force Aligned with Shareholders

The finance department is charged with preparing P&L statements by customer, rolled up to a sales professional view, which in turn rolls up through sales management. Once P&Ls are up and running, short training classes brief salespeople and sales directors on the details of the reports and how various elements affect the P&Ls and their individual pay.

The compensation plan is then changed to a model of net profit and profit quality.

Pillar III: Right-Level Decision Making

Flow charts along with the online decision logging systems are provided to sales personnel, to clearly show what types of decisions they are expected to make out in the field. The extraordinary power and momentum of empowering the professionals with the closest knowledge of the customer then kicks into high gear.

Pillars IV—VIII: Next Steps

Once the first three pillars are in place, momentum to add the remaining five pillars and related facets builds:

- Pervasive Sales Intelligence
- Comprehensive Logistics and Support
- Selling Readiness Operations
- Specialization of Sales Roles
- Unquestionable Commitment to Teamwork

All the concepts are introduced within the first year, with a goal of maturing the new sales force operations in year two.

Selecting the Right Team Leaders

Picking the right individuals for the key leadership roles in all the areas is the single most important decision the commander-in-chief of sales makes. The positions outside the core operational area VPs and sales directors that drive the final five pillars include:

- Captain of the Sales Intelligence Group (SIG)
    - Human Intelligence Chief
    - Electronic Intelligence and Analysis Chief

Implementing Semper Fortis on a Tight Budget

While not optimal, the model can be implemented on a tight budget by combining new functions with existing job slots within the organization.

For example, a sales director may take on two responsibilities - the management of his or her own area plus the role of the recruiting and retention specialist. Another might add the duty of being a thought-leadership consultant, developing material, publishing articles on a specific area while retaining his or her direct management duties. A third might become the selling readiness chief in addition to regular duties.

The one position that is perhaps the hardest to do on a part-time basis is implementing the SIG.

- Centralized Sales Support Desk Chief
- Captain of the Special Forces
- Recruiting and Retention Chief
- Captain of the SemperForte
- Training and Coaching Coordinator
- The Navigator (discussed in the next chapter)

Culture Building is Critical

As subsequent pillars and facets of the model are implemented, leadership must continue to focus first and foremost on culture. It often takes two years before the new culture becomes ingrained, and often requires pruning of bad apples and other somewhat painful measures along the way to demonstrate the company's resolve.

Culture is built with frequent and clear communication. The commander-in-chief of sales must set the tone, being seen by the troops often, preaching the merits of meritocracy and self-determination of success. The message is that there are no limits to a salesperson's achievements, if he or she is willing to stay and excel within the system.

Generally, cultural aspects such as meritocracy, responsibility, and right-level decision making are accepted quickly.

The key to the SIG's impact is to have pervasive knowledge of the ebb and flow of the sales effort across the organization. The top VP in sales is often in the position to know much of what is going on, but in my experience, never has the bandwidth to have to continuous in-depth conversations with CUBEs, sales directors, and others to keep the information current and catalogued. Therefore, even on a tight budget, my advice is to start the SIG with an energetic, respected, and dedicated leader and at least one prolific administrative assistant. Often, this can be accomplished by taking a senior salesperson that may be looking for a new challenge out of the field and into a key HQ staff slot.

Where there is a will there is always a way. As with many things however, asking one person to shoulder too many areas at once results in substandard efforts and focus in each area and the eventual demise of the program.
I would not advise giving all the roles in the Semper Fortis model to one or two individuals to pull off by wearing many hats at once.

Continuous planning, learning and coaching are accepted over a few months. Candid knowledge sharing and trust are accepted grudgingly. Leadership is the spark that keeps fusion going during the infancy and growth of the Semper Fortis program.

By adding leadership to the center, the pillars of the Semper Fortis model are fused together. The final version of the Semper Fortis model is complete:

Chapter 27: Implementing Measurement Gauges

Running a company, especially a large one, is a complex endeavor. As competition gets tougher, management must be able to see the situation and the variables clearly, using that insight to make good decisions. The speed of change has made it ever more difficult to successfully steer the company by gut feel, as might have been possible when the enterprise was small and the markets generally stable.

Most companies have terrible *management* measurement systems. They have systems that keep great financial score, generally a month or a quarter in arrears, which managers try to use for forward-looking purposes. The root cause of the problem is that nearly all of these measures originate in the finance and accounting departments. Relying on accounting numbers to help proactively manage a company or a sales force is much like flying through thick thunderstorms, at night, with no instruments other than a global positioning system (GPS) device that reports where your plane was a month ago.

The purpose of *management* measurements is to enable executives to make decisions to help the business perform better, not to keep score per se. This drives several key requirements of "good" measurements:

1. **Whatever is measured should be as broad as it can be, while small enough to be understood and acted upon.**

   Sales managers can understand a gauge such as competitive win share by area of the country, which measures how many wins competitors have in relation to each other in any given area, in relation to the country overall. Yet most companies define their measurement landscape much more broadly.

   For example, measuring overall market share is generally pointless for sales management—too many factors can be changed to effect market share gains and losses; therefore, market share belongs in the "scorekeeping" side.

2. **Measurements should be aligned with the strategic goals of the company.**

   Companies often have conflicting messages in play at the same time because of well-intentioned measurements.

   For example, a company may have a "corporate-level" goal of dramatically improving customer satisfaction regarding the reliability of its products, yet simultaneously incite the service representatives based upon speed of fixing hardware in the field, which is based upon a service department goal.

   Clearly, service reps in this scenario will not take additional steps to ensure quality, nor conduct any preventative maintenance that could decrease the total number of service calls, if they are primarily measured and promoted on a basis of speed. This conflict results in more break-downs and more service calls, directly torpedoing the primary goal of improving the perception of reliability by customers.

3. **Managers must understand all the options for action, and the likely results of the measurement that they are trying to improve.**

   If a sales manager has little idea of what action can be taken to affect a measure, the measure is informational at best, confusing at worst. An example is return on shareholder equity: few sales managers will have clear action steps in mind to make a direct, substantial change to this number.

4. **The inter-relationships between different measures must be understandable.**

   We work in a complex, multi-dimensional world. Rarely are any measures free-standing; rather, most tend to relate to one another, usually with only a few degrees of separation.

5. **Managers must be able to see the "big picture" effect—many times, improvement in one measure results in degradation of another.**

   If the visual presentation is confusing, with measures found across multiple screens and paper reports, the big picture and cause and effect of various changes becomes impossible to understand. Managers wind up trying to tweak operations in one big circle, rarely making breakthrough progress.

6. **Measures must face forward, helping anticipate future events and business flow.**

   Nearly every company in America still operates with most measures deeply rooted in the accounting discipline and therefore, looking backward into recent history. Forward-facing measurement requires designing measures for the management discipline, not finance.

7. **Measures must have a goal of presenting reality.**

   Some managers prefer their personal biases versus brutal reality. For example, a credit card issuer might believe that their pet frequent flyer points program is highly effective in driving card usage, but the facts may point to three other factors as more important in increasing usage.

   Only by facing and testing against the best discernable facts can managers make smart decisions most of the time. The data will never be perfect, but the less bias involved, the better.

   Business people, who have for most of their career operated by gut feel alone, must adopt discipline to first face reality, question the facts, evaluate their own biases, and only then start applying good judgment and intuition, rooted in the facts and an accurate situational awareness.

The Navigator

Measurement, in these forward-facing terms, is a challenging task, clearly separate in focus from accounting and finance. The Semper Fortis system advocates having a full-time measurement guru, called the Navigator, on the commander-in-chief of sales' immediate staff to monitor, tweak, and develop new measures while removing measurements that are no longer useful. This way, the pilots, the CUBEs, solution sales specialists, area VPs, and sales directors, finally have a navigator and good instruments on the flight-deck. Note that the commander-in-chief of sales serves primarily as the airplane, gauge, and system *designer*, not as the day-to-day pilot.

The Navigator often serves a dual role: designing internal gauges and measuring customer loyalty and retention. Customer loyalty is tricky, but is hugely important in ensuring a firm's steady climb to the top of its niche. The Navigator is a key resource for top managers, using constant, outward-facing programs to collect candid retention and loyalty data, serving as an important second set of eyes and opinion for the commander-in-chief of sales.

Getting Measure Design "Right"

The ten commandments for designing excellent measures for management and leadership purposes are:

1. Measures must be synchronized with corporate strategy, which in turn, is developed in light of shareholder goals. Within Semper Fortis, compensation is designed to ensure that the sales force is aligned with shareholder goals and corporate strategy.

2. Measures must be aligned with the customer and his or her reasons for doing business with the company.

3. Measures must be forward-looking, and must provide excellent situation awareness and early red-flag warnings when appropriate.

4. Measures should be as simple and straightforward as they can be. Present as few measures as possible to managers while still covering all the important bases. Be sure the measures are displayed in simple formats to ensure understanding.

5. The lowest level of detail must be saved in the decision-making databases, letting the company adjust gauges in the future without limitations.

6. All data should be presented in both graphical and numerical views, to appeal to all managers no matter what their personal display preference.

7. The big picture view should be presented first, allowing managers to drill down to the lowest level of detail if requested.

8. Each measure must allow flexibility for manager's queries, providing selectable variables regarding timeframes, products, geography, and elements to include and exclude, mapping trends over time.

9. Measures must offer feedback mechanisms, with logging and tracking of how they are being used, how often they are used, by whom, and any comments the users provide. An excellent feature is to provide integrated discussion group forums where users share tricks of using each measure in their work electronically, enabling group learning and sharing.

10. All gauges should offer highlighting of values that are far outside the norm, drawing management's attentions to and promoting investigation of dramatic anomalies.

Simplicity

Everything should be made as simple as possible, but not simpler.

- Albert Einstein

Simplicity is not always simple to design. Many products try to be simple but always wind up complicated. The Palm Pilot's wildfire success is testimony to the power of simplicity, especially when contrasted against the earlier but much more complex Apple Newton.

The trick to effectiveness and simplicity is to present "just enough" data in each view, then allow the manager or executive to drill deeper into the detail with a few clicks of the mouse.

It is smart to shoot for "just enough" accuracy: it is usually straightforward to produce an analysis that is considered accurate, plus or minus five or ten percent. Yet many companies fall into the trap of putting in many more times the analysis work to reduce the plus or minus variance. Typically, the added (and expensive) precision does not change management's decisions.

Rapid Prototyping

The Navigator uses surveys and feedback to model any new measure. Instead of finishing all the work to automate the data flow, the proposed measure is piloted using human effort to collect and present the data, enabling feedback from managers as to the usefulness and design of the gauge before investing in full development. By rapid prototyping, gauges tend to stay simple, and only gauges that are truly useful receive full funding.

Keeping Only the Useful

As any corporate executive is aware, traditional reports tend to multiply like rabbits, until few are useful, and often, only a few data elements of each are ever looked at by managers. To prevent this phenomenon, all Semper Fortis measures are presented online on an intranet portal, called the management instrument panel, with a "rate this management gauge" icon adjacent to every item.

If a manager rates a gauge poorly, pop-up windows immediately route feedback to the Navigator. The Navigator then surveys additional managers to decide if a gauge needs changes, a complete overhaul, or deletion from the management instrument panel. Additionally, the panel is designed to track use of features by manager, by job slot, and by area, helping the Navigator understand what features are being used daily, weekly, monthly, or rarely.

> A sample of the dynamic feedback system is available at www.SeizingShare.com/feed

Flexibility

When designing gauges, care must always be taken to present trends versus snapshots in time, allowing managers to dynamically look at any time period they choose, rather than providing only preconfigured views. Knowing for example, that currently proposed gross margins on the K27 product are 14% is less useful than knowing that the K27 had margins over 20% for two years, but suddenly plummeted to 18%, then 17%, and now 14% in just seven months time.

Learning from Peers

One of the most powerful features of gauges is the "proactive advice" postings provided per gauge. Area VPs and sales directors are encouraged to post comments for other managers to see under each gauge, providing insight on what worked and what didn't work for them.

> A simulation is available at www.SeizingShare.com/mip

This fosters organizational management learning, as managers have message-board-like discussion groups on how to do their jobs better with the data presented. The system draws attention to new postings with blinking indicators, letting a manager know a new comment has been posted.

An Ever-Changing World

While the Navigator's job is to present data as simply as possible, the underlying models tend to get a bit complex. One of the more perplexing issues is that the complex multi-dimensional reality is constantly changing. What worked only one or two years ago may no longer work today.

To stay flexible with changing conditions, the underlying lowest-level detail data is stored in a highly normalized relational database system. The data is front-ended with a powerful, state-of-the-art graphical query development toolset, such as the Microstrategy suite.

Keeping up with these dynamics and warning managers of possible aspect changes drives the organization to use one of their most perceptive associates in the Navigator role. The Semper Fortis Navigator designs "effectiveness quotients" into the models that can be continuously monitored and retested, drawing attention to the changes in the bigger picture.

Right-Leveling the Measures

In a great design, the management instrument panel has views by level of management, starting at the CUBE level, not the sales director level. CUBEs are microcosm general managers, and management aids that apply in this environment should be offered liberally.

One of the more powerful concepts is to offer comparison views of a sales franchise to the average franchise, comparison to a top 25% franchise, and comparison to a top 10% franchise. The CUBE then can see how he or she tracks versus the better half of the sales force, which in turn initiates self-disciplined change.

The same comparison to best-of-breed is used at all levels. Sales directors can compare themselves versus peers. This method has been successfully used for years in chain retailing, where stores compare their performance to similar stores, model stores, and average stores.

Keeping Individual Stats

Some companies find that calculating the measures on an individual's performance into indexes helpful. The NFL offers a great example of this in the quarterback rating, which combines a variety of stats such as pass completions, pass attempts, touchdowns, and interceptions into an index.

In depth player statistics help management rate the effectiveness of sales professionals to a point and are kept in a Semper Fortis organization as diligently as Major League Baseball tracks a pitcher's productivity in different situations. In the end, this hard data helps highlight who fits in what class, in the concept of keeping A players on the roster while rotating out the C players.

No Matter How Big a Company Is, It's About Individuals

Many executives foolishly lull themselves into believing that individuals are unimportant. Managers at one of the largest computer hardware manufacturers often refer to salespeople as “coin-operated.” They operate believing that all that needs to be done is to offer financial incentives on one product versus another, and voilá, the sales drones crank out the result. They clearly are not leveraging much of the potential of their sales force.

In any knowledge work, individuals are extremely important. This may be easier to see in a biomedical example than in professional selling, where a small team of top-notch researchers might discover a multi-billion dollar compound that redefines health care for arthritis.

The same is true in complex knowledge-based selling. Quality is built one person at a time, and each individual matters. In my experience, the only executives who argue against this point are the ones with a lot of "C" and "D" players in the field.

Suggested Measurement Gauges

Measurement gauges vary by industry. I have developed more than thirty suggested forward-looking management gauges, which are discussed in my Measurement Brief, available on the SeizingShare.com website (see link below).

None of these measures address mainstream operational issues like delivery. While operational gauges are also needed, they are not intrinsically within the scope of selling, but rather belong in support department structures.

Generally, the Semper Fortis gauges are grouped in the following areas:

1. Opportunity,
2. Sales activity level,
3. Individual effectiveness,
4. Culture participation,
5. Customer focused, and
6. Management and support effectiveness.

> A comprehensive brief on forward-looking measures available at www.SeizingShare.com/measures

Clearly, the single most important gauge for sales management is the Sales Radar, sometimes referred to as the sales funnel or the sales pipeline. The Sales Radar refers to a graphical representation of the progress of opportunity projects through various steps of the selling process. At any one time, the enterprise view of the radar gives sales management a great view of the opportunities being pursued.

Sales radar by opportunity project / over time.

The multi-dimensional Sales Radar tracks opportunity projects, offering multiple management views of the data.

The Sales Radar system can be viewed in terms of:

- progress through time,
- number of projects,
- revenue and projected profit of projects,
- speed of projects through the radar levels, and
- successful close rates,

on a variable time basis such as comparing

- current year versus previous year,
- current month versus previous year month,
- current quarter versus previous year quarter, and
- month to month progression,

by different organizational levels, such as

- by sales professional,
- by sales director,
- by area VP,

further subdivided by

- industry classification of the opportunities,
- product lines,
- services offerings, and
- source of leads.

A well-implemented Sales Radar system becomes the prime command center for all sales management.

In Summary…

Measurement for management is different than measurement driven by finance and accounting. Reports based upon financials are invariably rearward facing. Managers, on the other hand, need forward-looking gauges which help them make good decisions about upcoming events. The speed and complexity of most selling environments has increased to the point where running a company efficiently by intuition and gut feel alone is no longer feasible.

The Semper Fortis system sets up a number of gauges to help management tune the effort. The highly flexible opportunity Sales Radar is the center of the management instrument panel, allowing management to track the number and quality of opportunities on an enterprise level, or any sublevel, over time. When designing gauges, special care must be taken to not lose trust by creating a negatively perceived "big brother is watching" atmosphere.

Setting up good measures is critical to achieving excellent situation awareness, which in turn drives better decision-making based on fact not bias, which in turn delivers world-class results and ultimately, competitive advantage via a superior Sales Olympian force.

Chapter 28: Playing Chess Not Checkers

Having made the journey through the chapters of Semper Fortis, it should now be clear that both market share and competitive advantage are available for the taking. Unlike some programs, this one is very much attainable by any company with strong visionary leaders that possess discipline, courage, and tenacity.

The build-up of momentum has many small but crucial breakthrough moments along the way. None are more pivotal that convincing everyone in the sales organization that they are about to become professionals and somewhat independent entrepreneurs, approaching business as though they are playing chess, not checkers. The days of reacting to other vendors' agendas become rare. The Semper Fortis firm seizes the offensive, while others stay in a reactive mode, thinking only one or two moves ahead.

A Call for Action

Implementing Semper Fortis is not rocket science. The vision has been offered here. Outlining the specifics of the mission simply requires a bit of personalization to each company's environment, but the vast majority of the plan has been presented as well.

A company should not try to implement Semper Fortis if it is significantly outgunned regarding product or solution value-add. Its time and focus should first be invested in becoming competitive with its offered solutions. A company must first be competitive in its field, even if it is not a market share leader, to attract great players. A superior sales team simply will not stick with a company that has truly substandard offerings, and Semper Fortis requires having “A” players onboard.

Once the vision and mission are planned, the next steps are to summon the courage, initiative, and whole-hearted commitment to make it happen. Momentum for programs of this magnitude builds slowly and starting the boulder down the hill often takes great effort. Establishing the prime directive and focusing all energies to become best-of-class is a mission that must remain in the active foreground of daily thought. If the leaders falter, distracted and seduced by brightly burning tactical fires, the boulder will rock backwards and settle back into its original, comfortable resting place.

The final stretch of achieving fusion is marked by patience, discipline, and perseverance. The momentum builds slowly, the team starts seeing the fruits of its labors, empowerment forges confidence and creativity, and the entire company starts having fun, rooted first in success and second in camaraderie.

The first step is making the choice. Nothing in the Semper Fortis discipline conflicts with other corporate improvement programs. The core issue is whether a company's executive team has the will to become a champion and then stay a champion. Given that creating the momentum and establishing all the balanced Semper Fortis pillars and facets can take several years to achieve, moving first, before one's competitors, offers an opportunity to take a lead and seize share. Competitors will find that it is nearly impossible to catch up if they start three years behind because a Semper Fortis company guards hard-won customer ground fiercely.

I hope you and your sales force make the decision to "be all you can be." History has plenty of lessons that clearly show that a country with a strong military and a great state department has a much better chance for survival and growth than one having a token force. Unlike some cost-center departments, a superior sales group pays for itself many times over, making the Semper Fortis initiative financially justifiable.

I would say *good luck* but Semper Fortis doesn't need much luck (though a bit of luck doesn't hurt). Implementing Semper Fortis requires vision, tenacity, and discipline. Given that I live in Texas, I think ***"Vaya con Dios!"*** fits best.

Additional Information

Appendices

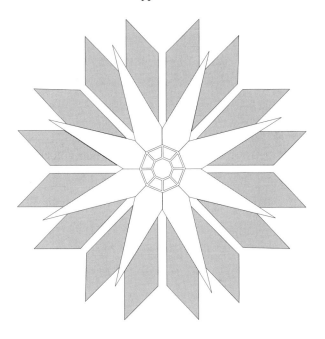

"The secret to success in life is for a man to be ready
for his opportunity when it comes."
- Benjamin Disraeli

Appendix A: Model Organization Chart

Please find a model Semper Fortis sales organization on the following page:

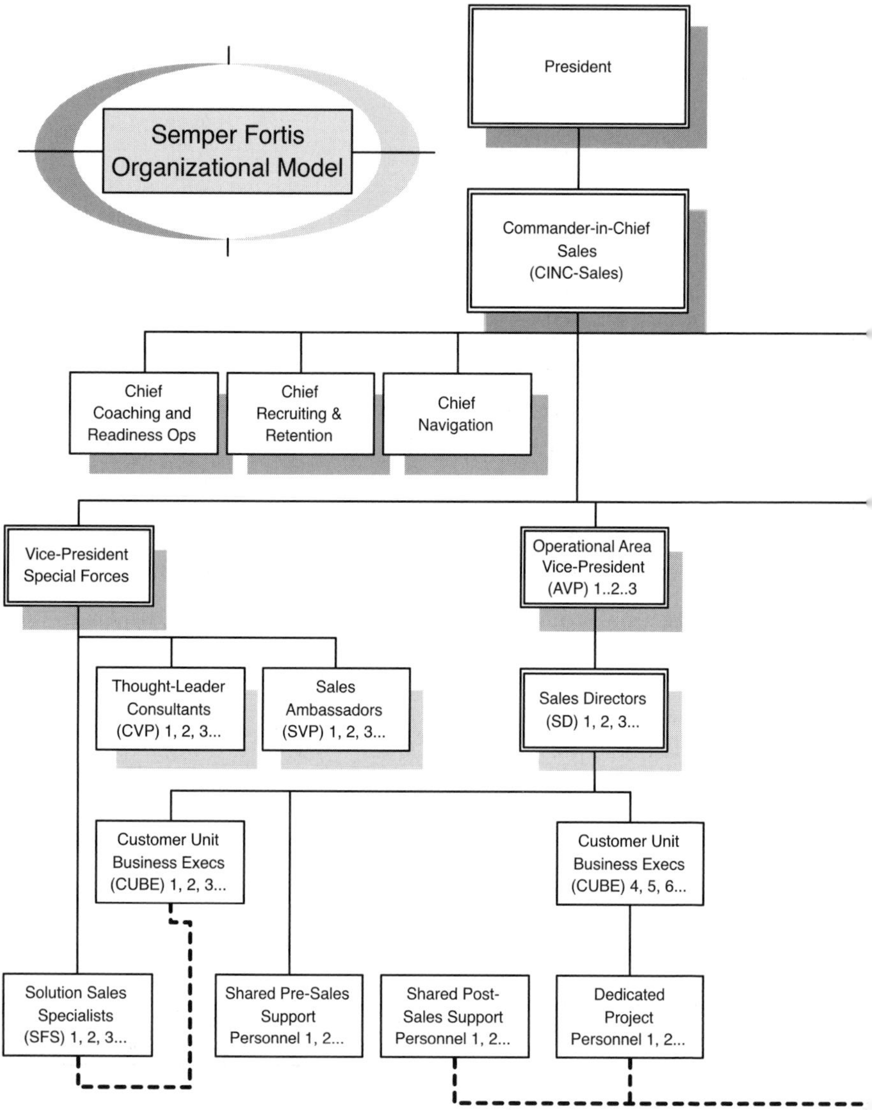
Semper Fortis
Organizational Model
President
Commander-in-Chief Sales (CINC-Sales)
Chief Coaching and Readiness Ops
Chief Recruiting & Retention
Chief Navigation
Vice-President Special Forces
Operational Area Vice-President (AVP) 1..2..3
Thought-Leader Consultants (CVP) 1, 2, 3...
Sales Ambassadors (SVP) 1, 2, 3...
Sales Directors (SD) 1, 2, 3...
Customer Unit Business Execs (CUBE) 1, 2, 3...
Customer Unit Business Execs (CUBE) 4, 5, 6...
Solution Sales Specialists (SFS) 1, 2, 3...
Shared Pre-Sales Support Personnel 1, 2...
Shared Post-Sales Support Personnel 1, 2...
Dedicated Project Personnel 1, 2...

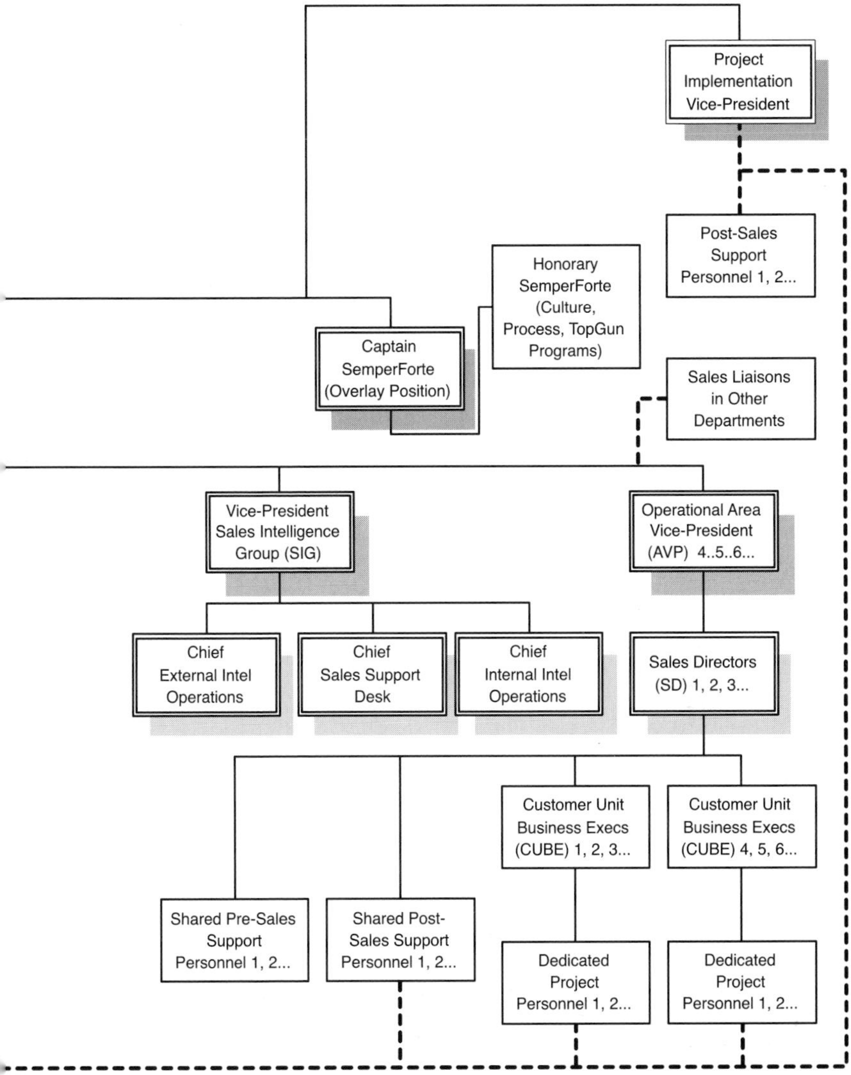
Project Implementation Vice-President
Post-Sales Support Personnel 1, 2...
Honorary SemperForte (Culture, Process, TopGun Programs)
Captain SemperForte (Overlay Position)
Sales Liaisons in Other Departments
Vice-President Sales Intelligence Group (SIG)
Operational Area Vice-President (AVP) 4..5..6...
Chief External Intel Operations
Chief Sales Support Desk
Chief Internal Intel Operations
Sales Directors (SD) 1, 2, 3...
Customer Unit Business Execs (CUBE) 1, 2, 3...
Customer Unit Business Execs (CUBE) 4, 5, 6...
Shared Pre-Sales Support Personnel 1, 2...
Shared Post-Sales Support Personnel 1, 2...
Dedicated Project Personnel 1, 2...
Dedicated Project Personnel 1, 2...

Appendix B: Glossary

A-Plan
A part of sales planning, the A-Plan is the Account level (strategic in nature) sales plan.

C-Plan
A part of sales planning, the C-Plan is sales Call level (tactical in nature) sales plan.

Complex Corporate Solutions (Selling) Environment (CCSE)
A selling environment that involves the following facets:

- Corporate-to-corporate selling,
- Complex, political selling environment,
- Consultative problem-solving,
- Often, but not always, customized solutions for each client,
- Often, but not always, complex solution sets.

Customer Unit Business Executives (CUBEs)
A sales professional who manages his own profit and loss, is paid as a percentage of profit, and is the responsible company person for a list of customers and prospects.

Customer Service Representative
Administrator charged with ordering, delivery logistics, and billing of products and services for a customer.

I-Plan
Implementation Plan for a customer project, produced by the Project Director.

I-Plan Portal
Secure web portal for consolidating information regarding an implementation project.

L-30
The L-30 checklist highlights the key leadership qualities required for managers working within the Semper Fortis formula.

Level-One P&L (L1)
A profit and loss accounting statement associated with a customer.

Level-Two P&L (L2)
A profit-and-loss accounting statement associated with a CUBE, typically combining a number of customers. The L2 includes the salesperson's overhead costs.

Level-Three P&L (L3)
A profit-and-loss accounting statement associated with a sales director, typically combining a number of CUBE P&Ls. The L3 includes the sales director's overhead costs.

Level-Four P&L (L4)
A profit-and-loss accounting statement associated with a area vice-president, typically combining a number of Sales Director P&Ls. The L4 includes the area VP's overhead costs.

Level-Five P&L (L5)
A profit and loss accounting statement associated with the commander-in-chief of sales, typically combining a number of area VP P&Ls. The L5 includes the commander-in-chief of sales' overhead costs, including support areas such as the SIG, Special Forces, and other staff.

O-Plan
A part of sales planning, the O-Plan is the Opportunity or project level sales plan.

Navigator
Key staff position that designs and monitors management reports and gauges used by the sales team.

Net Profit Model (NPM)
Compensation model in which the salesperson receives bonus as a percentage of net profit in his or her area.

Project Director
Project manager with sales awareness training, reporting to both the VP of Implementation and the CUBE over the account.

Revenue Quota Model (RQM)
Compensation model where the salesperson receives bonus by achieving a percentage of an arbitrarily set revenue target.

Right-Level Decision Making (RLDM)
A formula for company decision-making that places ultimate responsibility for customer-specific decision in the hands of the company's sales professional who is closest to the action.

Sales Director
First-Line sales manager who, in the Semper Fortis model, focused on coaching and resource allocation.

Sales Intelligence Group (SIG)
A department chartered with recording sales-related knowledge and making the data accessible on a timely basis in order to help selling at new prospects.

Semper Fortis
A formula for achieving competitive advantage through the development and deployment of a world-class selling organization. Translated from Latin, it means "Always Strong."

Solution Sales Specialists
Reporting to the VP of Special Forces, a solution sales specialist sells complex product or services offerings, manages his or her own profit and loss statement, and is paid as a percentage of profit, albeit often at a different rate than CUBEs. The specialist does not own the relationship with any accounts, unless there is not CUBE assigned to an account.

Systems Engineer (Pre-sales)
A field-based technical employee, chartered with ensuring technical aspects work as designed. In the Semper Fortis model, the system engineers are trained on professional selling and work on the sales team to assist the CUBEs and solution sales specialists, especially helping sell technical contacts on the customer side.

Endnotes

Chapter One

Index to Volume 71, *Harvard Business Review*, November-December 1993, pg. 209-211.

Index to Volume 72, *Harvard Business Review*, November-December 1994, pg. 194-196.

Index to Volume 73, *Harvard Business Review*, November-December 1995, pg. 214-217.

Index to Volume 74, *Harvard Business Review*, November-December 1996, pg. 196-200.

Index to Volume 75, *Harvard Business Review*, November-December 1997, pg. 193-198.

1998 Index – Titles by Subject, *Harvard Business Review*, November-December 1998, pg. 186-192.

1999 Index – Authors and Titles by Subject, *Harvard Business Review*, November-December 1999, pg. 203-211.

2000 Index of Articles – Titles by Subject, *Harvard Business Review*, November-December 2000, pg. 207-214.

2001 Index of Articles – by Subject, *Harvard Business Review*, January 2002, pg. 120 - 122.

2002 Index of Articles – by Subject, *Harvard Business Review*, December 2002, pg. 120 - 122.

Chapter Three

Michael Treacy and Fred Wiersema, *The Discipline of Market Leaders*
(PA, Harper Collins, 1995)

Chapter Four

Robert Miller, Stephen Heiman, and Tad Tuleja, *Strategic Selling*
(CA, Miller-Heiman, Inc. 1987)

Chapter Seven

Frederick F. Reichheld, *Loyalty Effect*
(MA, Harvard Business School Press, 1996)

Chapter Eight

Warren Buffet, *Berkshire Hathaway Owners Manual*
(www.berkshirehathaway.com)

Chapter Fourteen

Harvey MacKay, *Swim with the Sharks Without Being Eaten Alive*
(NY, Morrow, 1998)

Chapter Nineteen

Bradford D. Smart, *Topgrading*
(NY, Prentice Hall Press, 1999)

Chapter Twenty-Four

Kevin Freiberg and Jackie Freiberg, *Nuts*
(TX, Bard Books, 1996)

Why Register at SeizingShare.com

Registration at www.SeizingShare.com offers the following benefits:

- Access to all Seizing Share white papers, offering additional information on numerous topics found in this book;
- Access to interactive models of the overall Semper Fortis formula, pre-sales organization, model organization chart, opportunity radar, and decision logs;
- The ability to ask the author questions over e-mail;
- Access to future postings of new white papers, which will preview Bob's next book;
- Substantial electronic coupons for Bob's future publishing efforts,
- The ability to purchase copies of Seizing Share at corporate volume discounts for your sales force or Holiday list;
- An assurance that e-mails will be few (approximately once per quarter) and valuable; and
- An iron-clad privacy policy ensuring that your personal data is never sold or used in a way that you do not approve.

Please visit and register at www.SeizingShare.com.

When critical membership momentum is achieved, Sakalas plans to establish a networked club of executives and top-tier sales professionals working in the complex corporate solution-selling environment. The network will offer many new benefits including online discussion groups, a forum for world-wide networking and collaboration, a no-fluff monthly newsletter compilation of best-of-breed CCSE ideas, and great opportunities for community service.

Credits

This project has given me a tremendous appreciation for the efforts authors and their surrounding friends and associates pour into books. I could not have completed it with the help of many people. Above all, I would like to thank my wife Leslie and my daughters for all their patience and understanding.

Special thanks goes to Bruce W. Travis in Atlanta—Bruce was my Yoda when I got my first sales light saber and his lessons have served me well throughout my sales career. He remains my main sounding board, especially helping with the creation of the first *Seizing Share* outline many moons ago. I always appreciate his unique perspectives whenever I have a troubling sales strategy or tactics question.

I surveyed nearly one hundred career solution selling professionals to get their views regarding the organizational and sales environments found at the top vendors of the Fortune 500. To everyone that participated, sincere thanks.

I also would like to thank the many folks that helped with editing, especially Victoria Kiburas, Chris Ferrante, Zoe Rosenfeld, Tom St. John, and Ricky Nutt, all of whom went above and beyond the call of duty.

Lastly, I would like to thank Bob Loeffler for his suggestion that pushed me over the top and got me started in the first place. I have always had this project as a goal, but he was the catalyst that made me take that first step.

About the Author

Bob Sakalas has *"been there, done that"* in the high-end corporate solution selling environment of the Fortune 500.

After graduating from the University of Tulsa, Bob started his career at NCR Corporation, where he earned numerous honors over seven years, including NCR's Chairman Award, given to the top salesperson in the country. Sakalas expanded his quest for professional solution selling understanding and success with Teradata, the massively-parallel database pioneer specializing in decision support data mining.

Sakalas joined entrepreneurial, east-coast-based Kyrus Corporation in 1993 to lead its expansion west of the Mississippi River. Bob played a key role in fueling Kyrus' phenomenal growth into becoming IBM's largest value-added reseller and software partner targeting chain retailing. His team won the Top Revenue and Top Net Profit awards in different years, setting new company sales records while selling best-of-breed solutions from IBM, Symbol Technologies, HP, PSC / Spectra Physics, and others.

Bob left Kyrus to take a few years off, to enjoy the birth of his second child, and to write this book, a life-long dream.

Bob is currently Executive Vice-President of ACR Retail, a privately-held software company, and leads its innovation division RiverOak Interactive, the leader in customer interactive commerce systems for Fortune 1000 chain retailers (see www.RiverOakInteractive.com). He also serves as a board member of Capstrom Corporation, a technology incubation firm.

He resides in Dallas with his wife, Leslie, and two daughters.

Please visit www.SeizingShare.com for more information.